WORKBOOK / LAB MANUAL

PLAZAS

LUGAR DE ENCUENTROS

Second Edition

Jill Pellettieri
California State University, San Marcos

Silvia Rolle-Rissetto
California Sate University, San Marcos

Verónica Añover
California State University, San Marcos

THOMSON

HEINLE

Australia Canada Mexico Singapore Spain United Kingdom United States

THOMSON

HEINLE

PLAZAS

Second Edition

Workbook / Lab Manual

Pellettieri / Rolle-Rissetto / Añover

Editor-in-Chief: *PJ Boardman*
Publisher: *Janet Dracksdorf*
Acquisitions Editor: *Helen Alejandra Richardson*
Development Editor: *Viki Kellar*
Senior Production Project Manager:
  Esther Marshall
Editorial Assistant: *Ignacio Ortez-Monasterio*
VP, Director of Marketing: *Elana Dolberg*

Manufacturing Manager: *Marcia Locke*
Compositor/Project Manager:
  Pre-Press Company, Inc.
Cover Design: *Diane Levy*
Cover Illustration: © *2004, Simon Shaw/*
  IllustrationOnLine.com
Printer: *Globus Printing*

Printed in the United States of America.
1 2 3 4 5 6 7 8 9 10   09 08 07 06 05 04

ISBN: 0-8384-1062-6

Table of Contents

LAB MANUAL

PREFACE
to the
Workbook / Lab Manual

Workbook

The *Plazas* Workbook has been written and designed to accompany the *Plazas* textbook. Through a tightly structured instructional sequence that closely parallels the main text, the workbook leads students first through a set of highly contextualized form-focused activities (¡A practicar!) and then through more open-ended contextualized activities (¡Te toca a ti!) that foster the development of skills for creative expression in Spanish.

Each chapter of the *Plazas* Workbook contains activities targeted at vocabulary and grammar building, as well as the development of critical skills and strategies necessary for the comprehension and production of written texts. Following are some suggestions for the use of each of the chapters' sections:

¡A practicar!, and ¡Te toca a ti! parallel each vocabulary and grammar section of the main text and can be assigned as homework as these sections are covered in class. Many of the more open-ended ¡Te toca a ti! activities are easily adapted for in class pair and small group activity.

Síntesis: ¡A leer! mirrors the reading strategies of the main text and ask students to apply these strategies to a given Spanish text. Text types throughout the chapters range from magazine and newspaper articles to poems and pieces of short stories from the Spanish-speaking world. Topics of the readings reflect the chapter themes as well as today's students' interests. These activities are best completed after students have engaged in the chapter's themes so as to have sufficient background knowledge activated to maximize comprehension.

Síntesis: ¡A escribir! mirrors the writing strategies of the main text and guides students through the writing of their own composition in Spanish. Always contextualized and presented as an authentic writing task, the activities in these sections lead students through different types of written communication including personal letters, descriptive and expository writing, and the academic essay.

Laboratory Manual

The Plazas Laboratory Manual and Audio program have been written and designed to accompany the *Plazas* textbook. Each chapter is designed to help students improve their listening and speaking skills through vocabulary-based and form-based activities that parallel the analogous presentations in the main text. Listening tasks have been carefully contextualized in dialogs and conversations shaped to add cultural information, and to stimulate cultural awareness.

Like all of the components of *Plazas*, the Laboratory Manual embeds culture and provides examples of authentic oral expressions in the voice and accent of speakers from each country featured in the main text.

Vocabulario checks the core of the lexicon presented in each chapter of the main text, with listening comprehension and pronunciation activities, from closed-ended to open-ended.

Gramática and **Así se dice** parallel each structure and function presented in the main text. The activities in this section reinforce listening comprehension, as well as the handling of structures, forms and expressions from the aural perspective.

Pronunciación provides a complete review of sounds of the Spanish language. This portion is formed with pronunciation and listening activities targeting difficult sounds and pronunciation rules.

Acknowledgments

I would like to thank my family, colleagues, and friends, and in particular, Dr. Silvia Rolle-Rissetto and Dr. Verónica Añover, who are all of those rolled into one. In addition I would like to also thank Viki Kellar, Helen Richardson, Esther Marshall, and the rest of the Heinle Thomson team as well as all the freelancers involved with the production of this project. Their love, inspiration, and support throughout the development and production of this project was invaluable.

Dr. Jill Pellettieri

I would like to thank Heinle for their support during this project, my family and friends for putting up with me during the creation, process, and completion. First and foremost, I extend my sincere gratitude to my dear colleagues and friends: Dr. Verónica Añover and Dr. Jill Pellettieri. To the first, I thank her for having kindly and diligently shared her unparalleled expertise, time and efforts, making this final product possible. To Dr. Jill Pellettieri, undoubtedly one of the most talented applied linguists in the U.S. today, I am indebted for the opportunity of being on this author time in the first place, and above all, for the honor of working by her side. Thank you ladies; it is indeed a sheer honor to know people like you in this professions, and a true joy to call both of you "my colleagues."

Dr. Silvia Rolle-Rissetto

I would like to thank Heinle for supporting this project. I thank dearly my colleagues and friends, Dr. Jill Pellettieri and dr. Silvia Rolle, for allowing me to be part of the *Plazas* team, the World Languages team, and the "trio" team! I am eternally thankful to them for it.

Dr. Verónica Añover

Workbook

¡Mucho gusto!

VOCABULARIO Saludos y despedidas

¡A PRACTICAR!

WB P-1 **Saludos y despedidas** For each picture, circle the most appropriate of the three salutations or responses.

1.
- Buenas tardes, profesora.
- Buenos días, profesor.
- ¿De dónde es Ud.?

2.
Hola, ¿qué tal?
- Soy de Barranquilla.
- Encantada.
- Bastante bien. Y Ud., ¿cómo está?

3.
Adiós, Javier.
- Chao, Claudia. Nos vemos.
- Más o menos.
- Buenas noches, Claudia.

Presentaciones *(Introductions)* Your roommate wants to practice meeting and greeting people in Spanish. Help her by selecting from the second column the appropriate response to each expression in the first column. **¡OJO!** Some expressions may have more than one response.

_____ 1. ¡Encantada!   a. Bien, gracias.

_____ 2. ¡Hola! ¿Qué tal?   b. Muy bien, ¿y Ud.?

_____ 3. ¡Mucho gusto!   c. Soy de San Diego.

_____ 4. ¿Cómo se llama?   d. El gusto es mío.

_____ 5. ¡Buenas noches, Carolyn!   e. Nos vemos.

_____ 6. ¿Cómo está Ud.?   f. Bastante bien, ¿y tú?

_____ 7. ¿De dónde eres tú?   g. Felicia. Y Ud., ¿cómo se llama?

_____ 8. ¡Hasta luego!   h. ¡Buenas noches, señor Guzmán!

¡TE TOCA A TI!

WB P-3 **En una fiesta** You have just met Tomás from Puerto Rico and he asks you the following questions. Write appropriate responses to his questions.

1. ¿Cómo te llamas?

   _____

2. ¿Cómo estás?

   _____

3. ¿De dónde eres?

   _____

4. ¿Cómo se llama tu texto de español?

   _____

5. ¿Cómo se llama tu profesor(a) de español?

   _____

ESTRUCTURA I Talking about yourself and others: subject pronouns and the present tense of the verb *ser*

¡A PRACTICAR!

WB P-4   **¿Qué pronombre?** Which pronouns would Alberto Yáñez, a professor from Spain, use to address or talk about the following people? In the spaces provided below, write the most appropriate pronoun. **¡OJO!** Remember that Alberto is from Spain, which will affect the pronouns he selects in certain situations.

1. Referring to students Alicia and Cristina _____

2. Talking to Mr. Gutiérrez _____

3. Referring to his brother Carlos _____

4. Talking to Mr. and Mrs. Morán _____

5. Talking to his two sons _____

6. Referring to himself _____

7. Talking to his wife _____

8. Referring to his wife _____

9. Referring to himself and three friends _____

10. Talking to his two daughters _____

¡TE TOCA A TI!

WB P-5   **¿Qué piensas?** What do you think? Give your opinion by forming sentences with the words provided. Following the model, use the appropriate form of the verb **ser**.

MODELO: el presidente / sincero
El presidente es sincero.
o *El presidente no es sincero.*

1. Jerry Seinfeld / cómico

_____

2. Richard Simmons / energético

_____

3. yo / inteligente

_____

4. Julia Roberts / atractiva

_____

5. mis amigos (*friends*) y yo / interesantes

_____

¡A PRACTICAR!

WB P-6 **El sabelotodo** Juan Carlos is **un sabelotodo** (*know-it-all*) who doesn't always know it all. Mark each of Juan Carlos's statements with **C** for **cierto** (*true*) or **F** for **falso** (*false*). If a statement is false, rewrite the sentence correcting Juan Carlos's error. **¡OJO!** You will need to use both the verb form **hay** as well as numbers. Follow the model.

> MODELO: En el mes de septiembre hay 28 días (*days*).
> **F** *En el mes de septiembre hay 30 días.*

_____ **1.** En una semana (*week*) hay siete días.

_____

_____ **2.** Hay 13 huevos (*eggs*) en una docena.

_____

_____ **3.** Hay nueve números en un número de teléfono en los Estados Unidos.

_____

_____ **4.** En un año (*year*) hay 12 meses (*months*).

_____

_____ **5.** Hay 15 pulgadas (*inches*) en un pie (*foot*).

_____

WB P-7 **Problemas de matemáticas** Test your mathematical ability by completing the following equations. Note that **más** means *plus* and **menos** means *minus*. **¡OJO!** Write out the numbers. Follow the model.

> MODELO: Treinta menos dos son *veintiocho.*

1. Once más tres son _____.

2. Ocho menos ocho son _____.

3. Siete más tres son _____.

4. Catorce más quince son _____.

5. Veintiséis menos dos son _____.

6. Dieciocho más cuatro son _____.

¡TE TOCA A TI!

WB P-8 | **Guía telefónica** Your new "user-friendly" handheld computer won't let you input numerals! You can only store your friends' and family's telephone numbers by answering the software's questions and spelling out (number by number) these telephone numbers. Answer the software's questions below giving appropriate telephone numbers.

1. ¿Cuál es el número de teléfono de tu mejor amiga *(best female friend)*?

   _____

2. ¿Cuál es el número de teléfono de tu mejor amigo?

   _____

3. ¿Cuál es el número de teléfono de tus padres?

   _____

4. ¿Cuál es tu número de teléfono?

   _____

VOCABULARIO Palabras interrogativas

¡A PRACTICAR!

WB P-9 | **Tantas preguntas** You are meeting your date at his/her house, and your date's mother has many questions for you. Complete her questions by writing the appropriate question words below.

1. ¿_____ estás?
2. ¿De _____ eres?
3. ¿_____ estudiantes hay en la clase?
4. ¿_____ es tu número de teléfono?
5. ¿_____ son tus padres?
6. ¿_____ personas hay en tu familia?

¡TE TOCA A TI!

WB P-10 | **Más preguntas** After getting the "third degree" from your date's mother, you decide to ask her some questions. Write out the questions you would ask, using interrogative words.

1. ¿_____?
2. ¿_____?
3. ¿_____?
4. ¿_____?
5. ¿_____?

¡A PRACTICAR!

WB P-11 | **Entre amigos** Use the following words to form sentences with the verb **tener.** Follow the model.

MODELO: Carlos y yo / tener / 30 años
Carlos y yo tenemos 30 años.

1. Paqui / tener / 23 años

   _____

2. ellos / tener / 15 años

   _____

3. yo / tener / 22 años

   _____

4. tú / tener / 12 años

   _____

5. nosotros / tener / 21 años

   _____

6. Roberto, Silvia y Carlos / tener / 18 años

   _____

¡TE TOCA A TI!

WB P-12 | **¡Don Juan a la vista!** A friend has brought you to a Spanish-speaking party where you have met a Don Juan type. Write the conversation that takes place as this guest, Raúl, tries to talk to your friend Cristina. In this conversation, use as much of your new vocabulary as possible. **¡OJO!** Be sure to include the following: • a greeting and introduction • a request for a phone number • a discussion about where they are from • a good-bye • a discussion about how old they are.

_____

_____

_____

_____

_____

_____

_____

_____

Autoprueba

VOCABULARIO

WB P-13 **Una conversación típica** Below is a typical conversation likely to be heard during the first days of a new school year. Complete the conversation by supplying the appropriate vocabulary words or phrases.

MIGUEL: **1.** _____, Tomás. ¿**2.** _____ tal?

TOMÁS: Bien, Miguel. Tanto tiempo (*It's been awhile*). ¿Y cómo **3.** _____ tú?

MIGUEL: Bien, **4.** _____. Tomás, ésta es mi novia (*this is my girlfriend*), Elena.

TOMÁS: Hola, Elena, mucho **5.** _____.

ELENA: El gusto **6.** _____ _____.

TOMÁS: ¿De **7.** _____ eres, Elena?

ELENA: **8.** _____ de Puerto Rico.

TOMÁS: Muy bien. Bueno, ya me voy (*I've got to go*). **9.** _____.

ELENA: **10.** _____, Tomás.

MIGUEL: **11.** _____ vemos, Tomás.

WB P-14 **Números** Write out each of the numerals indicated below, as well as the numeral that precedes it. Follow the model.

MODELO: 28
       veintiocho / veintisiete

1. 15 _____ / _____

2. 1 _____ / _____

3. 30 _____ / _____

4. 17 _____ / _____

5. 25 _____ / _____

ESTRUCTURA

WB P-15 **Presentaciones** Complete the following conversation with the appropriate form of the verb **ser.**

PILAR: Me llamo Pilar. ¿Quién **1.** _____ tú?

LOLA: **2.** _____ Lola Araña Tellez. Y éste (*this*) **3.** _____ mi amigo, Carlos.

PILAR: Encantada. ¿De dónde **4.** _____ Uds.?

LOLA: Nosotros **5.** _____ de Cuba.

¿Sois de España? Ramón has come from Spain to the University of California to study engineering. Complete one of his campus conversations by supplying the appropriate subject pronoun. ¡OJO! Remember the difference between formal and informal subject pronouns, as well as the differences between Peninsular and Latin American Spanish with respect to pronoun usage.

RAMÓN: Perdón, ¿sois **1.** _____ de España?

DIANA (Y DIEGO):   No, **2.** _____ somos de México. **3.** _____ soy de
                    Guanajuato y **4.** _____ es de Morelia.

DIEGO: El profesor Carrazco es de España. ¿De qué parte de España
                    (What part of Spain) es **5.** _____, profesor?

PROFESOR CARRAZCO: **6.** _____ soy de Galicia.

RAMÓN: Mi mamá es de Galicia. **7.** _____ es de Vigo.

DIEGO: ¿De qué parte eres **8.** _____, Ramón?

RAMÓN: **9.** _____ soy de Toledo.

DIANA: Bueno, profesor y Ramón, **10.** _____ son compatriotas y van a
                    ser *(are going to be)* buenos amigos.

PROFESOR CARRAZCO: ¡Seguro!

¿Cuántos años tienen? You have just found your roommate's "little black book." In it he has listed his age and then all the new coeds and their ages. Surprise! Your sister, Carmen, is in his book, too! For each entry below, write out complete sentences telling how old each person is. Follow the model.

MODELO: Verónica (28)
         Verónica tiene veintiocho años.

1. Lourdes (21) _____

2. Olga y Nidia (19) _____

3. Mariana (18) _____

4. Carmen y tú (20) _____

En una clase de español: Los Estados Unidos

VOCABULARIO En la clase

¡A PRACTICAR!

WB 1-1 **Una de estas cosas no es como las otras** *(One of these things isn't like the others)* For each series, circle the word that does not form a set with the others and then write a Spanish word that could fit in that set.

1. el lápiz, la tiza, la pluma, la pizarra

   _____

2. el libro, el diccionario, la lección

   _____

3. la silla, el escritorio, el lápiz

   _____

4. la pizarra, el borrador, el bolígrafo, la lección

   _____

5. los compañeros, los novios, la profesora, los estudiantes

   _____

WB 1-2 **Asociaciones** Write in Spanish the color you usually associate with each of the following items.

MODELO: snow   *blanco*

1. a crow   _____   6. chocolate   _____
2. an orange   _____   7. a banana   _____
3. grass   _____   8. the sky   _____
4. cherries   _____   9. eggplant   _____
5. paper   _____

¡TE TOCA A TI!

WB 1-3 **En mi clase** Joaquín, a pen pal from Quito, Ecuador, is interested in how college classes are different in the U.S. from college classes in Ecuador. Answer his questions in complete sentences in Spanish.

1. ¿Cuántos estudiantes hay en tu clase de español?

   _____

2. ¿Cómo se llama tu libro de texto de español?

   _____

3. ¿Cómo se llama tu profesor(a) de español?

   _____

4. ¿Cuántos bolígrafos tienes?

_____

5. ¿Tienes computadora? ¿De qué marca *(what brand)*?

_____

WB 1-4 | **¿De qué color es?** You and your roommate have been living together too long and now you can't remember whose things belong to whom. State the color of each of your belongings listed below. Make sure that, when necessary, the color adjective agrees in number and gender with the noun. Follow the model.

MODELO: tu mochila
        Mi mochila es roja.

1. tu pluma favorita

_____

2. tu silla

_____

3. tu bicicleta

_____

4. tu teléfono

_____

5. tu libro de español

_____

6. tu coche *(car)*

_____

ESTRUCTURA I Talking about people, things, and concepts: definite and indefinite articles and how to make nouns plural

¡A PRACTICAR!

WB 1-5 | **Amigos raros *(Strange friends)*** Norma Vayaloca is a strange woman who likes to name every object that she owns with human names! Help Norma determine whether she needs to give the following items feminine or masculine names. For each of the nouns listed below, circle **F** for **femenino** or **M** for **masculino**. Then write the appropriate definite article needed to accompany the noun. **¡OJO!** Be sure that the definite articles agree with the nouns in number as well as in gender. Follow the model.

MODELO: Ⓕ/ M   la calculadora

1. F / M _____ diccionarios   **6.** F / M _____ computadoras

2. F / M _____ lápiz   **7.** F / M _____ calendario

3. F / M _____ luces   **8.** F / M _____ mesas

4. F / M _____ escritorio   **9.** F / M _____ relojes *(watches)*

5. F / M _____ mapa   **10.** F / M _____ pizarra

Nombre _____ Fecha _____

WB 1-6 | **¡Qué exagerada!** *(How exaggerated!)* Mari Bocazas is one of those people who often exaggerates. Whatever you do, she says she does it better, and whatever you have, she says she has more. What would Mari say if you were to tell her each of the statements below?

> MODELO: Yo tengo una mochila.
> *Yo tengo dos mochilas.*

1. Yo tengo un(a) novio(a).

_____

2. Mi amigo tiene una computadora Mac.

_____

3. Yo tengo una clase de español.

_____

4. Mi novio(a) tiene una pluma Cartier.

_____

5. Yo tengo un reloj *(watch)* Rolex.

_____

¡TE TOCA A TI!

WB 1-7 | **El descuento** Your roommate just got a job at the college bookstore and has told you that he can get a 50% discount on certain items. Look at the list of items below and take inventory of your school supplies. Then write what you already have and what you need. Follow the model.

> MODELOS: cuaderno
> *Tengo un cuaderno.*
> o *Necesito (I need) un cuaderno.*
> pluma
> *Tengo una pluma.*
> o *Necesito dos plumas.*

1. bolígrafo

_____

2. diccionario

_____

3. lápices

_____

4. mochila

_____

5. calendario

_____

6. computadora

_____

VOCABULARIO Las lenguas extranjeras, otras materias y lugares universitarios

¡A PRACTICAR!

WB 1-8 | **Intercambios *(Exchanges)* internacionales** Below is a list of the countries available for next year's Study Abroad programs. For each country indicate the language in which interested applicants must be minimally fluent. **¡OJO!** In Spanish, country names are capitalized, but the names of languages are not. Follow the model.

MODELO: Alemania
el alemán

1. Japón _____
2. China _____
3. Portugal _____
4. Italia _____

5. España _____
6. Francia _____
7. Rusia _____
8. Inglaterra _____

WB 1-9 | **Cursos** The following is the course list for the Universidad de Buenos Aires Semester Abroad Program. From the list, write the name of the major to which each course would normally pertain. Follow the model.

MODELO: Genética y evolución: *biología*

1. Fisiología animal: _____
2. Análisis de mapas: _____
3. Legislación y política ambiental: _____
4. Teoría literaria: _____
5. Oceanografía: _____
6. Historiografía de México: _____
7. Filosofía del derecho: _____
8. Literatura española: _____

WB 1-10 | **Lugares universitarios** Where on campus are you most likely to do each of the following activities? Use a different location in each sentence.

MODELO: practicar deportes
en el gimnasio

1. Comprar *(to buy)* un sándwich

_____

2. Hablar con mi profesor

_____

3. Estudiar

_____

4. Comprar libros

_____

5. Practicar baile

_____

6. Descansar *(to rest)* con mis amigos

_____

¡TE TOCA A TI!

WB 1-11 **Encuesta *(Survey)*** To enhance its international education program the Universidad de las Américas in Puebla, Mexico, is surveying students from around the world to see which courses are most interesting to them. Fill out their survey by writing the courses in the spaces that you consider **muy interesantes** *(very interesting)*, **un poco interesantes** *(somewhat interesting)*, or **no interesantes** *(not interesting)*.

UNIVERSIDAD DE LAS AMÉRICAS

Nombre: _____

Apellido: _____

Ciudadanía *(Citizenship):* _____

Lengua nativa: _____

Cursos muy interesantes	**Cursos un poco interesantes**	**Cursos no interesantes**
_____	_____	_____
_____	_____	_____
_____	_____	_____
_____	_____	_____
_____	_____	_____
_____	_____	_____

¡Gracias por su participación!

ESTRUCTURA II Describing everyday activities: present tense of regular *-ar* verbs

¡A PRACTICAR!

WB 1-12 **Conversando** Manu is an exchange student from Perú studying at the University of Massachusetts. Below is a conversation he has with Alicia and Tomás, two Mexican-American students. Complete their conversation by supplying the appropriate form of the verb in parentheses.

ALICIA: ¡Hola, Manu! ¿Qué tal? ¿Cómo está todo?

MANU: Muy bien, pero *(but)* **1.** _____ (tomar) muchos cursos y **2.** _____ (estudiar) mucho.

TOMÁS: ¿Cuántos cursos **3.** _____ (tomar) tú?

MANU: Seis. ¿Y Uds.? ¿Cuántos cursos **4.** _____ (llevar) este semestre?

TOMÁS: Nosotros... solamente dos. Alicia y yo **5.** _____ (tomar) los mismos *(the same)* cursos. **6.** _____ (Estudiar) fisiología y química.

ALICIA: Manu, ¿ **7.** _____ (trabajar) en la biblioteca?

MANU: No, mi compañero de cuarto **8.** _____ (trabajar) allí *(there)*. Yo no **9.** _____ (necesitar) trabajar.

ALICIA: Sí, entiendo *(I understand)*. Tú compañero... se llama Juan, ¿no? ¿Cómo es él? ¿Es simpático *(nice)*?

MANU: Sí, es muy simpático. Nosotros **10.** _____ (hablar) mucho y siempre **11.** _____ (mirar) «Baywatch» juntos *(together)* en nuestra casa. Y después del *(after the)* programa, nosotros **12.** _____ (practicar) inglés.

ALICIA: ¡Manu! ¿Uds. **13.** _____ (mirar) «Baywatch»? ¡Ese programa es horrible!

MANU: ¿Horrible? ¿Cómo que horrible *(What do you mean it's horrible)*? ¿Uds. aquí en los Estados Unidos no **14.** _____ (mirar) «Baywatch»?

ALICIA: ¿Yo? ¡Ni modo *(Not a chance)*!

TOMÁS: Pues *(Well)*...

¡TE TOCA A TI!

WB 1-13 **Mi rutina diaria** How much do you do in a typical day? Using the verbs and phrases you have learned so far, list as many of your daily activities as you can.

_____

_____

_____

_____

_____

_____

_____

Nombre _____ Fecha _____

ASÍ SE DICE Expressing personal likes and dislikes:
me gusta + infinitive

¡A PRACTICAR!

WB 1-14 **¿Qué te gusta?** For each of the following activities, write whether you like doing it or not. Follow the model.

> MODELO: practicar deportes
> *Me gusta practicar deportes.*
> o *No me gusta practicar deportes.*

1. descansar en la biblioteca

_____

2. hablar con mis padres por teléfono

_____

3. estudiar los viernes *(on Fridays)* por la noche

_____

4. bailar en las discotecas

_____

5. dibujar

_____

6. visitar a mis profesores

_____

¡TE TOCA A TI!

WB 1-15 **Cada cosa en su momento *(Everything in its own time)*** Go back to your daily activities that you listed in activity **WB 1-13.** Below indicate those activities that you like doing and those that you don't like doing. Follow the model.

> MODELO: *Me gusta hablar con mi novia. No me gusta estudiar.*

1. _____
2. _____
3. _____
4. _____
5. _____
6. _____

¡A PRACTICAR!

WB 1-16 **¿Qué cursos tomo?** Roberto Torres, an exchange student at your university, is having trouble reading the new course catalog for next semester. He has listed the courses he needs to take below and has asked that you write out in Spanish the time the course begins and the days of the week the course meets. Follow the model.

MODELO: la clase de psicología
Es a las dos de la tarde los sábados.

Course code	Course title	Units	Time	Days	Instructor
55940	Art 120	4	09:00–10:00	T/Th	Paredes
24965	Biology 10A	4	17:30–19:45	W	Smith
84804	Computer Science 101	3	15:00–16:00	M/W	Richardson
48997	Chemistry 7C	5	07:00–08:45	MWF	Nelson
94942	English 205	4	14:00–16:30	T	Hershberger
40900	Geography 10	3	09:00–10:00	Th/F	Cox
28817	Literature (American) 1A	3	10:00–11:50	T/Th	Rolle
38822	Mathematics 6C	4	13:00–14:00	MWF	Añover
99944	Music Appreciation 20	2	11:20–13:50	Sa	Frail
19902	Psychology 1C	4	12:00–14:45	T/Th	López
53229	Zoology 167	4	09:00–10:45	W/F	Clark

1. la clase de biología

_____

2. la clase de química

_____

3. la clase de geografía

_____

4. la clase de literatura

_____

5. la clase de matemáticas

_____

6. Roberto also wants to know if any of his course times conflict. If so, write out those courses along with their corresponding days and times.

_____

_____

_____

¡TE TOCA A TI!

WB 1-17   **Mi horario** Your Spanish instructor is planning a field trip and needs to know everyone's schedule to find the best time for the trip. Fill in the calendar page below, including the courses you take and the activities you do during the times and days indicated. **¡OJO!** Be sure to use the Spanish names of the courses you take.

	DÍA				
HORA	**lunes**	**martes**	**miércoles**	**jueves**	**viernes**
8:00					
9:00					
10:00					
11:00					
12:00					
13:00					
14:00					
15:00					
16:00					

¡A LEER!

RESEÑA Below you will find a short review of the movie *Austin Powers*. In order to understand any Spanish text, you will often need to read it several times using a range of strategies each time. In this reading activity, follow the steps below.

El rincón de los críticos:
Austin Powers

*A*ustin Powers es un auténtico fenómeno de la psicología de masas, además es un ícono de la cultura popular de la última década del milenio. El humor de la película es vulgar, grotesco e irreverente, y está dirigido básicamente a un público adolescente. La historia contiene mucha nostalgia de la sociedad norteamericana de los años sesenta: las imágenes retro, los colores psicodélicos, la música y los bailes. La película parodia no sólo los filmes típicos de espías al estilo James Bond, sino también varias películas populares, como *El Día de la Independencia* y *Apollo 13*. Seguramente, *Austin Powers* es una obra para ver y analizar, no por sus virtudes cinematográficas sino por sus alcances y su influencia social.

Strategy: Recognizing cognates

Cognates (**Cognados**) are words that belong to different languages but are identical or very similar to each other in spelling and meaning. There are many cognates in Spanish and English. Your ability to recognize them and guess their meaning will help you read Spanish more efficiently.

Paso 1: Before reading, thoroughly skim the passage and identify all the cognates that you can. What cognates can you find?

_____   _____

_____   _____

_____   _____

_____   _____

_____   _____

Paso 2: Now read the passage thoroughly for meaning. Don't look up any words in the dictionary, just try to get the gist of what the review is saying. If you had to state in one or two sentences what the text says (without worrying about reporting details), what would you say?

_____

_____

_____

_____

_____

_____

Paso 3: Read the review again and then answer the following questions.

1. How does the author describe the humor of the movie *Austin Powers*?

   _____

2. What are two examples of the North American nostalgia from the '60s that the author mentions?

   _____

   _____

3. What films does the author say that *Austin Powers* parodies?

   _____

4. Based on the vocabulary in the article, what are the Spanish equivalents for the following words and phrases?

   adolescent public: _____

   social influence: _____

   popular culture: _____

¡A ESCRIBIR!

EL MUNDO VERDADERO The Spanish language television network Telemundo has just announced on the local Spanish TV station that they are going to produce a new show and are looking for participants. This show will bring together five people who have never met to live for six months in a house in Miami's South Beach. In order for your application to be considered, you must submit a paragraph in which you introduce yourself and describe your daily routine.

Strategy: Organizing your ideas

A good way to improve your writing is to organize the ideas you want to express before you actually begin composing your document.

Paso 1: Start the paragraph that you would send by organizing your ideas before writing your first draft. Some of the following questions may help you to do so.

- What will you say about yourself? your name? where you are from? how old you are? what you study in school?
- What will you say about your daily routine? what days of the week you attend classes? what times of the day you study? where you study?

Paso 2: Now that you have all your ideas organized, write a first draft on a separate sheet of paper. Then, review it and write the draft of your paragraph below.

Functions: Describing people; Introducing; Talking about the present
Vocabulary: Countries; Languages; Studies; Arts
Grammar: Verbs: **ser, tener;** Prepositions: **de;** Personal pronouns: **él, ella;** Articles: indefinite: **un, una;** Articles: definite: **el, la, los, las**

Autoprueba

VOCABULARIO

WB 1-18 **Los cursos** Circle the course that does not belong in the category.

1. Letras: literatura / matemáticas / filosofía

2. Lenguas: alemán / inglés / historia

3. Ciencias sociales: zoología / sicología / economía

4. Arte: música / pintura / biología

WB 1-19 **¿Qué hora es?** What time is indicated in each digital display below? Write complete sentences and write out the times.

1. 2:45 p.m. _____

2. 1:22 p.m. _____

3. 12:31 p.m. _____

4. 5:15 a.m. _____

5. 9:30 a.m. _____

WB 1-20 **Está muy ocupada** Roberto is interested in getting to know Nancy and wants you to find out when she has free time to go out with him. Look at Nancy's busy study schedule below and explain to Roberto how busy she is. Tell him in Spanish what language she studies on each day of the week and at what time she studies. Follow the model.

Nancy's Study Schedule						
Monday	Tuesday	Wednesday	Thursday	Friday	Saturday	Sunday
Spanish 9:00 a.m.	German 3:45 p.m.	Chinese 12:45 p.m.	Russian 1:30 p.m.	Italian 5:15 p.m.	Portuguese 7:30 p.m.	Japanese 10:00 a.m.

MODELO: *Los lunes Nancy estudia español a las nueve de la mañana.*

1. _____

2. _____

3. _____

4. _____

5. _____

6. _____

WB 1-21 | **Los colores** Write in Spanish the color that you associate with each of the following items.

1. a lemon _____
2. Halloween _____
3. blood _____
4. dirt _____
5. a snowman _____
6. an American dollar bill _____

ESTRUCTURA

WB 1-22 | **Lupe y Lalo** To learn about Lupe's and Lalo's lives at the university, complete the following paragraphs with either definite or indefinite articles. ¡**OJO!** Remember that these articles must agree in number and gender with the nouns they modify.

Lupe Zarzuela es **1.** _____ persona inteligente. Ella estudia turismo, sicología y dos lenguas en **2.** _____ UNAM, que es **3.** _____ universidad enorme de **4.** _____ Ciudad de México. Para Lupe, **5.** _____ lenguas son fáciles, especialmente **6.** _____ inglés y **7.** _____ alemán.

Uno de **8.** _____ compañeros de clase de Lupe se llama Lalo Rodríguez, y es estudiante de ingeniería nuclear. Para Lalo, **9.** _____ inglés es **10.** _____ lengua muy difícil.

11. _____ clase de inglés de Lupe y Lalo es a **12.** _____ nueve de **13.** _____ mañana todos **14.** _____ días de **15.** _____ semana, excepto **16.** _____ sábados y domingos.

WB 1-23 | **Las actividades del día** Everyone who lives in Ramón's dorm has many activities and interests. Form sentences with the words provided to find out what everyone does each day.

1. Ramón / trabajar / todos los días

_____

2. Teresa y Evelia / estudiar / matemáticas / por la tarde

_____

3. yo / practicar / deportes / por la mañana

_____

4. nosotros / descansar / a las cuatro de la tarde

_____

5. tú / enseñar / ejercicios aeróbicos / por la noche

_____

6. Uds. / regresar / a la casa / a las seis de la tarde

_____

Nombre _____ Fecha _____

En una reunión familiar: México

VOCABULARIO La familia

¡A PRACTICAR!

WB 2-1 **La familia de Mariana** Mariana is telling her coworkers all about her family members. Complete her story by supplying the appropriate words from the list below.

sobrinos	hermana	perro	esposo	padre	hija	hijos

En mi casa somos cinco personas y un animal. Mi **1.** _____ se llama Paco. Tenemos

dos **2.** _____; se llaman Tomás y Miguelito. Tenemos una **3.** _____; se

llama Carolina. El **4.** _____ se llama Popeye.

Mi **5.** _____ se llama Jorge y es divorciado de mi mamá. Su nueva *(new)* esposa

se llama Maribel. Maribel tiene una hija, Magdalena. Ella es mi hermanastra.

Yo tengo una **6.** _____, Claudia. Su esposo se llama Jaime. Ellos tienen tres hijos,

Carlos, Jesús y Mateo. Ellos son mis **7.** _____. Paco no tiene hermanos.

WB 2-2 **El árbol genealógico de los Herrera Castellanos** Carlos Herrera Castellanos has just finished researching the paternal side of his family tree. Look at his family tree below, and then answer the questions on page 24 about his family members.

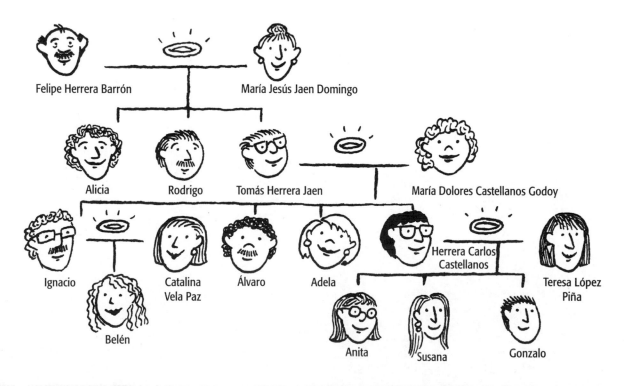

1. ¿Cómo se llama la esposa de Carlos? _____

2. ¿Cómo se llama la sobrina de Carlos? _____

3. ¿Cuántos hijos tiene Carlos? _____

4. ¿Cómo se llama el abuelo de Anita? _____

5. ¿Cómo se llama la nieta de María Jesús? _____

6. ¿Cómo se llama el esposo de Catalina? _____

7. ¿Cómo se llama el primo de Belén? _____

¡TE TOCA A TI!

WB 2-3 | **Una conversación con Helena «habladora»** *(talker)* **Masquetú** Your new, inquisitive pen pal from Guanajuato, Mexico, wants to know all about your family and has asked the following questions. Read and answer her questions.

1. ¿Tienes hermanos o hermanas? ¿Cómo se llama(n)?

   _____

2. ¿Estás casado(a) *(married)* tú? ¿Cómo se llama tu esposo(a)?

   _____

3. ¿Tienes sobrinos o sobrinas? ¿Cómo se llaman?

   _____

4. ¿Cómo se llaman tus padres?

   _____

5. ¿Tienes un gato o un perro? ¿Cómo se llama?

   _____

ASÍ SE DICE Indicating ownership and possession: possession with *de(l)* and possessive adjectives

¡A PRACTICAR!

WB 2-4 | **Nuestras familias** Francisco and his sister, Linda, are discussing families with their new friend, Antonio. Complete their conversation with the appropriate possessive forms. **¡OJO!** Pay attention to who is speaking to whom so that you will know which possessive form is necessary.

FRANCISCO: ¿Es grande **1.** _____ familia, Antonio?

ANTONIO: Sí, **2.** _____ familia es muy grande. Somos ocho personas. Y Uds., ¿es grande **3.** _____ familia?

FRANCISCO: No, **4.** _____ familia no es muy grande. Somos cinco.

LINDA: Pero **5.** _____ padres tienen familias grandes. Nuestra madre tiene seis hermanas y **6.** _____ padre tiene cuatro hermanos.

ANTONIO: Muy interesante. Linda, ¿de dónde es **7.** _____ madre?

LINDA: **8.** _____ madre es de México, de Zacatecas. Y tú, ¿de dónde son **9.** _____ padres?

ANTONIO: **10.** _____ padres son de Canadá, pero **11.** _____ padres y mis abuelos son de España.

¡TE TOCA A TI!

WB 2-5 | **Compañero ladrón** You and your roommates discovered that your other roommate has been "borrowing" your belongings without your permission. Identify the owner of each of the following items you found in his room by answering the questions as indicated. Follow the model.

MODELOS: ¿De quién es la foto de Ricky Martin? (Mariana)
La foto de Ricky Martin es de Mariana. Es su foto.
¿De quién es esta mochila? (yo)
Es mi mochila.

1. ¿De quién es el disco compacto de los Red Hot Chili Peppers? (Juan)

_____

2. ¿De quién es este bolígrafo? (tú)

_____

3. ¿De quién es la computadora? (Uds.)

_____

4. ¿De quién es el dinero? (nosotros)

_____

5. ¿De quién es la bicicleta? (Mariana)

_____

6. ¿De quién es la radio? (yo)

_____

ESTRUCTURA I Describing people and things: common uses of the verb *ser*

¡A PRACTICAR!

WB 2-6 **¡Mucho gusto!** Aníbal and Jaime, two exchange students from Spain, are trying to get to know all of the other Spanish speakers on their floor. Fill in the blanks with the appropriate form of the verb **ser** in their conversation.

ANÍBAL: ¿De dónde **1.** _____ Uds.?

CELIA: Nosotros **2.** _____ de Latinoamérica. Jesús **3.** _____ de Nicaragua. Felipe, Mabel y yo **4.** _____ de Cuba. Y tú, Aníbal, ¿de dónde **5.** _____?

ANÍBAL: Yo **6.** _____ de México, de Puerto Vallarta.

MABEL: Y tú, Jaime, ¿de dónde **7.** _____?

JAIME: De España, **8.** _____ de Córdoba.

CELIA: ¡Qué bueno! Y, ¿Uds. **9.** _____ hermanos?

JAIME: No, no **10.** _____ hermanos, **11.** _____ buenos amigos.

¡TE TOCA A TI!

WB 2-7 **Preferencias** Who are your favorite people? What are your favorite things? Complete the sentences below with the appropriate name or names, as well as the appropriate form of the verb **ser**. ¡OJO! Pay attention to whether each statement requires the verb in singular or plural.

MODELOS: *Jimmy Smits es mi actor favorito.*
Jennifer López y Julia Roberts son mis actrices favoritas.

1. _____ mi actor favorito.

2. _____ personas interesantes.

3. _____ mi comida favorita.

4. _____ mi profesor(a) de español.

5. _____ mis películas favoritas.

6. _____ mi restaurante favorito.

ASÍ SE DICE Describing people and things: agreement with descriptive adjectives

WB 2-8 **¡Qué familia tiene!** Ángel has a large family with very different relatives. Write out complete sentences to describe each of the relatives shown on the following page. Use the appropriate possessive form, as well as the adjective that best describes each person. Make sure the adjective agrees with the person/persons. Follow the model.

MODELO: *Su mamá es artística.*
o *La mamá de Ángel es artística.*

la mamá

Nombre _____ Fecha _____

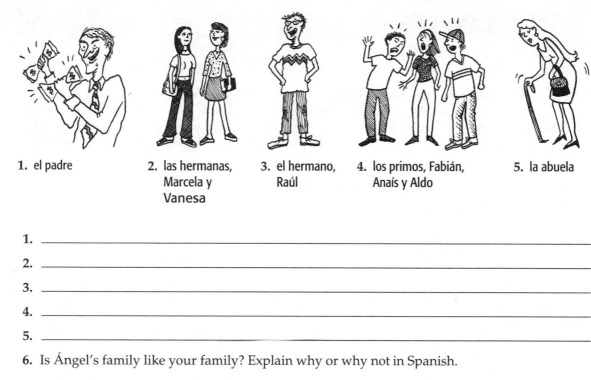

1. el padre

2. las hermanas, Marcela y Vanesa

3. el hermano, Raúl

4. los primos, Fabián, Anaís y Aldo

5. la abuela

1. _____
2. _____
3. _____
4. _____
5. _____

6. Is Ángel's family like your family? Explain why or why not in Spanish.

_____

_____

_____

¡TE TOCA A TI!

WB 2-9 **Personas interesantes** If you could meet anyone in the world, who would it be? Fill in the chart below with the names of the people you would enjoy meeting and at least one adjective that describes each of them. Be sure your adjectives agree in gender (masculine or feminine) and number (singular or plural). Follow the model. **¡OJO!** For a challenge, try to fill in the blanks with Latinos who fit those descriptions.

MODELO:

	Nombre	Adjetivo
An athlete	*Michael Jordan*	*simpático*
An actress	*Salma Hayek*	*bonita*

	Nombre	Adjetivo
An author		
Two local celebrities		
A political leader		
A movie director		
A talk or reality show host		

¡A PRACTICAR!

WB 2-10 | **¿De dónde son y qué lengua hablan?** You are organizing a directory of international students at your university that will list students by their nationality and native language. Begin your list by describing the following students. **¡OJO!** When giving someone's nationality, it must agree with the number and gender of the person or people being described. Follow the model.

MODELO: Alicia Ramos / España
Alicia Ramos es española. Habla español.

1. Teresita Sedillo / Honduras

   _____

2. Tomás Romero / Puerto Rico

   _____

3. Beatriz y Nancy Ruiz / Costa Rica

   _____

4. Helmut Schmidig / Alemania

   _____

5. Steven Ensley / Canadá

   _____

6. Madeline Depuy / Francia

   _____

7. Alejandro y Luis Villegas / Paraguay

   _____

¡TE TOCA A TI!

WB 2-11 | **Nuestra ascendencia** Most U.S. citizens can trace their roots to another country, and many speak or have family members who speak a language other than English. Reflect on your family and state the nationality and languages spoken by several of your family members. Follow the model. Be creative!

MODELOS: *Mi abuelo es italiano. Habla italiano.*
Mi padre es italiano y griego. Habla inglés.

1. _____
2. _____
3. _____
4. _____
5. _____
6. _____

ESTRUCTURA II Describing daily activities at home or at school: present tense of *-er* and *-ir* verbs

¡A PRACTICAR!

WB 2-12 | **Dos amigos** Tomás and Estela are students at the Universidad de Guadalajara. See how similar their lives are to yours by writing the appropriate form of the verb provided.

Estela y su familia **1.** _____ (vivir) en México, D.F. Estela es estudiante y

2. _____ (aprender) mucho en sus clases de la UNAM. Ella **3.** _____

(comprender), **4.** _____ (leer) y **5.** _____ (escribir) tres lenguas: español,

japonés e inglés. Estela trabaja mucho en sus clases porque quiere ser intérprete.

Tomás no **6.** _____ (vivir) con su familia. Sus padres, sus dos hermanas y su her-

mano **7.** _____ (vivir) en Mérida, la capital del Yucatán. Carlos le **8.** _____

(escribir) a su familia frecuentemente y él **9.** _____ (recibir) muchas cartas de ellos.

Tomás y Estela **10.** _____ (aprender) inglés por la mañana. Él

11. _____ (deber) estudiar más porque el inglés es difícil. Por la tarde Tomás y Estela

12. _____ (comer) en la cafetería de la UNAM. Ellos **13.** _____ (comer)

sándwiches y **14.** _____ (beber) sodas. Después de comer, ellos toman un café.

WB 2-13 | **Actividades diarias** In order to create a chore schedule, you and your roommates need to know who is available at what time. Make a chart of everyone's routines by using one element from each of the categories below and writing sentences that describe what each roommate does on a regular basis. Follow the model.

MODELO: Magaly
Magaly bebe café en el Café Roma por la mañana.

¿Qué?	¿Dónde?	¿Cuándo?
beber café	en un restaurante	por la mañana
comer	en el Café Roma	los domingos
deber estudiar	en casa	todos los días
escribir cartas	en el centro universitario	por la tarde
asistir a clases	en la universidad	por la noche
leer libros	en la biblioteca	los lunes
vender libros	en la librería	los fines de semana
¿?	¿?	¿?

1. Mi familia y yo _____

2. Teresa _____

3. Yo _____

4. Esteban _____

5. Tú _____

6. Nancy _____

7. Yo _____

| WB 2-14 | **Otro email de Marcia** You have just received another email from your Mexican pen pal, |

Marcia. Respond to her questions below by writing your answers in complete sentences in Spanish.

1. ¿Dónde vives? ¿Vives con tu familia o con tus amigos?

   _____

2. ¿Vives en apartamento, en casa o en una residencia?

   _____

3. ¿Qué lenguas hablan los miembros de tu familia?

   _____

4. ¿Qué lenguas lees o escribes tú?

   _____

5. ¿Qué aprendes en tus clases?

   _____

6. ¿Estudias mucho o poco? ¿Debes estudiar más?

   _____

7. ¿Lees novelas o poesía?

   _____

8. ¿Comes con tus amigos en los restaurantes del campus?

   _____

9. ¿Asistes a muchas actividades en la universidad? ¿Cuáles son?

   _____

10. ¿Crees en la importancia de la diversión (fun)?

   _____

ASÍ SE DICE Expressing possession and physical states: common uses of the verb *tener*

¡A PRACTICAR!

| WB 2-15 | **¡Algo tienen!** Alicia is talking about how strange her family is. Match each of her statements with the corresponding picture of her family members.

A   **B**   **C**   **D**

____ **1.** Siempre tenemos mucha hambre.

____ **2.** Mi hermano siempre tiene prisa.

____ **3.** Mi hermanita siempre tiene sueño.

____ **4.** Mi abuela siempre tiene sed.

WB 2-16   **Una conversación** Javier and Silvia are classmates who are getting to know each other better. Complete their conversation by using the appropriate form of the verb **tener. ¡OJO!** Remember that Javier and Silvia are classmates and would use the **tú** form.

JAVIER: ¿Cuántos años **1.** _____ , Silvia?

SILVIA: **2.** _____ 19 años. ¿Y tú?

JAVIER: Yo **3.** _____ 24.

SILVIA: ¿Cuántos hermanos **4.** _____ ?

JAVIER: **5.** _____ seis: tres hermanas y tres hermanos.

SILVIA: ¡Qué bueno! Yo no **6.** _____ hermanos. Pero mi mamá **7.** _____

un pájaro.

JAVIER: Pues, en mi casa nosotros no **8.** _____ mascotas. Pero mis abuelos

9. _____ tres gatos.

¡TE TOCA A TI!

WB 2-17   **Todos tenemos algo** In every family, different members have their peculiarities. Which of the following **tener** idioms are always or are never associated with your family members? Form sentences with each of the idioms by matching it with a family member listed below. **¡OJO!** Be sure to conjugate the verbs appropriately for the person or persons you describe. Follow the model.

MODELOS: Yo
Yo siempre tengo prisa por la mañana.
Mi hermano
Mi hermano nunca tiene éxito.

tener éxito   tener razón   tener hambre   tener sed   tener prisa   tener sueño

1. Yo _____

2. Mi hermano(a) _____

3. Mis abuelos _____

4. Mi padre y yo _____

5. Mi tío(a) _____

6. Mi madre _____

ASÍ SE DICE Counting to 100: *los números de 30 a 100*

¡A PRACTICAR!

WB 2-18 | **Números** Write the numerals that correspond to the following numbers.

MODELO: treinta y cinco
35

1. treinta y dos   _____

2. cincuenta y cinco _____

3. cuarenta y nueve _____

4. noventa y nueve _____

5. ochenta y uno   _____

6. setenta y siete   _____

7. sesenta y ocho   _____

8. cien   _____

¡TE TOCA A TI!

WB 2-19 | **Los gastos del mes** *(Monthly expenses)* Think of some of the purchases you make in a typical week. List each item and then write out the dollar amount of the cost of the item. Below is a list of some of the purchases you might make.

| café   comida   discos compactos   libros   películas   pizza   videos |

¿Qué?   **¿Cuánto?**

1. _____   _____ dólares

2. _____   _____ dólares

3. _____   _____ dólares

4. _____   _____ dólares

5. _____   _____ dólares

6. _____   _____ dólares

SÍNTESIS

¡A LEER!

Los anuncios de segunda mano The following are classified ads from a Mexican newspaper that advertise items people would like to sell second-hand.

Strategy: Skimming and scanning

Two useful reading strategies are skimming and scanning. Skimming reading material is useful for quickly getting the gist or general idea of its content, and scanning is used to find specific information in the same material.

Paso 1: ¡OJO! Before beginning, take a minute to think about how much you already know about classified ads. Think about the following:

- What kinds of things do people normally sell second-hand through classified ads?
- What types of information are normally included in these kinds of ads?
- What kind of descriptive words do you expect to see in these ads?

---

1. Rodrigo Salazar de México D.F.

Vendo órgano alemán. Sólo para coleccionistas. Perfecto estado. Valuado en $12,000 pesos. Comunicarse al 5 55 43 687 (noche), o dejar su mensaje en el 5 55 23 103.

---

2. Javier Ortiz Alavez de Ciudad de México, D.F.

Vendo televisión Sony Trinitron 15", control remoto, antena, buen estado. $1,100 pesos. Informes al 5 55 34 153.

---

3. Jorge Sánchez de Ciudad de México, D.F.

Vendo Celular Nokia 232. Batería de larga duración, 2 cargadores de viajero. $1200.00 pesos. Informes al 5 55 07 170.

---

4. Roberto Sosa de México D.F.

Vendo 13 diferentes películas de Walt Disney. Originales en formato VHS, semi nuevas a buen precio. Interesados, favor de comunicarse al 5 55 48 163, en la Ciudad de México.

---

5. Karina Ramírez, Aguas-calientes, México

Vendo Nintendo 64 en buenas condiciones, incluye: consola, dos controles, cartucho Goldeneye 007, aparato para conectarlo directa-mente a la TV sin necesidad de tener VCR. $2500 pesos o su equivalencia en dólares.

Paso 2: Scan the ads and answer the following questions.

1. From what country is Rodrigo Salazar's organ? What kind of condition is it in?

   _____

2. If you were interested in purchasing this instrument, what number should you call? What time of day is it recommended to call?

   _____

3. What countries are these ads from?

   _____

4. What phone number do you call to buy Disney movies?

   _____

¡A ESCRIBIR!

Anuncios personales One of your good friends has been having trouble in the romance department lately and has asked you to help write a personal ad. She/He is very interested in meeting Spanish-speaking people and wants you to write the ad in Spanish. Write the personal ad that will help your friend meet the **amor de sus sueños** (love of his/her dreams).

Strategy: Learning Spanish word order

Word order refers to the meaningful sequence of words in a sentence. The order of words in Spanish sentences differs somewhat from English word order. Some common rules of Spanish word order that were presented to you in the textbook are:

- Definite and indefinite articles precede nouns.
  Los gatos y **los perros** son animales.
  Tengo **un gato** y **un perro.**
- Subjects usually precede their verbs in statements.
  Mi gato es negro.
- Subjects usually follow their verbs in questions.
  ¿**Tiene usted** animales en casa?
- Adjectives of quantity usually precede nouns.
  ¿**Cuántos animales** tienes en casa?
- Adjectives of description usually follow nouns.
  El **perro pardo** (brown) se llama Bandido.
- Possession is often expressed by using **de** with a noun.
  Tigre es **el gato de Sara.**

Paso 1: Unscramble the words in the following sentences and then rewrite them in their correct sequence. Be sure to capitalize the first word of every sentence and end each one with a period. Begin and end each question with appropriate question marks.

> **Functions:** Wrtiting a letter (informal); Introducing; Describing people
> **Vocabulary:** Family members; Numbers; Animals; Domestic; Colors; University
> **Grammar:** Verbs: **ser, tener;** Possession with **de**; Adjectives: agreement, position

MODELO: es Carlos Rodríguez de México
         Carlos Rodríguez es de México.

1. es Ana López una madre

   _____

2. años tiene cuántos ella ¿?

   _____

3. Chino es padre su

   _____

Paso 2: Now think of your ideas for your ad and write a first draft on a separate sheet of paper. Then, review it and write the draft of your paragraph below. Remember to check for correct word order.

_____

_____

_____

_____

_____

_____

_____

Autoprueba

VOCABULARIO

WB 2-20 **Los miembros de la familia** Read the following statements and fill in each blank with a family-related vocabulary word.

1. Mi mamá es la _____ de mi papá.

2. El hijo de mi tío es mi _____.

3. Me llamo Antonio Casagrande. Casagrande es mi _____.

4. La hija de mi hermano es mi _____.

5. Los hijos de mi hija son mis _____.

WB 2-21 **Descripciones** Describe the following people and animals by completing each sentence with the appropriate form of the verb **ser,** as well as the appropriate form of the adjective in parentheses. Make any changes necessary so that the adjectives agree in number and gender with the person or animal they are describing.

1. Salma Hayek _____ una actriz _____ (mexicano).

2. Michael Jordan y yo _____ personas _____ (simpático).

3. Ace Ventura y Austin Powers _____ hombres _____ (tonto).

4. Tú _____ una persona _____ (atlético).

5. Hillary Rodham Clinton _____ una mujer bastante _____ (paciente).

WB 2-22 **Probablemente son...** Your new friend, Andrés, is describing different friends and family members. Read his descriptions and then write the adjective that best matches each description in the space provided. **¡OJO!** Do not use the same adjective more than once.

1. Iliana y Rafael trabajan diez horas al día. Probablemente son _____.

2. Eva estudia filosofía y las ciencias. Estudia y lee libros todo el día. Probablemente es

   _____.

3. Carlos tiene mucho dinero, pero nunca gasta dinero. Probablemente es _____.

4. Belén usa mucho su tarjeta de crédito, pero nunca paga sus facturas (*pays her bills*). Probable-

   mente es _____.

5. Mi hija nunca limpia su cuarto y nunca estudia. Probablemente es _____.

6. Adán y Lupe comen mucho y nunca hacen ejercicios (*exercise*). Probablemente son

   _____.

WB 2-23 **Los números** Write out the numbers that correspond to the following numerals.

1. 32 _____   5. 15 _____

2. 99 _____   6. 17 _____

3. 24 _____   7. 46 _____

4. 12 _____   8. 79 _____

ESTRUCTURA

WB 2-24 | **Una conversación** Complete the following conversation with the appropriate forms of the verb **tener**, as well as the appropriate possessive adjectives.

PILAR: ¿**1.** _____ tú una familia pequeña o grande, Lola?

LOLA: **2.** _____ familia es grande. Yo **3.** _____ cuatro hermanas.

PILAR: ¿No **4.** _____ hermanos?

LOLA: No, **5.** _____ padres **6.** _____ cinco hijas.

PILAR: Pues, tus padres también **7.** _____ un gato. ¿Cómo se llama

    8. _____ gato?

LOLA: **9.** _____ gato se llama Pipo.

PILAR: ¡Pipo! **10.** _____ razón. ¡Qué gato más lindo!

LOLA: Oye, Pilar. Yo **11.** _____ hambre. Vamos a (*Let's go*) comer algo.

    ¿**12.** _____ hambre tú?

PILAR: No, pero **13.** _____ sed. Yo voy contigo (*I will go with you*).

WB 2-25 | **En la universidad** Complete the following conversation between Diana and Tomás with the appropriate verb form.

creer	deberv	escribir	recibir	tener	vivir

TOMÁS: ¿Dónde **1.** _____, Diana?

DIANA: Yo **2.** _____ con mi tía aquí en D.F. pero mi familia **3.** _____ en Guadalajara.

TOMÁS: ¿Les **4.** _____ muchas cartas a tus padres?

DIANA: Sí, de vez en cuando (*once in a while*). Y tú, Tomás, ¿les **5.** _____ muchas cartas a tus padres?

TOMÁS: No, pero yo **6.** _____ muchas cartas de mis padres. Yo **7.** _____ escribir más.

DIANA: Tú **8.** _____ razón. ¡Yo **9.** _____ en la importancia de la correspondencia escrita!

El tiempo libre: Colombia

VOCABULARIO Los deportes y los pasatiempos

¡A PRACTICAR!

WB 3-1 | **Juanjo el increíble** *(the incredible)* Juanjo likes to do it all and tells us about it, too! Look at the pictures of Juanjo doing many of his favorite activities and write the letter of the picture that corresponds to each description.

_____ 1. Me gusta patinar en línea.	_____ 6. Me gusta caminar por las montañas.
_____ 2. Me gusta montar a caballo.	_____ 7. Me gusta jugar al golf.
_____ 3. Me gusta ir a la discoteca.	_____ 8. Me gusta hacer ejercicio.
_____ 4. Me gusta esquiar.	_____ 9. Me gusta visitar el museo.
_____ 5. Me gusta el ciclismo.	_____ 10. Me gusta ir de compras.

¡TE TOCA A TI!

WB 3-2 | **Pasarlo bien** Several of the new Spanish-speaking exchange students at your university want to know about day and evening leisure activities that you can do in your town. Write out these activities below. Follow the model.

Durante (*During*) **el día**	**Por la noche**
MODELO: *Dar un paseo*	*Ir a un concierto*

1. _____   _____

2. _____   _____

3. _____   _____

4. _____   _____

ESTRUCTURA I Expressing likes and dislikes: *gustar* + infinitive and *gustar* + nouns

¡A PRACTICAR!

WB 3-3 | **Gustos famosos** Alex Villalobos, manager of an exclusive hotel for the rich and famous, discusses the likes and dislikes of some of his most famous guests. Use the indirect object pronouns **me, te, le, nos,** or **les** to find out what he has to say.

Nuestro hotel sí es popular con la gente más conocida (*best known*) del mundo. A todos los

famosos **1.** _____ gusta pasar por lo menos (*at least*) una semana aquí. Tenemos

clientes políticos, como el vicepresidente. A él **2.** _____ gusta bailar en la discoteca

toda la noche. Pero él no es el único cliente político. El expresidente visita también. A él no

3. _____ gusta bailar en la discoteca, pues prefiere practicar deportes. Por ejemplo, a

él **4.** _____ gusta jugar al tenis.

　　A mí **5.** _____ gustan los clientes políticos, pero prefiero las estrellas de cine. A

ellos **6.** _____ gusta hacer muchas actividades divertidas conmigo (*with me*). Por

ejemplo, a Madonna y a mí **7.** _____ gusta montar a caballo, andar en bicicleta, pati-

nar en línea y pescar.

WB 3-4 | **Mis preferencias** Ignacio Casaverde is looking for a Spanish-speaking sports partner, and he posted the following message on your gym bulletin board. Complete his message by se- lecting the correct verb form.

Hola, soy Iggi. En general me **1.** (gusta / gustan) los deportes como el tenis y el baloncesto, pero

me **2.** (gusta / gustan) más el ciclismo y el hockey. No me **3.** (gusta / gustan) la pesca porque es

aburrida (*boring*). Los viernes por la mañana a mi hermano y a mí nos **4.** (gusta / gustan) ir al

gimnasio a levantar pesas. Los sábados por la mañana nos **5.** (gusta / gustan) jugar al fútbol. Por

la tarde a mí me **6.** (gusta / gustan) jugar al billar. A mi hermano le **7.** (gusta / gustan) más las

cartas (*cards*), pero no juega conmigo. Los domingos no me **8.** (gusta / gustan) practicar ningún

deporte porque a mi esposa le **9.** (gusta / gustan) ir de compras y no hay tiempo para jugar. Y a ti,

¿qué te **10.** (gusta / gustan) hacer?

¡TE TOCA A TI!

WB 3-5 | **Una carta para Iggi** Respond to Iggi's message in activity **WB 3-4** by describing some of the sports and pastimes that you do and do not like. Also tell him when and with whom you typically do those activities.

_____

_____

_____

_____

_____

VOCABULARIO Los lugares

¡A PRACTICAR!

WB 3-6 | **¿Adónde va uno (one) para... ?** Answer the following questions using the appropriate place names. Follow the model.

MODELO: ¿Adónde va uno para mandar una carta?
A la oficina de correos.

1. ¿Adónde va uno para ver una película *(movie)*?

_____.

2. ¿Adónde va uno para nadar?

_____.

3. ¿Adónde va uno para hacer las compras *(do shopping)*, hablar con amigos o tomar algo?

_____.

4. ¿Adónde va uno para sacar *(take out)* dinero?

_____.

5. ¿Adónde va uno para ver arte?

_____.

6. ¿Adónde va uno para bailar?

_____.

7. ¿Adónde va uno para comprar comida?

_____.

8. ¿Adónde va uno para jugar al fútbol?

_____.

9. ¿Adónde va uno para tomar café?

_____.

10. ¿Adónde va uno para cenar con amigos?

_____.

¡TE TOCA A TI!

WB 3-7 | **Para conocer *(to know)* la ciudad** A friend wants to know about interesting places in your town. Answer his questions in complete sentences in Spanish.

1. ¿Cómo se llama la calle principal de la ciudad?

   _____

2. ¿Cuántas películas hay en el cine de la ciudad?

   _____

3. ¿Hay una plaza en la ciudad? ¿En qué calle está?

   _____

4. ¿A cuántas cuadras *(blocks)* de tu casa está el mercado al aire libre?

   _____

5. ¿Cómo se llama el mejor restaurante de la ciudad?

   _____

6. ¿Tocan música en los cafés de la ciudad? ¿En cuáles?

   _____

ESTRUCTURA II Expressing plans with *ir: ir a* + destination, and *ir a* + infinitive

¡A PRACTICAR!

WB 3-8 | **Compañeros de cuarto** You and your roommates have busy lives. Based on the following calendar page, describe in complete sentences what everyone is going to do and when (day and time). Follow the model.

MODELO: Eugenia y Cati
Eugenia y Cati van al cine el lunes a las tres de la tarde.

lunes 17	jueves 20	sábado 22
Eugenia y Cati: cine, 3 p.m.	Ángel, iglesia: 9 a.m.–1 p.m.	Carlos y yo: cenar y bailar, 9:00 p.m.
Carlos: sacar fotos con Silvia, 11:00 a.m.		
martes 18	**viernes 21**	**domingo 23**
Alberto: plaza, 8 p.m.	Eugenia: mercado al aire libre, 5 p.m.	Ángel, Carlos y Eugenia: jugar cartas, 2 p.m.
miércoles 19		
Yo: comer con mis padres, 1 p.m.		

1. Carlos y Silvia

_____.

2. Alberto

_____.

3. Carlos y yo

_____.

4. Ángel, Carlos y Eugenia

_____.

5. Eugenia

_____.

6. Ángel

_____.

7. yo

_____.

¡TE TOCA A TI!

WB 3-9 **¿Qué va a hacer?** Using the space below, create a calendar page from the life of your favorite latino icon. Where will he or she go? What will he or she do? With whom will he or she do it? Fill out at least five dates with complete sentences. **Escribe estas actividades en oraciones completas.** ¡OJO! Use **ir a** + infinitive or **ir a** + destination.

Agenda personal de: _____		
FEBRERO		
lunes **10**	jueves **13**	sábado **15**
martes **11**	viernes **14**	domingo **16**
miércoles **12**		

ESTRUCTURA III Describing leisure activities: verbs with irregular *yo* forms

¡A PRACTICAR!

WB 3-10 | **El profesor excéntrico** Paco Empacanueces is the Colombian "Nutty Professor." Find out what his strange habits are by building sentences using the words below. Follow the model and be careful to add prepositions where necessary.

> Modelo: yo / traer / comida / mis clases
> *Yo traigo comida a mis clases.*

1. todos los días / yo / salir de la casa / cuatro de la mañana

   _____

2. yo / hacer ejercicio / el parque

   _____

3. allí *(there)* / yo / ver / a mis amigos

   _____

4. yo / traer / discos compactos / universidad

   _____

5. yo / poner / música de Metállica / mi oficina

   _____

6. yo / dar fiestas / por la mañana

   _____

7. yo / conocer / a todos mis colegas / la universidad

   _____

8. pero / yo / no saber / su nombre

   _____

WB 3-11 | **Los sábados** Mercedes likes to spend her Saturdays with friends. Complete the following paragraph with the appropriate form of the verb in parentheses to find out what she does.

Los sábados por la mañana me gusta pasear por la ciudad. Normalmente yo **1.** _____ (salir) de mi casa temprano para ir al mercado al aire libre. Allí **2.** _____ (ver) a mis amigos y todos **3.** _____ (hacer) las compras juntos.

Mi amiga Lilián siempre **4.** _____ (traer) a sus hermanos, Fabián y Santi. Ellos **5.** _____ (conocer) a todos los vendedores *(vendors)* del mercado y por eso nosotros compramos a muy buenos precios.

Después de ir al mercado mis amigos y yo **6.** _____ (dar) una vuelta (*go around*) por el centro. Muchas veces vamos al museo de arte. Mi amiga Silvia **7.** _____ (saber) mucho del arte y me gusta ir con ella. Otras veces vamos a un café muy especial que yo

8. _____ (conocer). En este café, el dueño (*owner*) siempre **9.** _____ (poner) música reggae y todos bailamos.

¡TE TOCA A TI!

| **WB 3-12** | **Entrevista** To practice your Spanish you decide to find a Spanish-speaking roommate. Your prospective new roommate is from Medellín and asks you the following questions. Respond in complete sentences.

1. ¿Sabe Ud. cocinar?

   _____

2. ¿Dan muchas fiestas Ud. y sus amigos?

   _____

3. Normalmente, ¿qué hace Ud. los fines de semana?

   _____

4. ¿Conoce a mucha gente hispana?

   _____

5. ¿Pone música en la casa por la mañana?

   _____

6. ¿A qué hora sale de la casa por la mañana?

   _____

¡A PRACTICAR!

WB 3-13 **Y ahora...** It's now your turn to interview your future Spanish-speaking roommate. Complete the following questions with the correct form of the verb **saber** or **conocer**. Since in many parts of Colombia the **usted** form is used instead of **tú,** make sure to use this form in the activity.

1. ¿_____a muchas personas aquí?

2. ¿_____jugar al tenis?

3. ¿_____cocinar bien?

4. ¿_____a los dueños *(owners)* del apartamento?

5. ¿_____qué tiendas están cerca *(close by)*?

WB 3-14 **Los abuelos de Camila** To find out what Camila's grandparents are like, complete the phrases with the correct form of **saber** or **conocer.**

CAMILA: Diego, Ud. **1.** _____ tocar muy bien la guitarra.

DIEGO: Gracias, Camila, pero también Ud. **2.** _____ tocar el piano y cantar muy bien.

CAMILA: ¡Gracias! Oiga, ¿quiere **3.** _____ a mis abuelos? Mi abuela toca el tambor en una banda de rock metálico y mi abuelo canta con un grupo de música punk.

DIEGO: Sí, con mucho gusto. Yo **4.** _____ que ellos tienen como 80 años, ¿no?

CAMILA: Sí, es cierto, ¡pero todavía *(still)* **5.** _____ vivir!

DIEGO: Bueno, quiero **6.** _____ a tus abuelos. ¡Voy a aprender mucho de ellos!

En tu opinión, ¿cómo son los abuelos de Camila? ¿Son como tus abuelos?

_____

_____

¡TE TOCA A TI!

WB 3-15 **Yo...** Are the following statements about you true (T) or false (F)?

_____ **1.** Yo sé hablar más de dos idiomas.

_____ **2.** Conozco a un deportista famoso.

_____ **3.** Mis amigos y yo sabemos jugar al jai-alai.

_____ **4.** Mi madre conoce a Shakira.

_____ **5.** Yo sé correr las olas.

ASÍ SE DICE Talking about the months, seasons, and the weather

¡A PRACTICAR!

WB 3-16 **Estaciones y meses** Write the season, the months of that season (in the Northern Hemisphere), and the weather that each drawing represents.

1. Estación: _____

Meses de la estación:

_____

El tiempo: _____

_____

2. Estación: _____

Meses de la estación:

_____

El tiempo: _____

_____

3. Estación: _____

Meses de la estación:

_____

El tiempo: _____

_____

4. Estación: _____

Meses de la estación:

_____

El tiempo: _____

_____

Las condiciones en el Tolima Consult the following
weather report for Tolima, Colombia, and answer the questions
in complete sentences.

Condiciones actuales: Tolima, Colombia	
Temperatura	77° F
Humedad	84%
Viento	0–6 mph
Condiciones	neblina
Visibilidad	6 millas

1. ¿Qué tiempo hace hoy en el Tolima?

   _____

   _____

2. ¿Hace mucho viento hoy en el Tolima?

   _____

   _____

3. ¿Es un buen día para esquiar? ¿Por qué?

   _____

   _____

4. ¿Qué tiempo hace hoy en tu ciudad?

   _____

   _____

¡TE TOCA A TI!

WB 3-18 | **¿Qué te gusta hacer en... ?** Using complete sentences, write out which activities you like to do in the months of the following seasons. Follow the model.

MODELO: En la primavera
En marzo me gusta patinar en línea.
En abril y mayo me gusta caminar en el jardín.

1. En el invierno

_____
_____
_____
_____

2. En la primavera

_____
_____
_____
_____

3. En el verano

_____
_____
_____
_____

4. En el otoño

_____
_____
_____
_____

SÍNTESIS

¡A LEER!

EL CARIBE COLOMBIANO In a travel agency you find the following brochure about Santa Marta, a tourist resort in the Colombian Caribbean.

Strategy: Using context to predict content

Efficient readers use effective strategies for guessing the meaning of unfamiliar words and phrases in a reading selection. Some of these strategies are:

• Readers rely on what they already know about the reading topic (background information).
• Readers guess what the selection will be about (prediction).
• Readers use the ideas they understand in the passage (context).

Paso 1: What type of information do tourist brochures usually contain?

_____

_____

Paso 2: Look at the brochure's graphics and titles. Based on what you see, make a list of the kind of information you expect to find in this brochure.

_____

_____

Paso 3: Now read the brochure over once. Then, go back and read it a second time, this time underlining the sections that provide information that answers any of the questions you listed in **Paso 2**.

Paso 4: Now check your comprehension by answering the following questions in Spanish.

1. Describe qué tiempo hace en Santa Marta normalmente.

   _____

   _____

2. ¿Qué actividades puede hacer el turista en Santa Marta?

   _____

   _____

3. ¿Qué actividades puede hacer el turista en el Rodadero?

   _____

   _____

4. ¿Qué otros sitios interesantes están cerca de Santa Marta?

   _____

   _____

5. ¿Dónde puede encontrar el turista más información sobre Santa Marta?

   _____

   _____

6. ¿Te va a gustar visitar Santa Marta? ¿Por qué?

   _____

   _____

Nombre _____ Fecha _____

¡BIENVENIDOS A SANTA MARTA!

Conocida internacionalmente, Santa Marta constituye, sin duda, una de las principales atracciones turísticas de Colombia. Como demuestra[1] el siguiente mapa, esta hermosa ciudad está situada al pie de la Sierra Nevada de Santa Marta y sobre una de las más hermosas bahías del Caribe. Esta ciudad tiene un clima privilegiado por las suaves brisas de la montaña. Es, además, punto de partida para visitar los numerosos sitios de interés de sus alrededores,[2] donde abundan las oportunidades para descansar, practicar deportes o hacer el turismo arqueológico, ecológico y de aventura.

PLAYA Y MAR

Muy cerca de Santa Marta el visitante tiene lugares ideales para la recreación y el descanso, algunos modernos y otros más primitivos. El principal centro turístico es El Rodadero, sólo a diez minutos de la ciudad. Es un lugar ideal donde las playas blancas y las aguas azules y transparentes se mezclan[3] con los colores vivos y la música de la costa caribe. En Rodadero vale la pena[4] visitar el Acuario y Museo del Mar.

OTROS PUNTOS DE INTERÉS

Parque Tairona

- Parque nacional con playas solitarias ideales para tomar el sol.
- En una de las playas hay diez «ecohabs», unas cabañas rústicas para acampar.

Vestigios arqueológicos

- La Sierra Nevada de Santa Marta constituye un ecosistema único en el mundo y es hábitat de comunidades de indígenas Kogis, Arhuacos y Arsarios.
- Aquí uno puede ver las reliquias arqueológicas más importantes de Colombia.

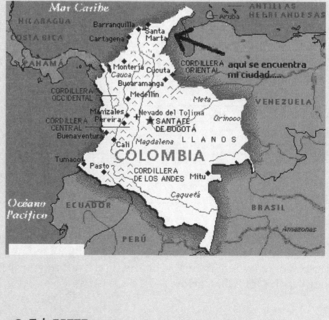

INFORMACIÓN ÚTIL

Temperatura promedio: 28° C
Indicativo telefónico: (954)
Acceso: Por vía aérea al Aeropuerto Simón Bolívar

INFORMACIÓN TURÍSTICA

Corporación Nacional de Turismo, Edif. del Claustro del Seminario, Carrera 2, Tel. 35773

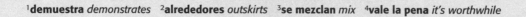

[1]**demuestra** *demonstrates*   [2]**alrededores** *outskirts*   [3]**se mezclan** *mix*   [4]**vale la pena** *it's worthwhile*

¡A ESCRIBIR!

MIS PLANES PARA EL VERANO Your friend Carlos wrote to tell you about his summer vacation plans, and he wants to know what you are doing. Write him back and tell him about all of your summer plans.

Strategy: Combining sentences

Learning to combine simple sentences into more complex ones can help you improve your writing style immensely. In Spanish, there are several words you can use as connectors to combine sentences and phrases.

y	*and* (**y** becomes **e** before **i, hi** or **y**)
que	*that, which, who*
pero	*but*
o	*or* (**o** becomes **u** before **o** or **ho**)
porque	*because*

Before you begin to write, follow these steps.

Paso 1: Write a few basic sentences about your plans for summer.

Este verano yo _____.

Este verano yo _____.

Este verano yo _____.

Este verano yo _____.

Este verano yo _____.

Paso 2: Connect some of these sentences with **y, o, pero,** or **que** to make more complex sentences.

_____

_____

_____

_____

_____

Functions: Writing a letter (informal); Describing people; Talking about the present *Vocabulary:* Sports; Leisure; Board games; Family members; Animals; Domestic; University *Grammar:* Verbs: **ser, tener, conocer,** and **saber;** Verbs: Future with **ir;** Article: contractions **al, del**

Paso 3: Now that you have all your ideas organized, write a first draft on a separate sheet of paper. Then, review it and write the final draft of your letter with complete sentences. You can begin with **Querido Carlos:**

Autoprueba

VOCABULARIO

WB 3-19 **Los meses y las estaciones** In the first column write the Spanish names for the months in which the following U.S. holidays are celebrated. In the second, write the season in which the holiday falls.

1. Christmas _____ _____

2. Valentine's Day _____ _____

3. New Year's Day _____ _____

4. Halloween _____ _____

5. Memorial Day _____ _____

6. Thanksgiving _____ _____

WB 3-20 **En la ciudad** Write the letter of the description next to the place where you would most likely do that activity.

_____ 1. un museo   a. aprender historia

_____ 2. una plaza   b. comprar comida

_____ 3. el mercado   c. mandar una carta

_____ 4. un banco   d. sacar dinero

_____ 5. la oficina de correos   e. comer algo

_____ 6. la piscina   f. nadar

_____ 7. el restaurante   g. hablar con los amigos

ESTRUCTURA

WB 3-21 **Pasatiempos** State your pastimes by matching a verb with an appropriate phrase in the second column and forming a complete sentence. Follow the model.

MODELO: hacer   ejercicio
        Me gusta hacer ejercicio.

ver	fotos
sacar	la guitarra
jugar	al tenis
tocar	a mis abuelos
bailar	con música rock
visitar	películas en video

1. _____

2. _____

3. _____

4. _____

5. _____

6. _____

WB 3-22 **Entre amigos** Complete the following conversation with the appropriate forms of the verb **ir.**

IRENE: ¿Adónde **1.** _____ tú este fin de semana?

CARLOS: **2.** _____ al parque para estudiar. ¿Por qué no **3.** _____ conmigo?

IRENE: No, gracias. Mi mamá y yo **4.** _____ de compras.

CARLOS: ¿No **5.** _____ tu papá con Uds.?

IRENE: No, porque mi papá, Raúl y Sara **6.** _____ al cine.

WB 3-23 **Un joven contento** Complete the paragraph with the **yo** form of the appropriate verb from the list.

conocer	saber	ver	dar	salir	estar	hacer	ir	poner

Yo **1.** _____ con mis amigos frecuentemente. **2.** _____ muchas cosas con ellos, y normalmente yo **3.** _____ a fiestas con estos amigos. También, a veces **4.** _____ fiestas en mi casa con ellos. **5.** _____ mucha música rock y todo el mundo baila. **6.** _____ a muchas personas y **7.** _____ que a todos mis amigos les gusta estar en mis fiestas. Los domingos **8.** _____ a mis abuelos y comemos juntos. La verdad es que *(the truth is that)* **9.** _____ muy contento.

WB 3-24 **¿Qué vas a hacer?** Match each verb with an appropriate phrase to form a complete sentence with **ir a** + infinitive. Follow the model.

MODELO: visitar un museo
         Yo voy a visitar un museo.

practicar   al tenis
jugar   a caballo
nadar   en la piscina
montar   pesas
levantar   deportes

1. _____

2. _____

3. _____

4. _____

5. _____

¿Qué tiempo hace? Describe the weather depicted in each of the following scenes.

A. _____

B. _____

C. _____

D. _____

E. _____

F. _____

En la casa: España

VOCABULARIO La casa

¡A PRACTICAR!

WB 4-1 **Sopa *(soup)* de letras** Unscramble the letters to reveal the name of a household item. Then write where in the house that item is typically found. Follow the model.

MODELO: MACA

Palabra	Lugar de la casa
cama	*dormitorio*

	Palabra	**Lugar de la casa**
1. MRRAIOA	_____	_____
2. ORDONIO	_____	_____
3. SEMA	_____	_____
4. ÁFSO	_____	_____
5. REBAÑA	_____	_____
6. NÓLISL	_____	_____
7. DAHUC	_____	_____
8. AMÓDOC	_____	_____

WB 4-2 **En la agencia de bienes raíces *(real estate)*** Which house will you rent? Match the letter of each picture with its description. Then, in each drawing write the names of the items mentioned in its description.

A

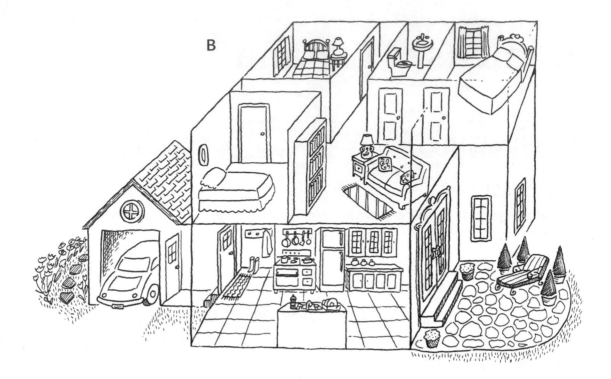

B

C

_____ 1. Esta casa tiene tres dormitorios, un baño y una sala que están en el segundo piso. La sala está amueblada *(furnished)* con un sofá y un estante para libros. En el primer piso, hay una cocina grande con una puerta muy elegante que da a un patio grande. La casa también tiene un jardín pequeño que está al lado del garaje.

_____ 2. Esta casa de dos pisos tiene tres dormitorios, un baño, una cocina y una sala. La sala está en el primer piso. Está amueblada con dos sillones, un sofá, una lámpara y una alfombra nueva. Una de las paredes de la sala tiene un espejo pequeño. También en la sala hay una escalera elegante para llegar al segundo piso. Los dormitorios y el cuarto de baño están en el segundo piso. La casa no tiene garaje, pero tiene un patio grande.

_____ 3. Esta casa tiene tres dormitorios, una cocina y un cuarto de baño con inodoro y lavabo. La casa también tiene una sala grande que está amueblada con tres sillones y una lámpara. Esta casa tiene muchas ventanas que dan al *(look out on the)* patio pequeño. Al lado del *(Next to the)* patio hay un jardín grande con muchas flores. La casa también tiene un sótano y un garaje pequeño.

WB 4-3 **¿Para qué es esto?** Select the name of the appliance described in each statement.

_____ 1. Es para preparar la comida rápidamente.

    a. la estufa   **b.** el horno de microondas   **c.** la tostadora

_____ 2. Es para limpiar la alfombra.

    a. la aspiradora   **b.** la plancha   **c.** la secadora

_____ 3. Es para quitar arrugas *(wrinkles)* de la ropa.

    a. el despertador   b. el refrigerador   c. la plancha

_____ 4. Es necesario usarla después de lavar la ropa.

    a. el lavaplatos   **b.** el horno de mircoondas   **c.** la secadora

---

WB 4-4 **Una venta** Stella and José are moving in together and trying to organize their things. They have several of the same items and will need to sell one. Help them organize their things by writing the name of the items under the appropriate category. Remember they will sell what they have two of. Follow the model.

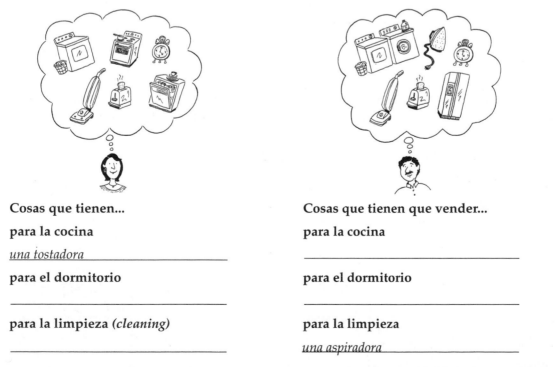

Cosas que tienen...

para la cocina

una tostadora _____

para el dormitorio

_____

para la limpieza *(cleaning)*

_____

Cosas que tienen que vender...

para la cocina

_____

para el dormitorio

_____

para la limpieza

una aspiradora _____

¡TE TOCA A TI!

WB 4-5 | **Decisiones** Look at the houses described in activity **WB 4-2**. Select the one you would most like to rent and make a list of the characteristics that you find most appealing.

1. La casa que más me gusta es _____.

2. Me gustan más las siguientes características:

_____

_____

_____

WB 4-6 | **¿Moderno(a)?** Just how modern are you? For each appliance below write a sentence using a word from the list provided to describe the frequency with which you typically use the appliance. Then, follow the instructions to measure your level of modernity. Follow the model.

MODELO: la aspiradora
Casi nunca uso la aspiradora.

a veces *(sometimes)* **casi nunca** *(almost never)* **nunca** *(never)* **todos los días**

1. la aspiradora

_____

2. el lavaplatos

_____

3. la secadora

_____

4. la plancha

_____

5. el refrigerador

_____

6. el horno de microondas

_____

Para cada electrodoméstico que usas todos los días, date *(give yourself)* 10 puntos. Para cada uno que usas a veces, date 6 puntos. Para cada uno que usas casi nunca, date 4 puntos y para cada uno que nunca usas, date 1 punto.

Suma *(Add)* tus puntos y busca tu medida de modernidad.

Puntos _____

50–70: Persona moderna
25–49: ¡Bienvenido(a) al siglo XIX!
7–24: Antimáquina total

Nombre _____ Fecha _____

ESTRUCTURA I Describing household chores and other activities: present tense of stem-changing verbs *(e → ie: o → ue: e → i)*

¡A PRACTICAR!

WB 4-7 **¡Qué compañeros!** Paqui lives in a colegio mayor *(dorm)* in Madrid and is always complaining about her roommates. To find out what she says, complete the following sentences with an appropriate form of a verb from the list below.

cerrar	comenzar	pedir	perder	regar	venir

1. Tomás siempre _____ favores *(favors)*.

2. El día de Santi _____ a las 3:00 de la mañana.

3. Lola y Eva siempre _____ sus llaves *(keys)*.

4. Carlos nunca _____ las plantas.

5. Los amigos de Amparo _____ a visitar muy tarde.

6. Belén nunca _____ la boca *(mouth)*.

WB 4-8 **Los Adanes** The Adanes are the Spanish version of the Addams family—a little creepy and kooky. Today the daughter, Miércoles, is giving an oral report on her family life. Form complete sentences with the words below to find out what she says.

1. mi papá / siempre / jugar / con una espada *(sword)*

_____

2. mi tío Fester / dormir / en una cama de clavos *(nails)*

_____

3. mi madre Morticia / siempre / volver a casa / con plantas muertas *(dead)*

_____

4. nosotros / almorzar / a las 2:00 de la mañana

_____

5. mi hermano Pugilio / poder / dormir con los ojos abiertos

_____

¡TE TOCA A TI!

WB 4-9 **Intercambio cultural** Your Spanish pen pal, Socorro, has a lot of questions for you about student life in the U.S. Answer her questions in complete sentences.

1. ¿A qué hora comienza tu primera clase? _____

2. ¿Prefieren Uds. (los estudiantes) vivir en una casa, un apartamento o una residencia

   estudiantil? _____

3. ¿Almuerzas en el campus? _____

4. ¿Pueden tomar alcohol en su campus? _____

5. ¿Cuántas clases tienes? _____

6. ¿Qué piensas de tus profesores? _____

ASÍ SE DICE Expressing physical conditions, desires, and obligations with *tener*

¡A PRACTICAR!

WB 4-10 | **La familia Ortega** To learn more about the Ortega family, complete the following sentences with the correct form of an appropriate **tener** expression. Note that you already know some of the **tener** expressions from **Capítulo 2.**

tener años	tener miedo	tener celos	tener paciencia	tener frío
tener prisa	tener ganas	tener sed	tener hambre	tener sueño

1. María Elena _____. Ella va a descansar en el sofá por media hora.

2. Chús está enferma, pero su mamá no sabe qué hacer. Ella _____.

3. Beti y Tomás son jóvenes. Ella _____ 14 _____ y

   él _____ 18 _____.

4. Juanjo _____ porque son las 8:45 y él debe llegar a su trabajo a las 9:00.

5. Esta noche Elena va a salir a comer con Eduardo, un viejo amigo del colegio. Ahora el novio

   de Elena _____ de Eduardo.

6. Carlos es un travieso *(rascal)*, pero su mamá _____ mucha _____ con él.

7. Silvia va al cine. _____ de ver la nueva película de Almodóvar.

¡TE TOCA A TI!

WB 4-11 | **Prueba de compatibilidad** Take the following compatibility test to find out if you and your best friend/girlfriend/boyfriend are truly compatible. Answer the questions in complete sentences and then calculate your points as indicated.

1. ¿Cuántos años tienes? ¿Cuántos años tiene tu novio(a) o compañero(a)?

   _____

2. ¿Siempre tienen Uds. muchas ganas de hacer las mismas cosas?

   _____

3. Cuando tienes hambre, ¿qué te gusta comer? ¿Y a tu novio(a) o compañero(a)?

   _____

4. ¿De qué tienen miedo Uds.?

   _____

5. ¿Tienes celos cuando tu novio(a) o compañero(a) pasa tiempo con otra persona?

   _____

6. ¿Tienen Uds. mucha paciencia?

   _____

Puntería Calcula tus puntos según las siguientes instrucciones.

Pregunta 1
25 puntos por tener la misma edad; 15 puntos por tener entre 1 y 5 años de diferencia de edad; 10 puntos por tener entre 6 y 10 años de diferencia de edad; 5 puntos por tener más de 10 años de diferencia

Pregunta 2
25 puntos si contestas que sí; 5 puntos si contestas que no

Preguntas 3 y 4
20 puntos (cada pregunta) si la respuesta es la misma para las dos personas; 10 puntos (cada pregunta) si la respuesta es diferente para las dos personas

Pregunta 5
20 puntos si contestas que no; 5 puntos si contestas que sí

Pregunta 6
25 puntos si contestas que sí; 5 puntos si contestas que no

Puntos en total: ____
100–135: ¡Prácticamente gemelos *(twins)*! Uds. son demasiado compatibles. ¡Cuidado!
  55–99: ¡Como anillo *(ring)* al dedo *(finger)*! Tienen una relación bastante equilibrada.
  45–54: ¡Adiós, amigo(a)! Tienes que buscar otro(a) novio(a), compañero(a) o amigo(a).

VOCABULARIO Los quehaceres domésticos

¡A PRACTICAR!

WB 4-12 | **Entrevista** Mariana is talking to her friend about her chores. Look at her answers and write the question that Mariana most likely asked. **¡OJO!** Remember some of the question words you have already learned. Follow the model.

> MODELO: ¿Cuándo te gusta barrer el piso?
> *Me gusta barrer el piso por la mañana.*

1. ¿_____?

  Sí, pongo la mesa todos los días.

2. ¿_____?

  No, no me gusta planchar la ropa.

3. ¿_____?

  Mi hermano riega las plantas.

4. ¿_____?

  No, no tenemos que lavar las ventanas.

5. ¿_____?

  Sí, hago mi cama todos los días.

De vacaciones Pedro asked you to house-sit for him while he is on vacation, but he left you an incomplete list of chores to do. Complete the list with the chores that he most likely wants you to do in each place indicated. Follow the model.

En la cocina

barrer el piso
_____

_____

En el dormitorio

_____

_____

En toda la casa

_____

_____

En el jardín

_____

_____

¡TE TOCA A TI!

WB 4-14 **En tu casa** Now you are going on vacation and need to make a list of chores for Pedro to do while watching your house. Also, let him know with what frequency he should do each chore (**todos los días, solamente los sábados, nunca,** etc.). Write your list below.

Tienes que...

_____

_____

_____

_____

_____

_____

_____

ESTRUCTURA II Expressing preferences and giving advice: affirmative *tú* commands

WB 4-15   **Las reglas** Ana has just moved into the sorority house and her house mother is telling her the rules of the house. To find out what she says, write **tú** commands with the following phrases.

MODELO: Llegar a casa antes de las once de la noche.
Llega a casa antes de las once de la noche.

1. Leer los anuncios del día.

   _____

2. Limpiar tu habitación una vez a la semana.

   _____

3. Hablar con tus hermanas.

   _____

4. Regar las plantas del jardín todos los lunes.

   _____

5. Cantar nuestra canción con tus hermanas.

   _____

WB 4-16   **Mari Mandona** Mari Mandona always has advice for all of her friends. For each of her friend's problems listed in the left-hand column, write the letter of Mari's advice listed in the right-hand column.

1. _____ Tengo que limpiar toda la casa hoy.

2. _____ No me gusta estar en casa.

3. _____ No me gusta mi nuevo compañero de casa.

4. _____ No tengo comida en la casa.

5. _____ Quiero visitarte.

6. _____ Soy muy mala.

7. _____ La universidad ya no tiene habitaciones disponibles *(available)* en la residencia.

8. _____ Tengo un secreto.

a. Ven a mi casa.

b. Dime

c. Haz un buen trabajo.

d Pon tu nombre en la lista de espera *(waiting list).*

e. Sé buena.

f. Sal de la casa.

g. Ve al supermercado.

h. Ten paciencia con él.

¡TE TOCA A TI!

WB 4-17 | **Y tú, ¿qué dices?** You have just been hired to write the advice column of your university's newspaper. What advice will you give to the following people? For each situation, write a different **tú** command. Follow the model.

> MODELO: Una mujer mayor que quiere conocer a hombre jóvenes.
> *Ve a muchos partidos de fútbol.*

1. Una chica que quiere vivir en la residencia estudiantil.

   _____

2. Un chico que quiere vivir en Argentina.

   _____

3. Un chico que quiere saber cómo sacar buenas notas.

   _____

4. Una chica que no sabe qué llevar a una fiesta latina.

   _____

5. Un chico que nunca dice la verdad.

   _____

WB 4-18 | **Pobre amigo** Think about some of your friends and the problems for which they sought your advice. Describe five problems and then write five **tú** commands to give as advice for each problem. Use different verbs each time. Follow the model.

> MODELO: Descripción de problema: *Juan nunca tiene dinero.*
> Tus recomendaciones para él/ella: *Trabaja más.*

Descripción de problema:	Tus recomendaciones para él/ella:
_____	_____
_____	_____
_____	_____
_____	_____
_____	_____

ESTRUCTURA III Talking about location, emotional and physical states, and actions in progress: the verb *estar*

¡A PRACTICAR!

WB 4-19 | **Pobre Antonio** Antonio is in Spain to film a movie without his wife, Marta. Help Antonio complete the following letter to Marta by filing in the blanks with the appropriate form of the verb **estar**.

> *Muy querida Marta:*
>
> *¿Cómo _____ tú? ¿Cómo _____ mi hija, Ana? Yo,*
> *pues, _____ muy triste porque tú no _____ aquí.*
> *Ahora _____ en las islas Canarias para filmar una escena de mi*
> *película, «Cinco noches de amor». Julia _____ aquí también y*
> *nosotros dos _____ muy ocupados. Nosotros _____ en*
> *la playa para filmar nuestra escena. Mañana voy a _____ en*
> *las islas Baleares con Victoria. Ella _____ muy guapa estos*
> *días. Como puedes notar, yo _____ muy ocupado. Bueno, me*
> *tengo que ir, pero espero verte a ti (see you) y a Ana muy pronto. Cuando*
> *Uds. no _____ conmigo no puedo vivir.*
>
> *Un beso,*
> *Antonio*

WB 4-20 | **Todos están trabajando** When you arrive at your friend's house, you find that everyone is working except one person. Describe what each person is doing in the pictures using the verb **estar** + the progressive form.

1. Patricio

   _____.

2. Paula

   _____.

3. Angelita

   _____.

4. Esteban

   _____.

5. Carlos

   _____.

6. Francisco y Stella

   _____.

¡TE TOCA A TI!

WB 4-21 **Una carta para Antonio** Now help Marta answer her husband's letter that you saw in activity **WB 4-19.** How is Marta doing after reading her husband's letter? How is she feeling about Antonio working with beautiful women? Describe how she is and feels as you write her letter below.

Hola, Antonio:

_____

_____

_____

_____

_____

_____

_____

_____

_____

_____

_____

Marta

WB 4-22 | **¡Sólo en los sueños (dreams)!** Imagine that you are watching a movie of your ideal life. Write complete sentences to describe what is happening in this movie. Don't forget to use an appropriate form of the present progressive.

_____

_____

_____

_____

_____

_____

ASÍ SE DICE Counting from 100 and higher:
los números de 100 a 1.000.000

¡A PRACTICAR!

WB 4-23 | **Matemáticas** Solve the following math problems. Write out the numbers in words. Follow the model.

MODELO: doscientos cincuenta + tres =
doscientos cincuenta y tres

1. trescientos cuarenta y ocho + quinientos setenta y nueve =

_____

2. doscientos cincuenta y ocho + mil cuatrocientos y tres =

_____

3. mil ochocientos catorce + cinco mil noventa y siete =

_____

WB 4-24 | **Pagando las facturas (bills)** Luis Ángel, an exchange student from Burgos, Spain, is leaving for a long vacation. Because he is such a shopaholic he has a lot of big bills that will come due and needs you to help him keep current with them. Following the notes he left for you, write out the checks to pay his bills.

Hola.
¡Gracias por ayudarme!
Luis Ángel

El Corte Inglés: $536.000 euros
Coches SEAT: $1.117.000 euros
Máximo Dutti: $762.000 euros

Luis Ángel Martín Elordieta	102
c/ Altamirano 9	
Burgos, España	Fecha _____

Páguese por este cheque a: _____

_____Euros.

002659870002687 6698 9897598 7889   *Luis Ángel Martín Elordieta*

Luis Ángel Martín Elordieta	103
c/ Altamirano 9	
Burgos, España	Fecha _____

Páguese por este cheque a: _____

_____Euros.

002659870002687 6698 9897598 7889   *Luis Ángel Martín Elordieta*

Luis Ángel Martín Elordieta	104
c/ Altamirano 9	
Burgos, España	Fecha _____

Páguese por este cheque a: _____

_____Euros.

002659870002687 6698 9897598 7889   *Luis Ángel Martín Elordieta*

¡TE TOCA A TI!

WB 4-25 | **El costo de la vida** Your Spanish pen pal wants to know how much it costs to be a university student in the U.S. Answer his questions using words in place of numerals.

1. ¿Cuánto es la matrícula universitaria, cada trimestre o semestre, en tu universidad?

   _____

2. ¿Cuánto gastas *(do you spend)* en libros cada trimestre o semestre?

   _____

3. ¿Cuánto es el alquiler *(rent)* por un apartamento en tu ciudad?

   _____

4. ¿Cuánto gastas en comida cada mes?

   _____

SÍNTESIS

¡A LEER!

EL COLEGIO MAYOR: CHAMINADE Many university students in Spain live in student residences called **colegios mayores.** Chaminade is the name of a **colegio mayor** at Madrid's Universidad Complutense.

Strategy: Clustering words

Reading one word at a time is inefficient because it slows down your reading speed. Reading one word at a time can also lead to a great deal of frustration, as in many instances you will not know the meaning of every word in a given passage. It is more efficient to read meaningful groups or clusters of words.

Paso 1: Read the following brochure once to get the gist of its content. ¡OJO! Remember to use the word clustering strategy you learned in your textbook. Try not to focus on each word individually, but rather look at groups of words to get the gist of what they are saying. When you are done, write down two or three main ideas that you got from your scanning of word clusters.

_____

_____

_____

_____

Paso 2: Now reread the ad at your usual reading speed and try to pull out information you may have missed during the first reading. Concentrate on reading clusters of three words. When you are done, write down some details about the main ideas you noted in **Paso 2.**

_____

_____

_____

_____

Paso 3: Read the brochure on Chaminade one more time, again trying to identify meaningful clusters of words. When you are done, answer the comprehension questions.

1. Is Chaminade a male or female dorm?

_____

2. Can you share a room but have your own private bathroom at Chaminade?

_____

3. Does a stay at Chaminade include food service seven days a week?

_____

4. What do you think the **portería** service is?

_____

5. How much does a month's stay at Chaminade cost in euros?

_____

6. What kinds of activities does Chaminade offer?

_____

_____

_____

_____

_____

_____

El colegio mayor Chaminade es una residencia estudiantil gestionada[1] por los Marianistas y está adscrito[2] a la Universidad Complutense de Madrid. Durante el año es un colegio masculino, pero permanece abierto durante los meses de julio, agosto y septiembre, ofreciendo alojamiento, tanto a mujeres como a hombres. Situado en la Ciudad Universitaria, tiene acceso a las líneas de autobús C, 45, 44 y 2, y a la línea 6 del metro.

Chaminade cuenta con los siguientes servicios e instalaciones:

- Habitaciones individuales con baño propio.
- Habitaciones individuales con baño compartido.
- Habitaciones dobles con baño propio.
- Desayuno, comida y cena excepto los domingos y festivos cuando no hay ningún servicio de comedor.
- Cambio de sábanas y toallas semanal.
- Uso de lavadora y secadora automáticas a precio módico.[3]
- Piscina, salas de TV, sala de estudio refrigerada, sala de periódicos, teléfonos públicos, cafetería.

Servicio de portería: Además de los servicios anteriormente mencionados, el colegio también cuenta con un servicio de portería que incluye despertar por la mañana a los colegiales, anunciar las visitas, repartir[4] el correo, atender los servicios telefónicos y llevar el registro de entradas y salidas.

Actividades culturales habituales: El colegio tiene otros servicios como un gimnasio, una pista deportiva, una sala de artes plásticas, una sala de arquitectura, una sala de electrónica, una sala de música, un laboratorio de fotografía, emisoras de radio, proyector de cine de 16 y 35 milímetros, estudio de fotografía y video, tuna,[5] coro colegial y celebraciones litúrgicas.

Costo: 646,81 euros al mes + 7% de IVA (aproximadamente)

DIRECCIÓN: Pº Juan XXIII, 9.–28040 MADRID (España)
Teléfono: 34–91.5545400 Fax: 34–91.5348157
Email: chaminade.es@mad.servicom.es
DIRECTOR: Sr. D. José Ignacio Gautier González

---

[1]**gestionada** _managed_ [2]**adscrito** _attached_ [3]**módico** _moderate_ [4]**repartir** _distribute_ [5]**tuna** _group of student serenaders_

¡A ESCRIBIR!

LAS VIVIENDAS ESTUDIANTILES You have been asked to write a short article on student residences in the U.S. for a magazine for international students. Before you begin to write, reflect on the writing strategy you learned in your text.

Strategy: Writing topic sentences

The first step in writing a well-structured paragraph is to formulate a clear, concise topic sentence. A good topic sentence has the following characteristics.

- It comes at the beginning of a paragraph.
- It states the main idea of the paragraph.
- It focuses on only one topic of interest.
- It makes a factual or personal statement.
- It is neither too general nor too specific.
- It attracts the attention of the reader.

Paso 1: Think about the types of quesitons you might answer in this article. For example:

- Where do the majority of students choose to live?
- What options are available for students?
- How much does each type of living arrangement cost?

> *Functions:* Writing an introduction; Describing objects
> *Vocabulary:* House: bathroom, bedroom, furniture, kitchen, living room
> *Grammar:* Verbs: **estar, tener**; Progressive tenses; Position of adjectives

Paso 2: On a separate piece of paper write a sentence about the most important idea you would want to communicate to international students about student living arrangements in the U.S. This will be your topic sentence. Then, write several sentences that support the point you make in your topic sentence. Organize these sentences and complete the first draft of your brief article.

Paso 3: Check over your paragraph, focusing on the characteristics of a good topic sentence and its relationship to the rest of the paragraph. You may use the following checklist questions as a guide: Does the topic sentence . . .

1. come at the beginning of the paragraph? _____ yes _____ no
2. state the main idea of the paragraph? _____ yes _____ no
3. focus on only one topic of interest? _____ yes _____ no
4. make a factual or personal statement? _____ yes _____ no
5. seem neither too general nor too specific? _____ yes _____ no
6. attract the attention of the reader? _____ yes _____ no

Paso 4: Make any necessary changes to your paragraph and write the final version below:

_____

_____

_____

_____

_____

_____

Autoprueba

VOCABULARIO

WB 4-26 **Los muebles** Complete the sentences with the names of the appropriate household items from the following list.

un armario	mi cama	un escritorio	el inodoro	el jardín

1. Escribo mis cartas en _____.
2. Pongo toda la ropa en _____.
3. Duermo bastante bien en _____.
4. En el baño limpio _____.
5. Miro las plantas en _____.

WB 4-27 **Los electrodomésticos** Complete the sentences with the names of the appropriate appliances from the following list.

un despertador	un horno de microondas	el refrigerador	una lavadora	una aspiradora

1. Siempre lavo mi ropa en _____.
2. Preparo la comida rápida en _____.
3. Limpio las alfombras con _____.
4. Para llegar a clase a tiempo uso_____.
5. Pongo la comida en _____.

WB 4-28 **Los quehaceres** Complete the following sentences with the names of the places where the chores described are normally done.

la cocina	el comedor	el jardín	la sala

1. Pongo la mesa en _____.
2. Lavo los platos en _____.
3. Corto el césped en _____.
4. Paso la aspiradora en _____.

ESTRUCTURA

WB 4-29 | **Entre novios** Complete the following conversation with the appropriate present-tense form of the verbs listed. **¡OJO!** You must use each of the verbs at least once.

comenzar	pensar	preferir	querer	tener

TOMÁS: ¿Qué **1.** _____ ganas de hacer hoy, Ceci?

CECI: **2.** _____ ganas de ir al cine. ¿Qué **3.** _____ hacer tú?

TOMÁS: Yo no **4.** _____ ir al cine. **5.** _____ ver videos en casa esta noche.

Pero, dime *(tell me)*, ¿a qué hora **6.** _____ la película en el cine?

CECI: **7.** _____ a las 6:00. Mi hermana y yo no **8.** _____ ver videos en

casa, **9.** _____ ir al cine.

TOMÁS: ¿Tú hermana va con nosotros? Yo **10.** _____ que no voy con Uds.

WB 4-30 | **La hora del almuerzo** Complete the following paragraph with an appropriate present-tense form of the verbs listed.

almorzar	decir	dormir	jugar	servir	volver

Normalmente, yo **1.** _____ con mi familia a las 2:00 durante la semana. Mis padres

preparan la comida, luego mi padre **2.** _____ la comida. Siempre como dos porciones

y mi padre siempre **3.** _____ que voy a estar gordo.

Después de **4.** _____, yo **5.** _____ la siesta por media hora. Después,

mis padres **6.** _____ a su trabajo y yo **7.** _____ a la universidad.

A veces, mis amigos y yo **8.** _____ al fútbol después de nuestras clases. Yo no

9. _____ muy bien, pero me gusta mucho practicar ese deporte.

WB 4-31 | **En otras palabras** Change the verb phrases in the sentences, using an expression with the verb **tener.** Some suggestions appear below. Follow the model.

MODELO: <u>Quiero dormir.</u>
Tengo sueño.

tener celos	tener paciencia	tener ganas de	tener prisa
tener hambre	tener sueño	tener miedo	

1. Quiero salir a bailar esta noche.

   _____

2. Siempre estoy enojado cuando estoy con los niños. Hacen demasiado preguntas.

   _____

3. No me gusta el nuevo novio de mi exnovia.

   _____

4. No me gusta estar en la casa solo.

   _____

WB 4-32 **¿Qué hago?** Tell your friend how to get along better with his roommates. Use the following verb phrases to form **tú** commands.

1. hacer tu cama todos los días

   _____

2. quitar la mesa después de comer

   _____

3. sacar la basura todos los días

   _____

4. ir al supermercado todos los sábados

   _____

WB 4-33 **¿Cómo están todos?** You are baby-sitting and the children's mother calls to find out how everyone is and what they are doing. Tell her, using the verb **estar** + adjective or the present progressive. Follow the model.

   MODELO: Tomás / furioso / pasando la aspiradora
           Tomás está furioso. Está pasando la aspiradora.

1. Lolita / emocionada / jugar en el patio

   _____

2. Teresita y Javi / ocupado / regar las plantas

   _____

3. Miguelín / aburrido / leer un libro

   _____

4. Ángel y yo / sucios / preparar un pastel

   _____

WB 4-34 **¿Cuántos son?** Solve these mathematical problems using words, not numerals.

1. doscientos treinta y cinco + mil quinientos tres =

   _____

2. seiscientos setenta y nueve + cuatrocientos ochenta y uno =

   _____

3. dos mil trescientos cincuenta y dos – novecientos treinta y seis =

   _____

5 | La salud: Bolivia y Paraguay

VOCABULARIO El cuerpo humano

¡A PRACTICAR!

WB 5-1 **El cuerpo humano** Look at the drawing below and write the names of the indicated body parts.

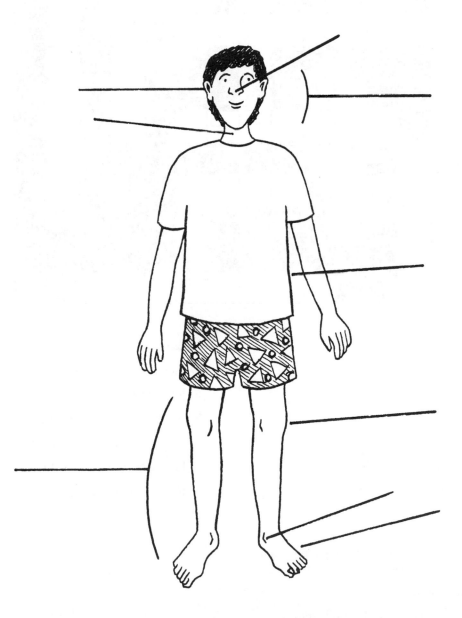

Vertical

1. Dumbo tiene ____ muy grandes.

2. Señalas *(Point)* con el ____.

3. Michael Jordan no tiene ____.

4. Ves con los ____.

5. La ____ tiene cinco dedos.

7. Cuando tomas algo, el líquido pasa por la ____.

9. La ____ es parte de la cara.

10. Si tienes la ____ blanca, te quemas *(you get burned)* al sol.

11. Comes con la ____.

13. El ____ está conectado con la mano.

15. Escuchas con el ____.

Horizontal

2. Tienes ____ en la boca.

6. Jennifer López tiene una ____ muy bonita.

8. Si comes mucho te duele *(hurts)* el ____.

12. El ____ es el símbolo del amor.

14. En medio del brazo está el ____.

16. Respiras con los ____.

Nombre _____ Fecha _____

¡TE TOCA A TI!

WB 5-3 **¡El extraterrestre!** Imagine that the Bolivian version of the *National Enquirer* reports about an extraterrestrial being that will conquer Earth. Read the description of this being and draw what he must look like.

El extraterrestre SondeBón tiene una cabeza pequeña y no tiene pelo. Tiene sólo un ojo grande justo en el medio de la cara. Tiene tres orejas pequeñas, dos en los dos lados de la cabeza y una encima de *(on top of)* la cabeza. Tiene una boca muy grande con tres dientes grandes que salen de la boca cerrada *(closed)*. No tiene nariz. Tiene un cuello muy largo y un estómago grande. No tiene brazos, pero tiene cuatro piernas largas. Sin embargo, tiene pies muy pequeños.

ESTRUCTURA I Talking about routine activities: reflexive pronouns and present tense of reflexive verbs

¡A PRACTICAR!

WB 5-4 | **La familia Soriana** The Soriana house is always very active and each family member has a different routine. Describe these routines by forming complete sentences with the following elements. Follow the model.

MODELO: MariPepa / acostarse / las 6:30 / la mañana
MariPepa se acuesta a las seis y media de la mañana.

1. Carmen / despertarse / 6:30 / la mañana

   _____

2. don Carlos y Miguel / afeitarse / por la noche

   _____

3. yo / lavarse / y después / cepillarse / los dientes

   _____

4. los niños / bañarse / por la mañana

   _____

5. doña Lucía y Luisita / maquillarse / y después / peinarse

   _____

6. Miguel / quitarse / la ropa / y acostarse / las 8:00 de la noche

   _____

WB 5-5 | **¿Compañeros?** Jerry wants to find Spanish-speaking roommates to practice his Spanish, so he interviews Elena from Bolivia, Jorge from Paraguay, and Lola from Miami. To find out if their routines are compatible, complete their conversation with the appropriate reflexive form of the verb in parentheses.

JERRY: Bueno, ya que hay sólo un baño, debemos hablar de cómo vamos a compartir el apartamento, ¿no?

JORGE: Pues, yo **1.** _____ (despertarse) a las 5:00 de la mañana porque trabajo muy temprano. **2.** _____ (Bañarse) en seguida *(right away)* y después **3.** _____ (secarme) y **4.** _____ (ponerme) la ropa. Y Uds., ¿a qué hora **5.** _____ (levantarse)?

ELENA: Yo aunque *(although)* **6.** _____ (dormirse) tarde, **7.** _____ (despertarse) a las 7:00 de la mañana porque tengo clase a las 8:00. ¿Y tú, Lola? **8.** _____ (Acostarse) tarde y **9.** _____ (despertarse) temprano también, ¿no?

LOLA: Sí, y **10.** _____ (ducharse), **11.** _____ (vestirse) y **12.** _____ (maquillarse) en el baño, así que paso mucho tiempo allí por la mañana.

Nombre _____ Fecha _____

ELENA: Ah, ¡no te preocupes! A mí me gusta **13.** _____ (pintarse) en mi cuarto. No paso mucho tiempo en el baño por la mañana. Parece que todo está bien entonces, ¿no?

JERRY: Un momento, por favor. Yo también **14.** _____ (levantarse) temprano, a las 7:30. Necesito **15.** _____ (bañarse) inmediatamente para **16.** _____ (despertarse). Después **17.** _____ (cepillarse) los dientes, **18.** _____ (peinarse) y **19.** _____ (afeitarse). Finalmente, **20.** _____ (ponerse) la ropa y salgo del baño a las 8:30.

JORGE: Este hombre **21.** _____ (cuidarse) bien, ¿no?

¿Van a ser compatibles estos cuatro? Explica tu respuesta usando oraciones completas.

_____
_____
_____
_____

¡TE TOCA A TI!

WB 5-6 **¿Cambias tu rutina?** Do you change your routine much on the weekends? Write a brief description of your routine during the week and then on the weekends.

_____
_____
_____
_____

ASÍ SE DICE Talking about things you have just finished doing: *acabar de* + infinitive

¡A PRACTICAR!

WB 5-7 **La vida sana** Dr. Ruiz is a Spanish doctor visiting a rural health clinic in Bolivia. He is talking to the Bodega family about a healthy lifestyle and asks them questions. Write the family members' responses by stating what they have just done, using **acabar de** + infinitive. Follow the model.

MODELO: A los niños: ¿Se cepillan los dientes todos los días?
         Sí, acabamos de cepillarnos los dientes.

1. A toda la familia: ¿Desayunan Uds. todos los días?

   _____

2. A la señora Bodega: ¿Descansa Ud. durante el día?

   _____

3. A Juanito: ¿Te bañas todos los días?

_____

4. A la señora Bodega: ¿Toman mucha agua los niños?

_____

¡TE TOCA A TI!

WB 5-8 | **¿Y tú?** Following the model, write a list of activities that you have just finished doing.

MODELO: *Acabo de lavarme las manos.*

1. _____
2. _____
3. _____
4. _____
5. _____

VOCABULARIO La salud

¡A PRACTICAR!

WB 5-9 | **Bienvenidos** Dolores Castellanos is giving some new volunteers a tour of the Clínica de Salud Rural Andina. Complete her description of the clinic choosing from the words provided. **¡OJO!** You will not use all of the words and you cannot use a word more than once.

enfermero(a)	mareado	receta	antibiótico	farmacia	médico
catarro	gripe	pacientes	sala de espera	enfermedad	jarabe
pastillas	síntomas				

Empezamos en la **1.** _____ donde los **2.** _____ esperan su cita *(appointment)* con el **3.** _____. Antes de ver al doctor Dardo Chávez, ellos comentan sus síntomas con el (la) **4.** _____. Durante el invierno, muchos de ellos tienen **5.** _____ y sus **6.** _____ son fiebre, escalofríos y dolor en todo el cuerpo. En estos casos el doctor Dardo Chávez les da una **7.** _____ para antibióticos, y los pacientes tienen que ir a la **8.** _____. Pero en otros casos los pacientes simplemente tienen **9.** _____, pues tosen y estornudan mucho. En estos casos el doctor Dardo Chávez les da **10.** _____ y **11.** _____.

WB 5-10 **¿Qué pasa?** Juan Carlos is observing what goes on in the clinic to prepare for his volunteer work. What does he see? What is wrong with each patient? What are their symptoms? Based on the drawings below describe in complete sentences what he sees. Follow the model.

MODELO: *El señor está enfermo. El señor...*

_____

_____

_____

_____

_____

_____

_____

Felipe Velarde

_____

_____

_____

_____

_____

_____

_____

Cecilia Dopazo Hernán

_____

_____

_____

_____

_____

_____

_____

_____

Tomás Casales García

¡TE TOCA A TI!

WB 5-11 **¿Qué deben hacer?** Juan Carlos is thinking about what to recommend for each patient in activity **WB 5-10**. Make a list of several suggestions. Follow the model.

MODELO: Felipe Velarde
Felipe debe tomar aspirina y guardar cama por varios días.

Felipe Velarde

_____

_____

Cecilia Dopazo Hernán

_____

_____

Tomás Casales García

_____

_____

WB 5-12 **¿Loco por la medicina?** David does not like pain and has all kinds of medicine to solve different painful problems. He is explaining to his friend Bea what kind of pain each medicine is for. Write what he says following the model.

MODELO: Tylenol
Usas Tylenol cuando te duele la cabeza.

1. Alka Seltzer

_____

2. Solarcane

_____

3. Vicks

_____

4. Sulfato de magnesio

_____

ESTRUCTURA II Describing people, things, and conditions: *ser* versus *estar*

¡A PRACTICAR!

WB 5-13 **¿Cuánto sabes?** Show how much you know about people, places, and events in Bolivia and Paraguay by writing the following sentences with the correct form of **ser** or **estar.** Follow the model.

MODELO: el boliviano Jaime Escalante ser/estar muy inteligente
El boliviano Jaime Escalante es muy inteligente.

1. Santa Cruz de la Sierra ser/estar en el este de Bolivia

_____

2. el parque Carlos Antonio López ser/estar en Asunción

_____

3. La Paz y Sucre ser/estar las capitales de Bolivia

_____

4. el guaraní ser/estar la moneda oficial de Paraguay

_____

5. la celebración de Achocalla ser/estar en La Paz

_____

WB 5-14 | **La doctora Reyes** Dra. Reyes is reviewing her notes about her patients. Complete them with the appropriate form of **ser** or **estar**.

Hoy **1.** _____ viernes, el 22 de febrero y **2.** _____ las 2:00 de la tarde.

La paciente **3.** _____ Aracelia Itzapú. Ella **4.** _____ casada y

5. _____ madre de tres hijos. Ella **6.** _____ de Asunción y

7. _____ paraguaya, pero su esposo **8.** _____ boliviano. Aracelia

9. _____ baja y delgada.

Hoy día Aracelia **10.** _____ muy enferma. **11.** _____ congestionada,

12. _____ tosiendo y estornudando mucho. Dice que **13.** _____ muy

cansada también. Además, dice que **14.** _____ un poco deprimida *(depressed)* por

varias razones: acaba de morir su padre y su esposo no **15.** _____ aquí. Él

16. _____ en La Paz y **17.** _____ buscando trabajo. Creo que

18. _____ necesario para Aracelia dormir más y tomar vitaminas. La próxima cita

para Aracelia va a **19.** _____ el primero de marzo.

¡TE TOCA A TI!

WB 5-15 | **Tu mejor amigo(a)** Write a description of your best friend. Include a physical description, a description of his/her personality, his/her place of birth, marital status, occupation, pastimes, etc. ¡**OJO!** Pay attention to your use of **ser** and **estar**. Follow the model.

MODELO: *Mi mejor amigo se llama Pedro. Él es alto, guapo y muy simpático. Es de Venezuela pero ahora está en Colombia...*

_____
_____
_____
_____
_____
_____
_____

ESTRUCTURA III Pointing out people and things: demonstrative adjectives and pronouns

¡A PRACTICAR!

WB 5-16 **¿Cómo funciona?** It is Leticia's first day volunteering at the health clinic and she has lots of questions about how to do a good job. Complete the questions with the correct demonstrative adjective: **este, esta, estos,** or **estas.** Follow the model.

MODELO: ¿Ayudo a _este_ señor?

1. ¿Hablo con _____ señora?

2. ¿Trabajo en _____ sala?

3. ¿Escribo sobre _____ síntomas?

4. ¿Todos los pacientes son de _____ pueblo?

5. ¿Tratamos aquí todas _____ enfermedades?

WB 5-17 **Algo boba** Poor Leticia is not doing too well on the job and all of her assumptions were wrong. How does her supervisor correct her? Based on Leticia's questions in **activity WB 5-16**, complete the supervisor's answers with the correct demonstrative adjective **(ese, esos, esa, esas)** or demonstrative pronoun **(ése, ésa, ésos, ésas).** Follow the model.

MODELO: No. Ayuda a _ese_ señor.

1. No. Habla con _____ señora.

2. No. Trabaja en _____ sala.

3. No. Escribe sobre _____.

4. No. Los pacientes son de _____ dos pueblos.

5. No. Aquí solamente tratamos _____.

¡TE TOCA A TI!

WB 5-18 **Ayuda para Leticia** Based on **activities WB 5-17** and **5-18** write out three more questions that Leticia would probably ask and three answers to those questions. Use demonstrative adjectives and pronouns.

1. ¿_____?

_____

2. ¿_____?

_____

3. ¿_____?

_____

SÍNTESIS

¡A LEER!

LOS KALLAWAYAS: CURANDEROS NÓMADAS DE BOLIVIA Below you will read an article about nomadic healers **(los curanderos)** in Bolivia.

Strategy: Recognizing Spanish affixes

An affix is added to the beginning (prefix) or to the end (suffix) of a word stem to create a new word. Knowing the meaning of Spanish affixes can significantly increase your ability to read Spanish effectively.

Paso 1: In English write the meaning of the following affixes.

1. im- (imposible)

   _____

2. -ción (acción)

   _____

3. -mente (especialmente)

   _____

Paso 2: In the reading you will see the following affixes:

- **pre-:** antes de
  prehistórico: pre- + histórico – prehistórico *(prehistoric)*

- **-ero:** significa la ocupación o la actividad de algo o alguien
  viajero: viaje + -ero = viajero *(traveler)*

- **-al:** hace un adjetivo de un sustantivo
  tradicional: tradición + -al = tradicional *(traditional)*

- **-eza:** expresa una cualidad abstracta del adjetivo
  belleza: bello + -eza = belleza *(beauty)*
  limpieza: limpio + -eza = limpieza *(act of cleaning)*

Based on this information, write the meaning of the following words.

1. preincaica _____   3. medicinal _____

2. curandero _____   4. naturaleza _____

Paso 3: Now you will read the article about the nomadic healers **(los curanderos)** in Bolivia. Use what you have learned about affixes to help you comprehend the text. When you are done, answer the following questions.

1. ¿De qué parte de Bolivia son los kallawayas?

   _____

2. ¿Por qué se llaman curanderos «nómadas»?

   _____

3. ¿Por qué prefiere la gente rural la medicina tradicional de los kallawayas?

   _____

4. ¿Cómo se conservan las tradiciones de los kallawayas en Bolivia?

Los kallawayas: Curanderos nómadas de Bolivia

En la provincia de Bautista Saavedra, al norte del lago Titicaca, viven los kallawayas, los sagrados[1] curanderos cuyos[2] hierbas y ritos tradicionales datan de la época preincaica. Con su chuspa, una bolsa llena de hierbas, y la bendición de los dioses aymara,[3] los kallawayas viajan desde esta región andina del noroeste de Bolivia hasta partes de Perú, de Argentina, de Chile, de Ecuador y de Panamá para tratar y curar a la gente. Vistiendo su colorido poncho de vicuña[4] y su lluchu (gorra de lana[5]), los kallawayas viajan a pie, como lo hacían hace siglos, a pesar de los medios de transporte modernos.

Los kallawayas, como la mayoría de los bolivianos de ascendencia indígena, guardan vínculos con la naturaleza y el entorno físico que los rodea.[6] Creen que los seres humanos deben respetar y vivir en armonía con su medio ambiente. Su enfoque holístico requiere una larga conversación con el paciente sobre su enfermedad y un examen del ambiente que lo rodea.

En algún momento de su vida, el 80 por ciento de bolivianos recurre a un curandero tradicional como el kallawaya. Y hasta el 40 por ciento de la población total de este país andino practica solamente la medicina tradicional. Esta cifra sube en las zonas rurales de Bolivia porque en muchas de estas zonas no existe la medicina moderna. Además, la medicina tradicional de los kallawayas es más barata que los servicios de salud modernos.

Tradicionalmente los conocimientos de los kallawayas se transmiten de padres a hijos mediante un idioma secreto conocido solamente por ellos. Sin embargo, muchos dicen que sus tradiciones están en peligro de perderse[7] si los kallawayas no comparten sus secretos con otros. Por ese motivo el gobierno boliviano mantiene un registro permanente de los conocimientos holísticos y aplicaciones prácticas de plantas medicinales de los kallawayas.

[1]**sagrados** *sacred* [2]**cuyos** *whose* [3]**aymara** *indigenous group still occupying Bolivia* [4]**vicuña** *relative to the llama* [5]**gorra de lana** *wool cap* [6]**que los rodea** *that surrounds them* [7]**peligro de perderse** *danger of being lost*

¡A ESCRIBIR!

ESCRIBIR POR EL INTERNET You have just made a new Paraguayan friend through the Internet. Her name is Alicia Veraní, and she wants to know all about you. Write her an email and tell her all about yourself.

Strategy: Using a bilingual dictionary

A bilingual dictionary is a useful tool that, when used properly, can enhance the quality, complexity, and accuracy of your writing in Spanish. It is very important, however, that you learn to use it correctly. Here are some suggestions to help you use your bilingual dictionary properly.

1. When you look up the Spanish equivalent of an English word, you will often find several meanings for the same word, sometimes appearing like this:

    cold: *n.* frío, catarro, resfriado

    adj. frío

2. In larger dictionaries, additional information may be given that will clarify meanings and uses.

    cold: *n.* frío *(low temperature)*; catarro *(illness)*; resfriado *(illness)*

    adj. frío

3. Pay attention to certain abbreviations in your dictionary that will tell you what type of word you have found. Notice the abbreviations *n.* and *adj.* in the examples above, indicating that the word is a noun or an adjective. Some of the more common abbreviations you will find are listed below. Their Spanish equivalents are in parentheses.

n. noun *(sustantivo)*

adj. adjective *(adjetivo)*

adv. adverb *(adverbio)*

conj. conjunction *(conjunción)*

prep. preposition *(preposición)*

v. verb *(verbo)*

4. Looking up a lot of different words in a bilingual dictionary when you are writing is inefficient. If you insist on looking up too many words as you write, you may become frustrated or feel like you want to give up altogether. It is wiser and faster to use the phrases you already know in Spanish as much as possible, rather than trying to translate too many new words you don't know from English to Spanish. You will learn more and more new words as you continue reading and listening to the language.

Paso 1: Add to the following list at least five important aspects for describing yourself.

- where you and your family are from
- your nationality
- your marital status
- where your house is located
- your personality traits and your family members' personality traits

Functions: Describing people; talking about the present
Vocabulary: Countries; Studies; Leisure; Family members; University
Grammar: Verbs: **ser** & **estar**

_____

_____

_____

_____

_____

Paso 2: Choose four aspects from above and, on a separate piece of paper, write several sentences to describe each aspect chosen. If you need to use the dictionary, remember the strategy you have learned for looking up words.

Paso 3: Write your first draft of your email letter on a separate piece of paper and review it to make sure your ideas are clearly stated and that your vocabulary usage is correct. Then, write your final draft below.

_____

_____

_____

_____

_____

_____

_____

_____

_____

_____

Autoprueba

VOCABULARIO

WB 5-19 | **El cuerpo humano** Write the name of each body part indicated in the drawing.

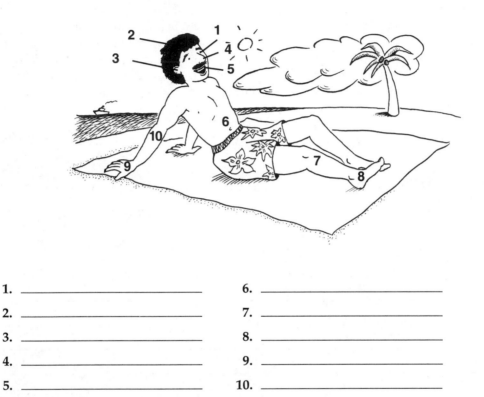

1. _____   6. _____
2. _____   7. _____
3. _____   8. _____
4. _____   9. _____
5. _____   10. _____

WB 5-20 | **Los problemas medicos** Complete the sentences with words from the list. ¡OJO! Use each word/phrase just once. You might need to conjugate verbs.

alergia	escalofríos	náuseas	catarro	estornudar
congestionado(a)	examinar	síntomas	enfermedad	fiebre
tomarle la temperatura	enfermo(a)	guardar	cama	sano(a)

1. En la primavera las flores me dan una _____ y yo _____ mucho.

2. Cuando alguien tiene _____, tose mucho.

3. El SIDA (*AIDS*) puede ser una _____ fatal.

4. Cuando alguien tiene alergia, a veces está _____.

5. El dolor del cuerpo y los _____ son _____ de la gripe.

6. Alguien que no está _____ está _____.

7. El médico _____ a sus pacientes antes de darles una receta.

8. Para saber si alguien tiene _____, el médico le _____.

9. Si alguien está mareado, puede tener _____ y por eso debe _____ para sentirse mejor.

Nombre _____ Fecha _____

ESTRUCTURA

WB 5-21 | **La rutina diaria** Look at the drawings of Beti Villalobos' daily routine, and describe in detail what she does each day. **¡OJO!** You will use reflexive and nonreflexive verbs.

1. _____
2. _____
3. _____

4. _____
5. _____
6. _____
7. _____
8. _____

WB 5-22 | **¡Cómo vuela el tiempo!** Now imagine that it's 8:00 a.m. in Beti Villalobos' life. Based on the drawings above, write a list of everything that she has just done this morning.

1. _____
2. _____
3. _____
4. _____
5. _____
6. _____
7. _____

WB 5-23 | **Lorena Bobada** Complete the following paragraph about Lorena using the appropriate forms of the verbs **ser** and **estar**.

Lorena Bobada **1.** _____ de Sucre, Bolivia. **2.** _____ estudiante de medicina y por eso **3.** _____ ahora en La Paz donde **4.** _____ la universidad.

Lorena ya no **5.** _____ casada; **6.** _____ divorciada y no tiene novio.

7. _____ soltera. Lorena **8.** _____ una mujer inteligente y

9. _____ bastante ocupada con sus estudios. Un día ella quiere **10.** _____ cirujana (*surgeon*). Para ella una carrera **11.** _____ muy importante y por eso ahora la vida académica **12.** _____ lo único (*the only thing*) para ella.

WB 5-24 | **Gemelos distintos** Roberto and Gustavo are twins, but have very different opinions on things. Roberto always wants one thing and Gustavo the other. Find out how they disagree by forming sentences using demonstrative adjectives and pronouns. Follow the model.

MODELO: Quiero ir a esta clínica.
         No quiero ésta, prefiero esa clínica.

1. Prefiero esta medicina.

_____

2. Quiero pedir a este médico.

_____

3. Prefiero guardar esta cama.

_____

4. Voy a pedir estos jarabes.

_____

5. Prefiero esto.

_____

¿Quieres comer conmigo esta noche?: Venezuela

VOCABULARIO La comida

¡A PRACTICAR!

WB 6-1 **Sopa de letras** Each of the following words names a part of a complete dinner. Using the vocabulary you learned in your text, decipher these words, then unscramble the circled letters to reveal the hidden idiom that the drawing illustrates.

1. ⬭ N ⬭ A ___ ___ D ___

2. C ___ ___ L ___ ⬭ ___ ⬭

3. ___ C E ___ ⬭ E

4. A ___ ⬭ PA ___

5. ___ ⬭ A N

6. C ⬭ ___ É

7. ___ E R ___ U ___ A ⬭

8. ___ I N ⬭

9. ___ A P ⬭ ___ ___

Frase idiomática: ¿Qué piensa esta mujer de su admirador?

___ ___ ___ Á HA ___ ___ A ___   N ___ ___   ___ ___ P ___.

WB 6-2 ¿«Cómo» come la gente? What kind of food do they serve in the restaurant in Maracaibo? To find out, look at the menu and answer the questions that follow.

1. Si quieres comida de mar, ¿qué puedes pedir?

   _____

2. ¿Tienen bebidas de fruta?

   _____

3. ¿Qué bebidas alcohólicas sirven?

   _____

4. ¿Qué platos de carne ofrecen?

   _____

5. ¿Qué bebidas no alcohólicas sirven?

   _____

6. ¿Qué platos ofrecen para los que no comen carne roja?

   _____

7. ¿Qué sirven de postre?

   _____

¡TE TOCA A TI!

WB 6-3 **Recomendaciones** A Venezuelan friend is coming to visit soon and has written you to ask about restaurants in your town. Answer her questions.

1. ¿Qué restaurante hace la mejor (the best) hamburguesa? ¿Con qué condimentos preparan la hamburguesa?

   _____

   _____

2. ¿Cuál es el mejor restaurante para desayunar? ¿Qué sirven allí?

_____

_____

3. ¿Qué restaurante hace los mejores sándwiches? ¿Qué tipos de sándwiches sirven?

_____

_____

4. ¿Cuál es el mejor lugar para comer postres? ¿Cuál es la especialidad de la casa?

_____

_____

5. ¿Cuál es tu restaurante favorito? ¿Qué te gusta comer allí?

_____

_____

ESTRUCTURA I Making comparisons: comparatives and superlatives

¡A PRACTICAR!

WB 6-4 **Encuesta** A marketing company wants to know your opinion about how certain things compare to one another. Write your answers in complete sentences using comparative structures **(más, menos, mejor, peor)**, and the adjective given. Follow the model.

MODELO: dos comidas: la hamburguesa / la ensalada (nutritivo)
La ensalada es más nutritiva que la hamburguesa.

1. dos programas: «Jerry Springer» / «Bernie Mac» (cómico)

_____

2. dos restaurantes: Jack in the Box / Pizza Hut (peor)

_____

3. dos actores: Denzel Washington / Brad Pitt (mejor)

_____

4. dos dulces: el chocolate / el caramelo (rico)

_____

5. dos frutas: la manzana / la naranja (dulce)

_____

WB 6-5 **¿Qué tienen en común?** Your favorite restaurant just opened up a second location and you have just eaten there. Your friend asks what the two have in common. Respond in complete sentences to the questions on page 92 using comparisons of equality. Follow the models.

MODELOS: ¿Es bonito el segundo restaurante?
El segundo restaurante es tan bonito como el primero.

¿Hay mucha gente en el segundo restaurante?
Hay tanta gente en el segundo restaurante como en el primer restaurante.

1. ¿Es barato el segundo restaurante?

_____

2. ¿Sirven mariscos en el segundo restaurante?

_____

3. ¿ Sirven muchas ensaladas en el segundo restaurante?

_____

4. ¿Es grande el segundo restaurante?

_____

WB 6-6   **La nueva novia** Robert is describing the family of his new girlfriend, Alicia, whose family owns a restaurant in Venezuela. To find out what he says, form phrases with superlative statements following the model.

MODELO: Alicia / simpática / todas mis novias
          Alicia es la más simpática de todas mis novias.

1. Alicia / menor / hijas

_____

2. José / mayor / hijos

_____

3. Tomás / alto / familia

_____

4. la familia / conocida / Maracaibo

_____

5. su restaurante / mejor / Maracaibo

_____

¡TE TOCA A TI!

WB 6-7   **Tus preferencias** You are creating a personal web page in Spanish. Write six sentences to describe your preferences in terms of the categories listed below. Follow the model.

MODELO: grupo musical / chévere *(cool)*
          Los Red Hot Chili Peppers es el grupo musical más chévere de todos.

1. deporte / divertido

_____

2. comida / deliciosa

_____

3. película / mejor / del año

_____

4. programa de televisión / peor

_____

5. novela / interesante

_____

WB 6-8 **Más preferencias** You continue to write your web page and now will describe your two favorite local restaurants. Write six sentences comparing these two restaurants. Use at least one comparison of equality, one of inequality, and one superlative.

_____

_____

_____

_____

_____

_____

VOCABULARIO El restaurante

¡A PRACTICAR!

WB 6-9 **¿Cómo lo dicen?** Your friend Hillary is going out tonight with some Spanish-speaking friends to a Venezuelan restaurant, but she doesn't speak Spanish. Help her select the most appropriate response to each statement or question.

_____ 1. Camarero, el menú por favor.

    a. Te invito.

    b. Sí, ¡cómo no!

    c. Gracias.

_____ 2. ¿Cuál es la especialidad de la casa?

    a. Está muy fresca esta noche.

    b. El menú.

    c. Arepas, ¡por supuesto!

_____ 3. ¿Qué quiere comer?

    a. No, gracias.

    b. Me encantan las arepas.

    c. Estoy a dieta.

_____ 4. ¿Desean ver la lista de postres?

    a. ¡Ay, no! No puedo comer más.

    b. Te invito.

    c. ¡Buen provecho!

_____ 5. Yo invito.

    a. ¡Salud!

    b. Está muy rica.

    c. Gracias, y yo voy a dejar una propina.

| **Ah, El Venezolano** Another friend knows the Venezuelan restaurant where Hilary is going and tells her about a Latin tradition. To find out what it is, complete the paragraph with the appropriate words from the list. **¡OJO!** Use the correct form of the verbs.

a dieta	desear	menú	propina	camarero	pedir
lista de postres	picar	rico	cuenta	ligero	recomendar

¡Me encanta ese restaurante! Tienen de todo y el servicio es excelente. Cuando voy, nunca tengo

que ver el **1.** _____ porque sé bien lo que voy a **2.** _____. Si no tienes

mucha hambre, sabes, cuando sólo quieres algo para **3.** _____, puedes pedir algo

4. _____. Yo **5.** _____ la sopa de chipichipi. No es para nada pesada.

Pero si realmente tienes mucha hambre y **6.** _____ algo muy **7.** _____,

tienes que pedir pabellón. ¡Es para chuparse los dedos! Siempre pido pabellón. Después de

comer, el **8.** _____ te pregunta que si deseas ver la **9.** _____. ¡Tienen hela-

dos y tortas muy, pero muy, ricos! Siempre estoy **10.** _____, pero no me importa (*it*

doesn't matter to me) —en ese restaurante siempre pido un helado.

    Ahora, los restaurantes latinos son un poco diferentes de los restaurantes norteamericanos.

Uds. tienen que pedir la **11.** _____ cuando todos estén listos para salir. Los camareros

no la traen (*bring it*) a la mesa automáticamente. Sé que te va a gustar mucho este restaurante. A

propósito, el servicio es tan bueno que tienes que dejar una buena **12.** _____, ¿sabes?

¿Qué consejo le da a Hillary?

_____

_____

_____

¡TE TOCA A TI!

| **¿Qué haces?** Answer the following questions about cooking and dining out.

1. ¿Cuál es la especialidad de tu casa cuando cocinas? ¿Es un plato ligero o pesado?

_____

_____

2. ¿Qué comida preparas cuando sólo quieres algo para picar?

_____

_____

3. Cuando quieres un postre ligero, ¿qué comes?

_____

_____

4. Cuando vas a un restaurante, ¿siempre dejas una buena propina? ¿Cuánto dejas?

_____

_____

ESTRUCTURA II Describing past events: regular verbs and verbs with spelling changes in the preterite

¡A PRACTICAR!

WB 6-12 **Una fiesta de sorpresa** Doña Carmen is telling her friend all about a surprise party her family threw for her. To find out what she says, form sentences using the preterite with the following elements. Follow the model.

MODELO: Tere / pensar / en la lista de compras
Tere pensó en la lista de compras.

1. Amalia / comprar / toda la comida

_____

2. Carlos y Lupe / preparar / empanadas

_____

3. Enrique / invitar / a todos mis amigos

_____

4. los invitados / llegar / a las 8:30

_____

5. yo / llegar / a las 9:00 / y / yo / empezar a bailar / inmediatamente

_____

6. nosotros / comer / empanadas y otras cosas

_____

7. nosotros / no nos salir de la fiesta / hasta las 3:00 de la mañana

_____

WB 6-13 **¿Algo más para tomar?** Paco is talking to his friends about his birthday celebration last night. To find out what happened, fill in the blanks with the appropriate form of the verb in the preterite.

MARICARMEN: Pues, ¡qué buena fiesta la de anoche!, ¿no?

VERÓNICA: Sí, sí, y yo **1.** _____ (comer) un montón en esa fiesta. Pero tú no

2. _____ (comer) nada. ¿Por qué?

MARICARMEN: Bueno, ayer a la 1:00 yo **3.** _____ (almorzar) con mi novio, Jorge. Él

me **4.** _____ (invitar) a ese restaurante italiano que tanto me gusta. Yo

5. _____ (decidir) pedir el pescado frito y él **6.** ____ (decidir) pedir los

camarones al ajillo. Después, nosotros **7.** _____ (decidir) pedir un

postre y no **8.** _____ (salir) del restaurante hasta las 3:30 de la tarde.

VERÓNICA: Ah, entiendo ahora. Bueno, no solamente comí mucho, sino que *(but)* también yo

9. _____ (beber) tres cervezas anoche.

MARICARMEN: ¡Ay, mujer, eso no es nada! Tú no 10. _____ (beber) nada comparada

con el pobre Paco. Yo 11. _____ (oír) que él 12. _____

(tomar) muchas cervezas y estaba *(he was)* bastante borracho *(drunk)* anoche.

VERÓNICA: Ya lo sé. Yo 13. _____ (llevar) a Paco a su casa. ¡Qué suerte la que

tengo!

MARICARMEN: ¿Tú 14. _____ (llevar) a Paco a casa? Ahhh, ¡por eso! A las 2:00 de la

mañana yo 15. _____ (decidir) ir a casa y yo 16. _____

(buscar) a Paco para llevarlo a su casa, pero yo no lo 17. _____ (en-

contrar) por ningún lado. ¿A qué hora 18. _____ (volver) Uds. a casa?

VERÓNICA: Pues, Paco 19. _____ (llegar) a su casa a la 1:30, pero yo no

20. _____ (llegar) a mi casa hasta las 4:00 de la mañana.

MARICARMEN: ¡Vero! ¿Hasta las 4:00? ¿Por qué?

VERÓNICA: Pues, porque a la 1:30 cuando Paco y yo 21. _____ (llegar) a su casa,

él 22. _____ (comenzar) a hacer tonterías *(stupidities)*.

Él 23. _____ (leer) y 24. _____ (cantar) poesía medieval

en voz alta. Claro, yo 25. _____ (comenzar) a gritar *(yell)*, pero él no

me 26. _____ (oír) porque él 27. _____ (salir) de la casa.

MARICARMEN: Vero, pobrecita. ¿Cuándo 28. _____ (regresar) Paco a la casa?

VERÓNICA: Una hora más tarde.

MARICARMEN: ¡Qué increíble!

¡TE TOCA A TI!

WB 6-14 **¿Un buen día?** Your Venezuelan pen pal has just written and inquired about what you have been doing. Write back and tell him all about your day yesterday. For example, what time did you get up?, what did you have for breakfast?, what did you do with your friends?, etc.

MODELO: *¡Fue un día excelente! Me desperté a las 10:00 de la mañana...*

_____

_____

_____

_____

_____

_____

_____

_____

_____

_____

ESTRUCTURA III Giving detailed descriptions about past events: verbs with stem changes in the preterite

¡A PRACTICAR!

WB 6-15 **¿Una cita divertida?** Last night Patricio went out with a new friend, Laura. Now he is talking to Silvina about the date. Complete their conversation with the correct preterite form of the verb in parentheses, and then indicate whether you think Patricio had fun with Laura.

SILVINA: ...pues, dime Patricio, ¿**1.** _____ (divertirse) anoche con Laura?

PATRICIO: Bueno, sí y no. Ella sí **2.** _____ (divertirse) conmigo, pero no sé si yo realmente **3.** _____ (divertirse) con ella, ¿sabes?

SILVINA: Pues, cuéntame, ¿qué pasó?

PATRICIO: Mira, yo **4.** _____ (conseguir) mi primera tarjeta de crédito y para impresionar bien a Laura yo **5.** _____ (sugerir) que fuéramos (*that we go*) a ese restaurante muy caro del centro. Ella dijo que sí. Esa noche yo **6.** _____ (vestirme) muy elegantemente y...

SILVINA: ¿También **7.** _____ (vestirse) Laura elegantemente?

PATRICIO: Sí, Laura estaba muy linda. Bueno, llegamos al restaurante y el mesero nos **8.** _____ (servir) unos vasos de vino tinto. Pero entonces Laura **9.** _____ (pedir) una botella de champán muy caro.

SILVINA: ¿Qué hiciste?

PATRICIO: Pues, en ese momento **10.** _____ (preferir) no decir nada así que simplemente **11.** _____ (sonreír) y no dije nada.

SILVINA: ¿Qué **12.** _____ (pedir) tú para comer?

PATRICIO: Yo **13.** _____ (pedir) el pollo asado, pero ella **14.** _____ (preferir) comer la langosta y el bistec.

SILVINA: ¿La langosta y el bistec? Esa chica sí tiene gustos muy caros, ¿no? Pues, hablaron mucho durante la cena?

PATRICIO: Sí, hablamos mucho y ella **15.** _____ (reírse) mucho. Yo diría (*would say*) que durante la cena nosotros sí **16.** _____ (divertirse) mucho. Pero cuando el mesero me trajo la cuenta, yo **17.** _____ (morirse) de susto (*fright*).

SILVINA: ¿Cuánto costó la cena?

PATRICIO: ¡Casi 200 dólares!

SILVINA: ¡Caray!

PATRICIO: Sí, y después de pagar la cena, Laura **18.** _____ (sugerir) ir a tomar copas y escuchar música en algún bar. Pero cuando yo le dije que mi tarjeta de crédito ya no podía más, ella dijo que se sentía (*she felt*) enferma, así que **19.** _____ (tener) que volver a casa.

SILVINA: ¡No me digas!

PATRICIO: Sí. Es la pura verdad. Entonces, nosotros **20.** _____ (despedirse) y yo fui a

casa y **21.** _____ (dormirse) en seguida.

SILVINA: ¿Y la pobre tarjeta de crédito?

PATRICIO: ¡Yo creo que la pobre tarjeta ya **22.** _____ (dormirse) para siempre!

¿Se divirtió Patricio con Laura? ¿Por qué sí o por qué no?

_____

_____

¡TE TOCA A TI!

WB 6-16 | **La última vez** Answer the following questions about the last time you did the following things. Use the preterite.

MODELO: ¿Cuándo fue la última vez que pediste comida rápida?
Yo pedí una chalupa en Taco Bell la semana pasada.

1. ¿Cuándo fue la última vez que tú y tus amigos se divirtieron en una fiesta?

_____

2. ¿Cuándo fue la última vez que alguien que conoces se durmió durante una película?

_____

3. ¿Cuándo fue la última vez que todos los estudiantes se rieron en la clase de español?

_____

4. ¿Cuándo fue la última vez que una estrella de cine se murió?

_____

5. ¿Cuándo fue la última vez que un(a) escritor(a) hispana recibió un premio literario?

_____

SÍNTESIS

¡A LEER!

Strategy: Improving your reading efficiency: organizational features of a passage and skimming

Reading efficiently involves a great deal of guessing. By considering several organizational features of a passage, you can often make intelligent guesses about the content of the passage even before you begin reading it. You should use all the information available to you, including titles, subtitles (if any are present), and pictures, to help you get an idea of the topic of the reading. You should also skim over the passage before reading it in order to get the gist of the reading.

Paso 1: Read the title of this article below and then write down the ideas you associate with the title.

_____

_____

_____

_____

_____

_____

_____

Paso 2: Now briefly skim the article, noting words that jump out at you. Do not stop to look up words in the dictionary. When you are done, make a list of the ideas that you have about this article from your skimming of its content.

_____

_____

_____

_____

Paso 3:
Now read the article and answer the comprehension questions that follow.

La comida rápida en Venezuela

En Venezuela, como en otros países del mundo, la comida rápida ya ha empezado a integrarse en la gastronomía de los grandes centros urbanos. Pero esta tradición sumamente *(extremely)* norteamericana no se limita *(is not limited)* a los restaurantes típicos del paisaje estadounidense, como McDonald's, Wendy's y Pizza Hut. En Venezuela uno puede encontrar varias cadenas *(chains)* propias de ese país, cada una con su especialidad. Éstas incluyen *Chipi's, Arturo's, Pecos Bill* y *Churro Manía.*

Como en todas las metrópolis, estos restaurantes de comida rápida sirven a la población trabajadora que tiene limitación en su horario para el almuerzo. También sirven a la gente joven que los fines de semana disfruta comer allí y divertirse con sus amigos. Aunque en Venezuela (como en otros países latinos) es mucho más común comer en el sitio que pedir la comida para llevar, estos restaurantes también tienen servicio para llevar. Además, muchas de las cadenas grandes, como McDonald's, Wendy's, Pizza Hut y Subway, ofrecen servicio a domicilio con motorizados.

Seguramente la comida rápida se está haciendo cada vez más *(more and more)* común en las grandes ciudades venezolanas como Caracas y Maracaibo. Sin embargo, hay que reconocer que mucha gente no se puede dar el lujo *(can't permit themselves the luxury)* de comer en estos sitios a menudo *(frequently)*. En un país donde el salario mínimo es de aproximadamente US$ 250.00 mensuales, estos restaurantes son accesibles sólo para la clase media y alta.

Comprehension questions

1. ¿Cómo se llaman algunas de las cadenas venezolanas de comida rápida?

   _____

2. ¿Cuáles son las similitudes *(similarities)* entre la comida rápida de Venezuela y de los Estados Unidos?

   _____

3. ¿Cuáles son dos diferencias entre la comida rápida de Venezuela y de los Estados Unidos?

   _____

¡A ESCRIBIR!

LA DIETA DEL ESTUDIANTE UNIVERSITARIO One of your favorite Spanish websites is soliciting short essays about the typical diet of American college students. Write a short paragraph on this topic to submit to this site.

Strategy: Adding details to a paragraph

In **Capítulo 4,** you learned how to write a topic sentence for a paragraph. The other sentences in the paragraph should contain details that develop the main idea stated in the topic sentence. The following procedure will help you develop a well-written paragraph in Spanish:

1. Write a topic sentence about a specific subject.

2. List some details that develop your topic sentence.

3. Cross out any details that are unrelated to the topic.

4. Number the remaining details in a clear, logical order.

5. Write the first draft of a paragraph based on your work.

6. Cross out any ideas that do not contribute to the topic.

7. Write the second draft of your paragraph as clearly as possible.

Paso 1: List a series of questions that people in Spanish-speaking countries might ask about the diet of an American college student. Some possibilities are:

- ¿Es una dieta equilibrada?
- ¿Es una dieta variada?
- ¿Es una dieta de comida rápida?

> *Functions:* Appreciating food; Describing objects; Stating a preference
> *Vocabulary:* Food; Food: restaurant
> *Grammar:* Verbs: **gustar, ser, tener;** Present tense of verbs

Paso 2: Now choose the most interesting of the questions you listed and answer it. Your answer will serve as the topic sentence for your paragraph.

Paso 3: Write a list of details that support the opinion (the answer to your question) you present in your topic sentence. For example, if your topic sentence is **La dieta del estudiante estadounidense no es muy equilibrada**, some examples of supporting details include: **Los estudiantes comen mucha comida rápida. La comida de las residencias universitarias es muy mala...**

Paso 4: Now write the first draft of your paragraph, incorporating your topic sentence and the sentences you wrote with supporting details. Only include details that truly demonstrate the point you make in your topic sentence.

Paso 5: Read over your first draft and correct any errors. Then write a final draft below.

_____

_____

_____

_____

_____

_____

_____

_____

_____

_____

_____

_____

Autoprueba

VOCABULARIO

WB 6-17 | **La comida** Put the names of the following foods into the most appropriate category.

vinagre	cerveza	vino	pollo
jugo	chuletas de cerdo	flan	camarones
banana	manzana	res	lechuga
jamón	té helado	sal	aceite
queso	mantequilla	papas	naranja
calamares	agua mineral	leche	bistec
pimienta	pavo	café	

Carnes: _____

Pescado/Mariscos: _____

Bebidas: _____

Postres: _____

Frutas: _____

Verduras: _____

Condimentos: _____

WB 6-18 | **En el restaurante** Write the letter of the word or phrase that best completes each sentence.

_____ 1. Antes de pedir la comida, el camarero nos trae...

   a. la cuenta.

   b. la propina.

   c. el menú.

_____ 2. Antes de comer con otros amigos, les decimos...

   a. ¡Cómo no!

   b. ¡Estoy a dieta!

   c. ¡Buen provecho!

_____ 3. Antes de tomar una bebida con nuestros amigos, les decimos...

   a. ¡Salud!

   b. ¡Estoy satisfecho(a)!

   c. ¡Está para chuparse los dedos!

____ **4.** Si no tienes mucha hambre, pides algo...

  a. para picar.

  b. para chuparse los dedos.

  c. pesado.

____ **5.** Si alguien te ofrece más comida y ya no quieres comer más, puedes decir...

  a. No gracias, deseo ver la lista de postres.

  b. No gracias, estoy satisfecho(a).

  c. ¡Buen provecho!

____ **6.** Si quieres pagar la cuenta para tu amigo, puedes decir...

  a. Te invito.

  b. Voy a dejar una propina.

  c. La cuenta, por favor.

ESTRUCTURA

WB 6-19 | **¡Viva la igualdad!** Beti and her cousin Martín have a lot in common. Use the information given to compare the two using **tan, tanto, tanta, tantos,** and **tantas**.

  MODELOS: tener años: *Beti tiene tantos años como Martín.*

  ser inteligente: *Beti es tan inteligente como Martín.*

1. comer verduras: _____

2. almorzar en restaurantes: _____

3. estar a dieta: _____

4. ser amable: _____

5. tomar café: _____

WB 6-20 | **El más...** Write sentences using the superlative. Follow the model.

  MODELO: dos hermanas: Beti (22 años) / Lorena (19 años) / menor
    Lorena es la hermana menor.

1. dos hijos: Tomás (8 años) / Guillermo (10 años) / mayor

_____

2. dos primos: Alejandro (super paciente) / Alberto (paciente) / paciente

_____

3. dos bebidas: la leche / el jugo / dulce

_____

4. dos jugadores: Michael Jordan (super bueno) / Dennis Rodman (bueno) / mejor

_____

WB 6-21 | **Un sábado por la tarde** Complete the following conversation using the preterite of the verbs in parentheses.

JULIO:　Gloria, ¿ya **1.** _____ (almorzar) Juan Carlos?

GLORIA:　Sí, yo **2.** _____ (almorzar) con él a las 2:00. Nosotros **3.** _____ (comer) un sándwich y una ensalada. Yo **4.** _____ (tomar) un cafecito y él **5.** _____ (beber) té caliente. ¿Ya **6.** _____ (terminar) tu novela?

JULIO:　Sí, **7.** _____ (terminar) ésa y **8.** _____ (comenzar) otra. En la última hora **9.** _____ (leer) 40 páginas.

GLORIA:　Ah, ésa es la novela que **10.** _____ (leer) Gonzalo el mes pasado. Yo **11.** _____ (buscar) ese libro la semana pasada para ti.

JULIO:　Pues, yo **12.** _____ (comprar) este libro esta mañana.

WB 6-22 | **Padre e hijo** Complete the following paragraph with the correct form of the preterite of the following verbs.

> pedir　servir　dormirse　divertirse

Anoche Julio y Juan Carlos **1.** _____ mucho mirando un video de Disney. Mientras lo miraban, el niño **2.** _____ un refresco y su padre le **3.** _____ una Coca-Cola. Más tarde el niño **4.** _____ en el sofá.

7 De compras: Argentina

VOCABULARIO La ropa

¡A PRACTICAR!

WB 7-1 **La ropa adecuada** Choose the clothing item that would be most appropriate to wear to the following events.

_____ **1.** ir a clase

_____ **2.** ir a un concierto de música ranchera *(country)*

_____ **3.** ir a una boda *(wedding)*

_____ **4.** esquiar

_____ **5.** pasar el día en la playa

a. un traje de baño

b. unas botas de cuero

c. un vestido de seda

d. un suéter de lana

e. una camisa de algodón

WB 7-2 **¡Emergencia de moda!** You would like to get several of your friends in for a fashion makeover. Look at the pictures of these friends and describe in detail what they are wearing. Mention the items of clothing, as well as the fabrics and styles.

1.

_____

_____

_____

_____

María Inés

2.

_____

_____

_____

_____

Francisco Javier

¡TE TOCA A TI!

> **WB 7-3** **¡De compras!** You've just won a thousand-dollar shopping spree at your favorite clothing store, but you must spend all the money at one time. What will you buy? **¡OJO!** Don't go over the thousand-dollar limit.

Tienda: _____

Prenda   **Precio**

_____   _____

_____   _____

_____   _____

_____   _____

_____   _____

ASÍ SE DICE Making emphatic statements: stressed possessive adjectives and pronouns

¡A PRACTICAR!

> **WB 7-4** **¡Fuera, compañero nuestro!** Alejandro, an exchange student from Argentina, is moving out of his place. Complete the conversation among the roommates with the appropriate possessive pronoun or adjective as they divide up their things.

TERE: ¿De quién es esta bufanda de lana? Alejandro, ¿es **1.** _____?

ALEJANDRO: No, no es **2.** _____. No llevo bufandas. Pero estos guantes sí son

3. _____. Los compré el año pasado.

CARLOS: Oye, Alejandro, ¿por qué tienes ese televisor en tu caja (*box*)? Es de Tere y mío. No es

4. _____ y tú lo sabes.

ALEJANDRO: ¡No es de Uds.! ¡No es **5.** _____! El televisor **6.** _____ está

en su habitación.

TERE: Esta vez Alejandro tiene razón, Carlos. Pero, Alejandro, ¿qué haces con esas gafas de

sol? Son de Carlos.

ALEJANDRO: No, ¡no son **7.** _____! ¡No son de Carlos! Perdió sus gafas de sol la

semana pasada.

CARLOS: No recuerdo. Pero Alejandro, ¿por qué tienes esas medias en tu maleta (*suitcase*)?

¿No son de Tere?

ALEJANDRO: Ah... ah... pues, este, pues, sí. Son de Tere. Son unas medias **8.** _____.

Yo no sé cómo se metieron (*they got in*) en mi maleta. ¡Qué extraño!

TERE: ¡Sí! ¡Qué curioso!

¡TE TOCA A TI!

WB 7-5   **¿Cuál es mejor?** In each case state who has the better item according to your personal opinion. Follow the model and write your answers in complete sentences.

MODELO: Analí tiene una bicicleta «Huffy» y tú tienes una «Cannondale».
La mía es mejor.

1. Tomás y Adolfo tienen un coche Jeep y tú y tu hermano tienen un Range Rover.

_____

2. Yo tengo un traje de baño «Speedo» y tú tienes un traje de baño «Nike».

_____

3. Yo tengo unas gafas de sol «CK» y Patricio tiene unas gafas «Ray Ban».

_____

4. Nosotras tenemos un par de zapatos «Bruno Magli» y tú tienes un par de zapatos «Payless».

_____

ESTRUCTURA I Talking about singular and/or completed events in the past: verbs irregular in the preterite

¡A PRACTICAR!

WB 7-6   **Una fiesta** Gloria is telling you all the gossip from the party you missed last night. To find out what she says, form complete sentences using the elements below and putting the verb in the preterite.

MODELO: Ledia / saber / de la fiesta / tarde
Ledia supo de la fiesta tarde.

1. muchas personas / venir / a la fiesta

_____

2. haber (hay) / casi 70 personas / en mi casa

_____

3. Marcos y su novia / traer / mucho vino

_____

4. yo / ponerse / contenta / y / ser / la reina de la fiesta

_____

5. Antonio / le / dar / un beso / a la novia de Óscar

_____

El viaje a Argentina It seems that Bea and her boyfriend had a slight problem during their recent trip to Argentina. To find out what happened, complete Bea's letter with the appropriate preterite form of the verbs in parentheses.

Querida Eva:

Pues, ¿qué te puedo decir? ¡1. _____ (Ser) un viaje maravilloso! Yo 2. _____ (ir) primero a Buenos Aires y 3. _____ (estar) sola allí cuatro días. Mi novio, Rafael, 4. _____ (venir) el quinto (fifth) día y nosotros 5. _____ (hacer) varias cosas juntos, pues 6. _____ (haber\hay) muchísimas actividades para hacer en Buenos Aires.

   Después nosotros 7. _____ (ir) a Mendoza. Tú 8. _____ (decir) una vez que tu madre nació allí, ¿verdad? Bueno, nosotros 9. _____ (estar) en Mendoza tres días y el último día yo le 10. _____ (dar) a Rafa una sorpresa. Yo 11. _____ (hacer) reservaciones para ir a Bariloche para esquiar. Rafa no 12. _____ (saber) de mis planes hasta la última noche en Mendoza. Yo le llevé los boletos (tickets) de avión esa noche en el hotel. Pero, Eva, ¿sabes qué? Rafa no 13. _____ (querer) ir.

   Él 14. _____ (decir) que los boletos habían costado demasiado. Yo le 15. _____ (decir) que no habían costado mucho, pero él 16. _____ (ponerse) enojado (angry). Yo no podía creerlo. Yo 17. _____ (hacer) todo lo posible para convencerlo, pero nada. Pero después de dos horas de discusión, yo 18. _____ (saber) por qué. Él también me 19. _____ (dar) una sorpresa: había comprado boletos para visitar las cataratas (falls) del Iguazú. ¡Qué romántico! Pues, tú sabes, ¡al final nosotros 20. _____ (tener) que ir a los dos sitios!

   Bueno, ya te cuento más en otro momento.

Un beso,
Bea

1. ¿Qué problema tuvieron Bea y Rafa en este viaje?

   _____

2. ¿Cómo solucionaron este problema?

   _____

¡TE TOCA A TI!

WB 7-8 | **¿Qué hicieron Uds.?** Write complete sentences to describe what you and others did last week. Follow the model.

MODELO: anoche / tú / no querer...
Anoche yo no quise hacer mi tarea.

1. la semana pasada / tus amigos / tener que hacer...

   _____

2. un día de fiesta el año pasado / tú y tu madre / hacer...

   _____

3. ayer para ir a clase / tú / ponerte...

   _____

4. las vacaciones del verano / tu mejor amigo / ir...

   _____

5. el año pasado / tú / saber...

   _____

VOCABULARIO De compras

¡A PRACTICAR!

WB 7-9 | **En la tienda** Write the letter of the word or phrase that best describes each picture.

_____ **1. a.** la talla

   b. un descuento del 20 por ciento

   c. el cheque

_____ **2. a.** una rebaja

   b. la talla de Michael Jordan

   c. el número que usa Michael Jordan

_____ **3. a.** Es una ganga.

   b. Es muy cara.

   c. Está de última moda.

_____ **4. a.** No le quedan bien.

   b. Cuestan mucho.

   c. Hacen buen juego.

_____ **5. a.** una tarjeta de crédito

   b. un cheque

   c. dinero en efectivo

WB 7-10 | **¡Qué ganga!** Felicity Shagwell is in Argentina trying to buy a special gift for her boyfriend, Austin Powers. To find out what that is, put the sentences of the conversation she has with the store salesperson in order. Two have been done for you.

_____ Ah, pues sí, ese traje es del estilo «retro», de los años 60. En su momento estuvo de última moda.

_____ ¡Me parece bárbaro! ¡Qué ganga!

_____ Muy bien, aquí está mi tarjeta de crédito.

_____ Quisiera comprar un traje nuevo para mi novio, Austin.

_____ Gracias, y aquí está el traje. Hasta luego.

_____ No, gracias. Entonces, ¿cuánto le debo?

_____ Muy bien, señorita. Por aquí tenemos los trajes de última moda.

_____ ¡Qué bueno! ¿Cuánto cuesta ese traje?

_____ No sé su talla, pero creo que esa talla que Ud. tiene por allí le va a quedar muy bien.

_____ Bien, ¿necesita algo más, señorita?

_____ Sí, señorita, es una ganga. ¿Sabe Ud. qué talla necesita su novio?

_____ A ver, el traje cuesta 1.400 pesos.

_16_ Gracias. Chao.

_____ Pues, normalmente ese traje cuesta unos 2.000 pesos, pero le puedo hacer un pequeño descuento. ¿Qué le parece un descuento del 30 por ciento?

_1_ Buenas tardes, señorita, ¿en qué puedo servirle?

_____ Bueno, creo que le va a gustar ese traje de cuadros y lunares que Ud. tiene por allí. ¡Qué lindo es!

¡TE TOCA A TI!

WB 7-11 | **¡Gasta ese dinero!** Write the conversation that takes place between a clothing salesperson and a client in the following situation. Try to use all the clothing-related words and phrases you learned in your text.

DEPENDIENTE: He/She works on commission. If he/she sells lots of clothes, he/she earns a lot of money. He/She needs to persuade his/her clients to buy lots of clothes.

CLIENTE: He/She is a conservative person with a lot of money and wants to buy a bathing suit and several shirts.

_____

_____

Nombre _____ Fecha _____

_____

_____

_____

_____

_____

_____

ESTRUCTURA II Simplifying expressions: direct object pronouns

¡A PRACTICAR!

WB 7-12 | **La vida de una super modelo** Imagine that an Argentinean newspaper has the following interview with supermodel Carolina Peleritti. Find out what she has to say about life as a supermodel by selecting the most appropriate answer. **¡OJO!** Pay attention to the direct object pronouns. Follow the model.

MODELO: ¿Levantas pesas con frecuencia?
_____ Sí, la levanto con frecuencia.
_X_ Sí, las levanto con frecuencia.
_____ Sí, me levanto con frecuencia.

1. ¿Tienes que hacer muchos ejercicios todos los días?

_____ Sí, no tengo que hacerlas todos los días.

_____ Sí, tengo que hacerla todos los días.

_____ Sí, tengo que hacerlos todos los días.

2. ¿Te llama todos los días tu entrenador personal?

_____ Sí, me llama todos los días.

_____ Sí, te llama todos los días.

_____ Sí, la llama todos los días.

3. ¿Compras la ropa de última moda?

_____ Sí, las compro cada mes.

_____ Sí, lo compro cada mes.

_____ Sí, la compro cada mes.

4. ¿Conoces a Donna Karan?

_____ Sí, las conozco.

_____ Sí, lo conozco.

_____ Sí, la conozco.

5. ¿Puedes tomar muchas vacaciones?

_____ Sí, las puedo tomar cada verano.

_____ Sí, lo puedo tomar cada verano.

_____ No, la puedo tomar cada verano.

6. ¿Te invitan a muchas fiestas los diseñadores famosos?

_____ Sí, los invitan a muchas fiestas.

_____ Sí, me invitan a muchas fiestas.

_____ Sí, nos invitan a muchas fiestas.

WB 7-13 | **De compras** Amalia and Elvia are talking about what they want to buy. Complete their conversation by writing answers to the questions and using direct object pronouns. Follow the model.

MODELO: AMALIA: Elvia, ¿vas a comprar esa blusa?
ELVIA: *Sí, la voy a comprar.*
o *Sí, voy a comprarla.*

1. ELVIA: Amalia, ¿tienes ahí tu tarjeta de crédito?

   AMALIA: _____

2. AMALIA: Elvia, ¿quieres comprar esas bufandas?

   ELVIA: _____

3. ELVIA: Amalia, ¿conoces a estos diseñadores?

   AMALIA: _____

4. AMALIA: Elvia, ¿vas a gastar tanto dinero?

   ELVIA: _____

¡TE TOCA A TI!

WB 7-14 | **¡A trabajar!** Answer the following questions in complete sentences using a direct object pronoun. Follow the model.

MODELO: ¿Con quién estudias español?
Lo estudio con mis compañeras de casa.

1. ¿Por qué estudias español?

   _____

2. ¿Vas a estudiar alemán?

   _____

3. ¿Tienes que hacer tu tarea todos los días?

   _____

4. ¿Ves muchas películas de Pedro Almodóvar?

   _____

5. ¿Con qué frecuencia limpian su casa o apartamento tú y tus compañeros(as) o tu familia?

   _____

ESTRUCTURA III Describing ongoing and habitual actions in the past: the imperfect tense

¡A PRACTICAR!

WB 7-15   **Cómo cambiaron los tiempos** Complete Ana María's memories of her past by using the elements below to write complete sentences using the imperfect tense. Follow the model.

MODELO: Hoy la gente siempre está ocupadísima.
en el pasado / la gente / no estar tan ocupada
En el pasado la gente no estaba tan ocupada.

1. Hoy los jóvenes comen mucho en restaurantes de comida rápida.
en el pasado / los jóvenes / comer / en casa

_____

2. Hoy siempre llevas la ropa de última moda.
en el pasado / tú / nunca llevar / la ropa de última moda

_____

3. Hoy la ropa cuesta muchísimo.
en el pasado / la ropa / no costar / mucho

_____

4. Hoy nosotros vemos muchas películas en casa.
en el pasado / nosotros / ir al cine / más

_____

5. Hoy tus padres trabajan diez horas al día.
en el pasado / tus padres / trabajar / sólo ocho horas al día

_____

6. Hoy la gente joven no lee mucho.
en el pasado / la gente joven / leer / más

_____

WB 7-16   **Cuando yo era niño** Carmen told her grandfather all the things she does on Saturdays, and he told her that he used to do the same things when he was a child. What did he say? Follow the model.

MODELO: CARMEN: Los sábados me levanto a las 8:00 y...
RAMÓN: *Los sábados me levantaba a las 8:00 y...*

CARMEN: Los sábados me levanto a las 8:00 y luego voy al baño. A veces, tengo mucho sueño. Después, desayuno mientras miro la televisión por media hora. Entonces me baño y me visto. Luego juego un poco en casa o, cuando veo a mis amigos en la calle, jugamos juntos. Tengo muchos amigos y somos un grupo muy unido. A veces vamos todos a la plaza para hablar con otros amigos y otras veces vamos al cine. Nunca gastamos mucho dinero, pero siempre nos divertimos mucho.

RAMÓN:

_____
_____
_____
_____
_____
_____
_____
_____
_____
_____

WB 7-17 | **Recuerdos de Mallorca** Elena is on vacation in Mallorca, Spain, and wants to send her boyfriend, Tomás, a letter but she needs your help. Decide whether the verbs should be in the preterite or the imperfect and then rewrite the letter. **¡OJO!** Read the letter through once to understand the context before deciding on the appropriate verb form.

Querido Tomás:

Lo estamos pasando muy bien en Mallorca. Rita, Simón, Toño, Amalia y yo (llegar) a la isla a mediodía y ya (hacer) calor. ¡Qué bonito día (ser), Tomás! Nosotros (ir) directamente a nuestro hotel donde (tener) una reserva por una semana. ¿Sabes cuál (ser) la primera cosa que (hacer)? ¡(Ponernos) el traje de baño y (nadar) en el Mediterráneo! El agua (estar) maravillosa. Después, (cambiarnos) de ropa y (tomar) un taxi al Restaurante Torremolinos. Allí, (haber) un papagayo en la terraza. Creo que Rita (enamorarse) de él porque le (dar) muchas galletas saladas.

Elena

¡TE TOCA A TI!

¡Cómo cambian los tiempos! Write complete sentences to describe what the following people and things were like when you were younger. Follow the model.

MODELO: tu rutina diaria los días de escuela
Me levantaba a las 6:00 de la mañana y desayunaba con mi familia.

1. tu casa o apartamento

_____

2. la ropa que llevabas

_____

3. tu escuela y tus maestros

_____

4. los programas de televisión que veías

_____

5. tu cantante favorito

_____

6. lo que hacías después de la escuela

_____

SÍNTESIS

¡A LEER!

EL TANGO: BAILE, CANCIÓN, MÚSICA, POESÍA In your textbook you have already learned a little about the tango. The following article will provide you with more information about the origins of the tango dance and song.

Strategy: Using background knowledge to anticipate content

The better you can anticipate what you will read, the more easily you will be able to understand the main ideas in reading a passage. In addition to looking at the pictures, titles, and subtitles that accompany a text, you should also think about what you already know about the topic.

Paso 1: Take a few minutes to think about what you have learned. Write some ideas below, and if you can, write them in Spanish.

_____

_____

_____

Paso 2: Now look at the title of the text on the following page and make a list of a few things you anticipate learning in this reading.

_____

_____

Paso 3: Before reading the article in detail, scan the following questions you will have to answer after reading it. You can then look for this information as you read.

1. ¿Dónde originó la música del tango?

_____

2. ¿Por qué dice el artículo que el tango es un hecho cultural?

_____

3. ¿Qué le da al tango su sonido único?

_____

4. ¿Por qué al principio el tango era de clase baja?

_____

5. ¿Dónde originó el nombre «tango»?

_____

El tango: baile, canción, música, poesía

El tango surgió de los suburbios de la ciudad de Buenos Aires a fines del siglo XIX cuando, por razones de inmigración y progreso, la ciudad se transformaba en un inmenso centro urbano. Este mosaico cultural incluía por un lado inmigrantes españoles, italianos, alemanes, árabes, judíos y negros, y por otro, gauchos e indios del interior del país. Esa mezcla hizo del tango un producto cultural único en el mundo y capaz de resaltar[1] en él todas las características de los habitantes de Buenos Aires.

En sus primeros años de vida el tango era ejecutado y bailado en prostíbulos[2] y se comenzó a bailar de un modo muy provocador, cercano, explícito: en pocas palabras, de una forma socialmente poco aceptable. Por eso el tango permaneció durante muchos años como algo marginal y de clase baja. Todo esto cambió, sin embargo, cuando el fenómeno del tango llegó a París, capital de la moda y cuna[3] del chic. Allí el tango triunfó y desde entonces ha entrado en los salones de baile más nobles de mundo.

En sus comienzos musicales, las canciones del tango eran solamente instrumentales, ejecutadas por tríos de guitarra, violín y flauta. Más tarde se incorporó un instrumento procedente de Alemania llamado el bandoneón. Éste le dio al tango su sonido característico por el cual hoy es reconocido en todo el mundo. Al principio las letras de las canciones del tango también fueron de un contenido vulgar y grotesco, pero todo esto cambió en segunda década del siglo XIX. Es cuando los grandes poetas de la música ríoplatense[4] comenzaron a escribir canciones sobre el amor y el amor perdido, así elevando el prestigio de la música del tango.

Aunque no cabe duda que Buenos Aires es el lugar de nacimiento del tango, el origen del nombre mismo es todavía un misterio. Algunos creen que es de origen español, pues en el siglo XIX se usaba el término para un palo flamenco. Otros creen que su origen es africano ya que la geografía africana cuenta con algunos topónimos[5] de ese nombre. Además, en varios documentos coloniales españoles se usa el nombre «tango» para referirse al lugar en que los esclavos negros celebraban sus reuniones festivas. Lo que no es misterio, sin embargo, es el completo fenómeno cultural que es el tango —baile, música, canción, poesía— que por una u otra razón atrae a tanta gente.

[1]**resaltar** *emphasize* [2]**prostíbulos** *houses of ill repute* [3]**cuna** *origin* [4]**ríoplatense** *from Río de la Plata, Argentina* [5]**topónimos** *place names*

¡A ESCRIBIR!

A REPORT ON CHANGING FASHION HABITS You will write a short report to describe what fashion was like when you were younger and how it has changed over time in your opinion.

Strategy: Editing your writing

Editing your written work is an important skill to master when learning a foreign language. You should plan on editing what you write several times. When checking your compositions, consider the following.

1. Content
   a. Is the title of your composition captivating? Would it cause readers to want to read further?
   b. Is the information you wrote pertinent to the established topic?
   c. Is your composition interesting? Does it capture reader interest?

2. **Organization**
   a. Does each paragraph in the composition have a clearly identifiable main idea?
   b. Do the details in each paragraph relate to a single idea?
   c. Are the sentences in the paragraph ordered in a logical sequence?
   d. Is the order of the paragraphs correct in your composition?

3. **Cohesion and style**
   a. Does your composition as a whole communicate what you are trying to convey?
   b. Does your composition "flow" easily and smoothly from beginning to end?
   c. Are there transitions between the different paragraphs you included in your composition?

4. **Style and accuracy**
   a. Have you chosen the precise vocabulary words you need to express your ideas?
   b. Are there grammatical errors in your composition (i.e., subject-verb agreement; adjective-noun agreement; errors with verb forms or irregular verbs, etc.)
   c. Are there spelling errors in your composition (including capitalization, accentuation, and punctuation)?

If you consider these factors as you edit your written work, the overall quality of your compositions can increase drastically!

Paso 1: Before you begin to write, answer the following questions in Spanish on a separate piece of paper.

Functions: Talking about past events; Talking about recent events
Vocabulary: Clothing; Fabrics; Colors; Stores and products
Grammar: Verbs: irregular preterite, regular preterite; Personal pronouns: direct, indirect

• How has fashion changed since you were in high school? Or since your parents were in high school?
• What clothes did people wear that they don't wear now?
• What shops and designers were popular then but are not now?

Paso 2: Now write a first draft on scrap paper, and then revise it using the strategy you have just learned.

Paso 3: Write your revised draft below.

_____

_____

_____

_____

_____

_____

_____

_____

_____

Autoprueba

VOCABULARIO

WB 7-19 **La ropa** Write the name of each of the appropriate clothing items listed in their appropriate category.

MODELO: Para las manos: *los guantes*

a blusa	el impermeable	el traje	las botas	las medias
el traje de baño	los calcetines	los pantalones	el vestido	la corbata
las sandalias	los zapatos	la falda	el sombrero	

1. Para nadar: _____

2. Para la cabeza: _____

3. Para los pies: _____

4. Para las mujeres: _____

5. Para los hombres: _____

6. Para la lluvia: _____

WB 7-20 **En la tienda** Complete the following conversation with appropriate words and phrases from the list. **¡OJO!** You don't have to use all the words and phrases.

en qué puedo servirle	moda	rebaja	número
talla	hace juego	probarme	tarjeta de crédito
le debo	queda bien	ganga	

DEPENDIENTE: Buenas tardes, señor. ¿**1.** _____?

CLIENTE: Buenas tardes. Busco un traje nuevo. ¿Puedo **2.** _____ este traje?

DEPENDIENTE: Sí, por aquí.

CLIENTE: Ay, este traje no es mi **3.** _____. No me **4.** _____.

DEPENDIENTE: Lo siento, señor. Aquí está otro.

CLIENTE: Sí, éste es mejor. Y esta camisa, ¿qué opina? ¿**5.** _____ con el traje?

DEPENDIENTE: Sí, hace juego perfectamente. Además, es de última **6.** _____.

CLIENTE: Muy bien, ¿cuánto **7.** _____?

DEPENDIENTE: En total son 200 dólares.

CLIENTE: ¡Qué **8.** _____! Puedo pagar con **9.** _____?

DEPENDIENTE: ¡Claro que sí!

Nombre _____ Fecha _____

ESTRUCTURAS

WB 7-21 | **¿Son tuyos?** Your friend Carlos is asking you for the fifth time to whom the following things belong. You are fed up with his forgetfulness and respond with very emphatic answers. Write them out using possessive adjectives or pronouns. Follow the model.

> MODELO: ¿De quién es esta mochila? / yo
> *¡La mochila es mía!*
> o *Ésta es una mochila mía.*

1. ¿De quién es este sombrero? / tú

_____

2. ¿De quiénes son estos cinturones? / Tomás y Ricardo

_____

3. ¿De quiénes son estos zapatos? / Uds.

_____

4. ¿De quién son estas gafas de sol? / yo

_____

5. ¿De quién es este paraguas? / Teresa

_____

WB 7-22 | **A la hora de la cena** Complete the conversations with the appropriate direct object pronouns.

1. —Preparaste una cena muy buena, Julio. ¡Eres tan simpático!

—Gracias, Gloria. _____ preparé porque sé que estás ocupada hoy.

2. —Juan Carlos, ¿ya comiste tu pescado?

—Pues... no, papá. El gato _____ está comiendo.

3. —¿_____ quieres, mamá?

—Sí, tu papá y yo _____ queremos mucho, Juan Carlos.

4. —De postre quiero una de esas naranjas, papá.

—Bien, Juan Carlos. Acabo de comprar_____ en el mercado.

WB 7-23 | **La pequeña Elena** Complete the following paragraph about Elena Navarro's childhood using the imperfect of the appropriate verbs from the list.

comer comprar gustar ir limpiar sacar tener vivir

De niña yo **1.** _____ cerca de Buenos Aires. (Yo) **2.** _____ algunos quehaceres en casa. Por ejemplo, **3.** _____ la basura y **4.** _____ mi dormitorio.

Todos los sábados mi mamá y yo **5.** _____ de compras al centro. A veces ella no **6.** _____ nada, pero nos **7.** _____ mirar las cosas de las tiendas. Por la tarde nosotras **8.** _____ en un café pequeño.

Paca y Peca Complete the following conversation with the appropriate form of either the preterite or the imperfect of the verbs in parentheses.

PACA: Anoche mientras nosotras **1.** _____ (trabajar) en la cocina, Marcos me

2. _____ (llamar) por teléfono.

PECA: ¿Marcos? ¿El hombre que **3.** _____ (conocer) en el supermercado? Pues, qué

4. _____ (querer) él, Paca?

PACA: Pues, Marcos me **5.** _____ (invitar) a salir a bailar el próximo sábado.

6. _____ (Ser) una sorpresa para mí.

PECA: Oye, ¡qué sorpresa más buena **7.** _____ (recibir) tú! ¿Y qué le

8. _____ (decir) a Marcos?

PACA: Le **9.** _____ (decir) que no **10.** _____ (poder) salir con él el sábado

porque ayer mis tíos nos **11.** _____ (invitar) a Rita y a mí a su casa.

PECA: Luego, ¿qué te **12.** _____ (decir) Marcos cuando **13.** _____ (oír) tu

respuesta?

PACA: Pues, Marcos **14.** _____ (ser) tan simpático. Me **15.** _____

(invitar) a bailar el domingo y yo **16.** _____ (aceptar) su invitación.

Fiestas y vacaciones: Guatemala y El Salvador

VOCABULARIO Fiestas y celebraciones

¡A PRACTICAR!

WB 8-1 **¿Qué pasó en la fiesta?** Paulino didn't go to Luci's surprise party last night, but he heard rumors about what happened. Based on the drawings below put the details in order and then, using your own words, write a paragraph about what happened at Luci's party.

____ Juan Carlos le gritó a Javi y Javi se asustó.

____ Todos lo pasaban bien, menos su novio, Juan Carlos.

____ Anoche se reunió toda la familia de Luci.

____ Juan Carlos reaccionó mal cuando vio que Javi, el ex novio de Luci, estaba en la fiesta.

____ Luci cumplió 20 años y su familia le dio una fiesta de sorpresa.

____ Luci lloró y le dijo a Juan Carlos que se portaba muy mal.

____ Todos los invitados le trajeron regalos.

¿Qué pasó?

_____

_____

_____

_____

_____

WB 8-2 **¡Qué dramáticos!** How do students react when their professor announces a surprise exam? Form sentences using an appropriate form of **ponerse** + the adjective provided. Remember to make the adjectives agree with the persons they describe. Follow the model.

MODELO: Teresa y Gabriel / triste
Teresa y Gabriel se ponen tristes.

1. Carolina / enojado

   _____

2. Javier y Silvia / asustado

   _____

3. tú y Verónica / horrorizado

   _____

4. yo / frustrado

   _____

5. tú / contento

   _____

6. nosotros / nerviosos

   _____

¡TE TOCA A TI!

WB 8-3 **Y tú, ¿qué haces?** Irene is new to the U.S., and she wants to know more about the holidays we celebrate here. For each day listed below, write a sentence to describe what you did last year. Follow the model.

MODELO: el día de la madre
Hice una fiesta en mi casa para mi mamá.

1. las navidades (*Christmas*)

   _____

2. el día de los enamorados (*Valentine's Day*)

   _____

3. tu cumpleaños

   _____

4. la noche vieja (*New Year's Eve*)

   _____

5. el día de las brujas (*Halloween*)

   _____

WB 8-4 **¿Cómo reaccionas?** Write a sentence to describe how you react in the following situations. Follow the model.

MODELO: al ver una película de comedia
Me pongo alegre.

1. al escuchar la música de los Red Hot Chili Peppers

_____

2. al recibir una mala nota

_____

3. al estar en la lluvia

_____

4. al ver una película cómica

_____

ASÍ SE DICE Inquiring and providing information about people and events: interrogative words

¡A PRACTICAR!

WB 8-5 **Una llamada a mamá** Mónica makes her weekly call home to her mother in El Salvador, and as usual, her mother has a million questions for her. Complete their conversation with the appropriate interrogative words. **¡OJO!** Remember that these words always have a written accent.

SEÑORA LÓPEZ: ¡Bueno!

MÓNICA: ¡Hola, mamá! Soy yo, Mónica.

SEÑORA LÓPEZ: ¡Mónica! ¿**1.** _____ estás, hija?

MÓNICA: Bien, mami, bien.

SEÑORA LÓPEZ: Me alegro. Oye, ¿**2.** _____ estás ahora? ¿Estás en la residencia?

MÓNICA: Sí, mami. ¿Y papi, **3.** _____ está? ¿Está en casa?

SEÑORA LÓPEZ: Sí, pero ya se durmió. ¿**4.** _____ hora es allí?

MÓNICA: Son las once. Dentro de poco voy a una fiesta.

SEÑORA LÓPEZ: Mónica, ¿**5.** _____ quieres ir a una fiesta tan tarde? ¿No tienes clases mañana?

MÓNICA: Ay, mami. Sí, tengo clases, pero está bien. No pasa nada.

SEÑORA LÓPEZ: ¿**6.** _____ vas? ¿Con **7.** _____ vas?

MÓNICA: Mami, no te preocupes. No vamos a salir de la residencia. Voy con mi amiga Carola.

SEÑORA LÓPEZ: ¿**8.** _____ es Carola? ¿**9.** _____ es ella? ¿Es de Nueva York? ¿**10.** _____ tiempo hace que la conoces?

MÓNICA: ¡Mami! Tranquila. Es mi amiga y es de Manhattan, pero habla español muy bien. Es muy buena gente y vamos a estar bien. Dime, mami, ¿11. _____ pasa allí? ¿Alguna novedad?

SEÑORA LÓPEZ: Pues, sí. ¡Nació (was born) tu primera sobrina!

MÓNICA: ¿De verdad? ¿12. _____ nació? ¿13. _____ se llama?

SEÑORA LÓPEZ: Se llama Verónica y nació anoche.

MÓNICA: ¿14. _____ pesa?

SEÑORA LÓPEZ: Unas ocho libras. Es grande.

MÓNICA: ¡Qué alegría, mami! Mira, voy a tener que irme, pero quería preguntarte, ¿te acuerdas (do you remember) del libro que me recomendaste la semana pasada?

SEÑORA LÓPEZ: ¿15. _____ libro?

MÓNICA: El libro de cuentos. ¿16. _____ era el título?

SEÑORA LÓPEZ: Ay, mi amor, ya soy tan vieja que no puedo recordar.

MÓNICA: Bueno, mami. Tal vez la próxima vez. Mira, ya me tengo que ir. Un beso para papi, y dos para mi nueva sobrina. Chao.

SEÑORA LÓPEZ: Te quiero mucho. Chao, Mónica.

¡TE TOCA A TI!

WB 8-6 **Entrevista** You work in a travel agency and are helping Mr. Muñoz plan a trip to Central America. What questions do you ask him to prepare his trip? Write eight different questions using interrogative words. ¡OJO! A travel agent would use the **usted** form of the verb with the client.

1. _____

2. _____

3. _____

4. _____

5. _____

6. _____

7. _____

8. _____

ESTRUCTURA I Narrating in the past: the preterite vs. the imperfect

¡A PRACTICAR!

WB 8-7 **Traducciones** Translate the following sentences into Spanish. **¡OJO!** Each sentence requires one verb in the preterite and one in the imperfect.

1. My grandmother was preparing food when the guests arrived.

   _____

2. My little brother was behaving poorly and he had to go to his bedroom.

   _____

3. My girlfriend called while I was watching television.

   _____

4. Teri and Juan remembered the party while they were at the office.

   _____

5. It began to rain as Santi was leaving the house.

   _____

WB 8-8 **Un cuento de hadas** Complete the fairy tale on page 128 by filling in the blanks with the appropriate form of the verb in the preterite or the imperfect. **¡OJO!** Read the story through once to understand the context before you try to decide on the verb form. When you finish, guess which fairy tale it is.

1. _____ (Haber) una vez un rey que 2. _____ (tener) cinco hijas. De todas ellas, la más joven 3. _____ (ser) la más bonita. La princesa 4. _____ (tener) una pelota (*a ball*) y siempre 5. _____ (ir) a jugar a solas con esta pelota al lado de un estanque (*pond*) cerca del castillo. Un día la princesa 6. _____ (perder) su pelota en el agua del estanque. La pobre princesa no 7. _____ (saber) nadar y por eso no 8. _____ (poder) recoger su pelota favorita. La princesa 9. _____ (estar) muy triste y 10. _____ (empezar) a llorar. De repente la princesa 11. _____ (oír) una voz. La voz le decía, «Princesa, ¿qué 12. _____ (pasar) aquí? ¿Por qué lloras?» La princesa no 13. _____ (saber) de dónde 14. _____ (venir) la voz, pero pronto ella 15. _____ (ver) un sapito (*little frog*). En este momento el sapo 16. _____ (volver) a hablar y 17._____ (decir): «Yo te puedo devolver (*return*) tu querida pelota si me haces un favor». La princesa 18. _____ (preguntar) cuál 19. _____ (ser) el favor y el sapo 20. _____ (contestar) que él 21. _____ (querer) un beso. La princesa 22. _____ (tener) que pensar un minuto: ella 23. _____ (querer) su pelota, pero no 24. _____ (saber) si 25. _____ (poder) darle un beso al sapo. Al final 26. _____ (decidir) que sí. Ella 27. _____ (ir) a darle un beso al sapo.

En ese momento el sapo se zambulló (*dove*) en el agua y le 28. _____ (devolver) la pelota a la princesa. Ahora la princesa 29. _____ (tener) que besarlo. Ella 30. _____ (cerrar) los ojos y lo 31. _____ (besar). Un segundo después la princesa 32. _____ (saber) por qué el sapo quería el beso.

¿Cómo se llama el cuento?

_____

¡TE TOCA A TI!

| WB 8-9 | **Termina el cuento** Now it is your turn to write the fairy tale. Write several sentences to complete the fairy tale on page 128. Pay attention to your use of the preterite and the imperfect. You can be creative!

_____

_____

_____

_____

_____

_____

_____

_____

_____

_____

VOCABULARIO La playa y el campo

¡A PRACTICAR!

| WB 8-10 | **¿Qué sabes y qué quieres aprender?** Look at the drawings below and on the next page and write whether or not you know how to do the indicated sport, or whether or not you have a desire to learn that sport. Following the model, name the sport in each drawing.

MODELO: *Sé pasear en canoa.*
     o *No sé pasear en canoa.*

       Quiero aprender a pasear en canoa.
     o *No tengo ganas de aprender a pasear en canoa.*

1. _____

_____

2. _____

_____

3. _____

_____

4. _____

_____

5. _____

_____

¡TE TOCA A TI!

WB 8-11 | **Fin de semana ideal** You have won a week-long beach resort vacation for you and two friends at Los Chorros in El Salvador. The resort offers all the sports and activities that you could want. With whom will you go? What activities will you do there? What will you bring there? Write a brief paragraph to answer these questions and describe all that you and your friends will do.

_____

_____

_____

_____

_____

_____

_____

_____

ESTRUCTURA II Stating indefinite ideas and quantities: affirmative and negative expressions

¡A PRACTICAR!

WB 8-12 **Conversaciones en el café** While in a café in San Salvador, you hear parts of different conversations. For each question that you hear, select the appropriate answer from the list and complete it with the correct affirmative or negative expression. Follow the model.

MODELO: ¿Quieres tomar algo más?
No, no quiero tomar nada.

No, no lo quiero hacer...	No prefiero...
No, no conozco a...	No, no vamos a hacer...
No, no lo tomo con leche...	No, no vi...

1. ¿Siempre tomas café con leche?

_____

2. ¿Conoces a alguien de esa compañía?

_____

3. ¿Quieres hacer camping este fin de semana?

_____

4. ¿Prefieres este pastel o esta torta?

_____

5. ¿Viste algo interesante en la tele anoche?

_____

6. ¿Van a hacer Uds. algún viaje este verano?

_____

WB 8-13 **Bienvenida, abuelita** Rafa's grandmother has just arrived and Rafa thinks she's brought him presents. To find out whether she did or not, complete their conversation with an appropriate word from the list.

algo algún algunas algunos ningún ninguna siempre tampoco

RAFA: ¿Me trajiste **1.** _____ regalo, abuelita?

ABUELA: ¡Claro! **2.** _____ te traigo regalos, ¿verdad?

RAFA: Sí. ¿Me trajiste **3.** _____ libros de Disney?

ABUELA: No, Rafa. No te traje **4.** _____ libro.

RAFA: ¿Me trajiste **5.** _____ para comer?

ABUELA: **6.** _____, niño.

RAFA: Pues, ¿qué me trajiste, abuelita?

ABUELA: Te traje 7. _____ camisas...

RAFA: ¡Ay, no quiero 8. _____ camisa!

ABUELA: ...y un juego electrónico.

RAFA: ¡Gracias, abuelita!

¡TE TOCA A TI!

WB 8-14 | **¿Cómo eres?** You will spend the summer with the Suárez family in Guatemala. Lola, your host mother, wants to know more about you and has written to ask you the following questions. Answer her questions using affirmative and negative expressions.

1. ¿Ya sabes algo de Guatemala?

   _____

2. ¿Te gusta hacer algún deporte acuático? ¿También te gusta caminar por las montañas?

   _____

   _____

3. Para el primer día de tu visita, ¿prefieres ir a la playa o ir a las montañas?

   _____

4. ¿Tienes algunas preguntas para nosotros?

   _____

ASÍ SE DICE Talking about periods of time since an event took place: *hace* and *hace que*

¡A PRACTICAR!

WB 8-15 | **¡Tanto tiempo!** Juan's family is very monotonous: they never change their routine. How long have his family members done the following activities? Following the model, put the elements together in complete sentences using **hacer** + time expression.

MODELO: Teresa: estudiar alemán / cuatro años
Hace cuatro años que Teresa estudia alemán.

1. doña María: trabajar de dependiente en una tienda / 20 años

   _____

   _____

2. don José: tomar copas con sus amigos después del trabajo / 30 años

   _____

   _____

3. Olivia y su hermana: jugar con las muñecas Barbie / dos años

   _____

   _____

4. toda la familia: acostarse a las 11:00 de la noche / mucho tiempo

_____

_____

5. la abuela: no salir de la casa los domingos / diez años

_____

_____

¡TE TOCA A TI!

WB 8-16 **¿Cuánto tiempo hace?** Answer the following questions and indicate how long the following people have been doing the indicated activities, or how long it has been since the last time they did the indicated activities. Follow the models.

MODELOS: ¿Cuándo fue la última vez que tus amigos hicieron una fiesta?
Hace dos días que mis amigos hicieron una fiesta.

¿Cuánto tiempo hace que estudias español?
Hace dos años que estudio español.

1. ¿Cuándo fue la última vez que viste una película extranjera?

_____

_____

2. ¿Cuándo fue la última vez que tus padres se vistieron elegantemente?

_____

_____

3. ¿Cuánto tiempo hace que no compras nada nuevo?

_____

_____

4. ¿Cuánto tiempo hace que Carlos, Tere y tú son amigos?

_____

_____

5. ¿Cuándo fue la última vez que tu y tu familia fueron de vacaciones?

_____

_____

¡A LEER!

LA SEMANA SANTA EN GUATEMALA You are going to read an article about Semana Santa, or Holy Week, in Guatemala.

Strategy: Guessing meaning from word roots

Up to this point, you have learned a large number of new Spanish words. You are also able to recognize a large number of cognates, even if these words are new to you. Using this knowledge, you can guess the meaning of even more new Spanish words if you know the meaning of their roots.

Paso 1: Guess the meaning by matching the definition to the word.

_____ **1.** bañado   **a.** to travel through

_____ **2.** guatemalteco   **b.** Guatemalan

_____ **3.** recorrer   **c.** bathed

_____ **4.** conmemorar   **d.** to commemorate

Paso 2: Now read the article through once and note below several of the words that you do not know.

_____

_____

_____

_____

Paso 3: Think about whether any of these words remind you of other Spanish words you have learned, or whether they look like English words you know. Below, write your best guess at the meaning of the words you listed in **Paso 2.**

_____

_____

_____

_____

Paso 4: Now read the article a second time. Keep in mind the meanings you believe the above words have. Try to confirm or reject these guesses based on the context of the reading this time.

Paso 5: When you are done, look up the actual definition of the words in a dictionary. Below, write the definitions of the words whose definition you guessed incorrectly.

_____

_____

_____

_____

Nombre _____ Fecha _____

Paso 6: Read the article once more and answer the following comprehension questions.

1. ¿Qué se conmemora durante la Semana Santa? ¿La celebramos también en los Estados Unidos?

   _____

2. ¿Cuáles son dos actividades de las celebraciones?

   _____

   _____

3. Según el artículo, ¿cuál es la función de las alfombras?

   _____

   _____

4. ¿Dónde se puede ver ejemplos de las alfombras de las celebraciones de Semana Santa?

   _____

La Semana Santa en Guatemala

La Semana Santa es una de las tradiciones más importantes en Guatemala y una de las épocas más bellas del país. Conmemorar el Sufrimiento y la Resurrección de Jesucristo, es una tradición que tiene sus orígenes en la religión católica.

Sin embargo, después de tantos años de repetirse, las celebraciones se han convertido en una expresión más cultural que religiosa del pueblo guatemalteco.

Durante Semana Santa se vive un fascinante ambiente pacífico, bañado en el sol de media tarde, los árboles de jacaranda en flor y un olor místico, mezcla de corozo[1] e incienso. Las actividades que se llevan a cabo también añaden a este ambiente espiritual. Llenos de fervor, los guatemaltecos tienen procesiones que recorren las calles para conmemorar a Jesús y María y para vivir la Pasión de Cristo.

Otra actividad importante de esta semana es la elaboración de alfombras de aserrín,[2] flores y frutas, entre otras cosas. Estas alfombras se utilizan para el paso de las procesiones y tienen su origen en la creencia de que lo sagrado no debe tocar el suelo. Las alfombras son ofrendas que unen a la familia y a los vecinos. Se trata de un arte popular efímero[3] que se originó en Guatemala y se difundió hacia el mundo. Las alfombras cada vez son más largas y elaboradas.

Unas de las más impresionantes se puede observar en San Bartolomé Becerra en La Antigua Guatemala.

Sin duda alguna, pasar una Semana Santa en Guatemala es vivir no solamente los colores y olores de la temporada, sino también la esencia de la cultura guatemalteca.

[1]**corozo** *a type of palm* [2]**aserrín** *sawdust* [3]**efímero** *ephemeral*

¡A ESCRIBIR!

LAS CELEBRACIONES FAMILIARES In this section you will write a summary of a favorite holiday or celebration.

Strategy: Writing a summary

A good summary tells the reader the most important information about an event. The following is a list of important data that one should include in a summary.

- An interesting title or topic sentence
- Description of the setting: when and where the action took place, who was involved, any special conditions that were in existence
- What made the situation interesting or unique
- What actions took place, expected or unexpected
- How the event or situation ended or was resolved

Paso 1: When you were young, what was your favorite holiday or celebration? How long has it been since you last celebrated? How did you celebrate? Did something special/funny/interesting happen? Answer these questions below in Spanish.

Functions: Writing about past events; Writing about theme, plot, or scene
Vocabulary: Family members; Religious holidays; Time expressions
Grammar: Verbs: Preterite & Imperfect

_____

_____

_____

_____

_____

Paso 2: Based on your responses above, write a descriptive paragraph to summarize these details. Since you will describe in the past, you will need to pay attention to your use of the preterite and the imperfect. Refer to your text to review the use of these verb forms.

Paso 3: Revise your first draft, making sure your ideas are organized and that your verb forms are accurate, and then write your final draft below.

_____

_____

_____

_____

_____

_____

_____

_____

_____

_____

Autoprueba

VOCABULARIO

WB 8-17 | **Una celebración especial** To find out how Ana's party was last night, complete the following description with the appropriate words from the list. **¡OJO!** If you use a verb, you may have to conjugate it.

anfitriona	llorar	brindis	máscara	celebrar	pasarlo
cumplir	pastel	disfraz	disfrazarse	recordar	invitados
entremeses	regalos	felicidades	reunirse	gritar	velas

Ayer Silvia **1.** _____ 30 años y Ana le hizo una fiesta divertida. Había mucha cerveza, vino y sodas. También Ana preparó varios **2.** _____ y todos comieron un montón.

Todos los **3.** _____ tuvieron que **4.** _____ de su personaje histórico favorito. Ana se puso una **5.** _____ de Marie Antoinette y su esposo, Jorge, llevó un **6.** _____ de Simón Bolívar. Después de que llegó Silvia, todos desfilaron (*paraded*) para seleccionar al que estaba mejor disfrazado.

A las 11:00 de la noche, a la misma hora en que nació Silvia, todos **7.** _____ para **8.** _____ el momento. Hicieron un **9.** _____ y todos **10.** _____, «¡**11.** _____!». Luego, empezaron a comer el **12.** _____ de cumpleaños. Esta vez no tenía **13.** _____ porque Silvia no quería **14.** _____ cuántos años cumplía. A la medianoche Silvia abrió sus **15.** _____. Su novio, Raúl, le dio un anillo de diamantes y Silvia empezó a **16.** _____.

La fiesta acabó a las 3:00 de la mañana. Todos **17.** _____ muy bien y antes de salir todos le dieron las gracias a la **18.** _____ que había preparado (*had prepared*) tan buena fiesta.

¡La celebración fue un éxito total!

WB 8-18 | **En la playa y en el campo** Write in the blank the letter of each activity described.

____ **1.** nadar debajo del agua con un tubo   **a.** bucear

____ **2.** nadar debajo del agua con un tanque   **b.** acampar

____ **3.** jugar en el agua con una tabla   **c.** tomar el sol

____ **4.** navegar en bote de vela en el mar   **d.** correr las olas

____ **5.** descansar tranquilamente en la playa   **e.** pasear en canoa

____ **6.** cocinar carne al aire libre   **f.** hacer esnórquel

____ **7.** dormir bajo las estrellas   **g.** hacer una parrillada

____ **8.** navegar por los ríos en un bote   **h.** pasear en velero

ESTRUCTURAS

WB 8-19 **Más preguntas** A new Internet pen pal asks you the following questions. Complete his questions with the appropriate interrogative word.

1. Soy de la Ciudad de Guatemala. ¿_____ eres tú?

2. Ahora estoy en la universidad. ¿_____ estás tú ahora mismo?

3. A mí me encanta la música de Pink Floyd. ¿_____ es tu música favorita?

4. Paso mucho tiempo en la selva con mis amigos. ¿_____ vas tú para divertirte?

5. Salimos a bailar mucho. ¿_____ haces tú para divertirte en tu ciudad?

6. Tomo tres clases este semestre. ¿_____ clases tomas tú?

7. Estudio relaciones internacionales. ¿_____ estudias tú?

WB 8-20 **Un viaje inolvidable** Read the following story about one of Guillermo's most memorable trips. Then fill in the blanks with the appropriate form of the verb in the preterite or the imperfect.

Cuando yo **1.** _____ (ser) más joven, **2.** _____ (hacer) una vez un viaje a

Belice. **3.** _____ (Ir) con toda mi familia. Mi hermanito **4.** _____ (tener)

tres años y yo **5.** _____ (tener) 14. Después de pensarlo mucho, mis padres

6. _____ (decidir) hacer el viaje a Belice porque quedaba tan cerca de donde nosotros

7. _____ (vivir) en Guatemala en esos años.

　　Recuerdo todo de ese viaje. El lugar **8.** _____ (ser) tan limpio y bonito y en las

playas **9.** _____ (haber) muchos pájaros y otros animales bonitos. Yo sí

10. _____ (poder) nadar, pero mi hermanito todavía no **11.** _____ (saber)

nadar. Un día yo **12.** _____ (ir) a bucear sin él y él **13.** _____ (empezar) a

llorar. ¡Pobre Juan! En realidad, pobre de mí, porque ese día mientras yo **14.** _____

(nadar) en el mar un pez grande me **15.** _____ (morder) *(to bite)*. En un instante yo

16. _____ (sentir) un dolor tremendo y **17.** _____ (gritar), «¡Mamá,

ayúdame!».

　　Mi mamá **18.** _____ (meterse) al agua y me **19.** _____ (salvar) la

vida. Después de salir del agua yo **20.** _____ (tener) que ir al hospital. Al final no

21. _____ (ser) nada serio, pero de todas formas toda la situación me

22. _____ (asustar) mucho.

WB 8-21 **Significados especiales** Remember that certain verbs have special meanings if used in the preterite or the imperfect. Complete the following with the appropriate form of the verbs according to the meaning of the phrase.

1. Anoche nosotros _____ (tener) que asistir a una reunión muy aburrida. No salimos de allí hasta las 10:00 de la noche.

2. El año pasado Elisa _____ (saber) que Esteban tenía una hermana. No lo _____ (saber) antes.

3. Anita quería llevarme a una celebración familiar pero yo no _____ (querer) ir. Me quedé en casa.

4. La semana pasada Dolores trató de sacar dinero del banco pero no _____ (poder). El cajero automático (la máquina «ATM») estaba descompuesto (broken) y el banco estaba cerrado.

5. Cuando yo era más joven _____ (tener) que estudiar mucho.

WB 8-22 **En el mercado** Complete the following conversation with the appropriate word from the following list.

algo	ni... ni	algún	ninguna	algunas	nunca	algunos	también	nada	tampoco

VENDEDOR: ¿Quiere **1.** _____, señor?

CLIENTE: Sí, quiero **2.** _____ tomates, por favor.

VENDEDOR: Bien. ¿Quiere **3.** _____ naranjas **4.** _____? Están muy frescas.

CLIENTE: No, no quiero **5.** _____ porque no como frutas.

VENDEDOR: ¿Necesita **6.** _____ huevos frescos, señor?

CLIENTE: No, **7.** _____ como huevos.

VENDEDOR: ¿Verdad? Mi esposa no come **8.** _____ frutas **9.** _____ huevos. ¡Qué coincidencia! ¿Necesita pan hoy?

CLIENTE: No, gracias, no necesito **10.** _____ más.

VENDEDOR: Muy bien... 20 pesos, por favor.

¿Cuanto tiempo hace? How long has it been since the following people have done the following things? Write the answers using the expression **hacer** + time.

MODELO: Juan: no comprar un traje nuevo / dos años
Hace dos años que Juan no compra un traje nuevo.

1. Lucía: no trabajar / tres meses

_____

2. Santi y Silvina: no estar casados / un año

_____

3. nosotros: no ir al centro comercial / una semana

_____

4. yo: (no) tener novio(a) / demasiado tiempo

_____

5. tú: no estar en la secundaria / ¿?

_____

De viaje por el Caribe: La República Dominicana, Cuba y Puerto Rico

VOCABULARIO Viajar en avión

¡A PRACTICAR!

WB 9-1 **Crucigrama** Use the horizontal and vertical clues on page 142 to solve this crossword puzzle about travel.

Horizontal

1. Conjunto de maletas con cosas para viaje
4. Donde guardas la ropa para un viaje
6. Un viaje directo de Miami a Puerto Rico es un vuelo sin ___.
9. El momento en que el avión sale del aeropuerto
10. Para saber cuándo sale un vuelo tienes que consultar un ___.
11. Para comprar un boleto de avión, vas a una ___ de viajes.

Vertical

2. Un boleto de San Francisco a Puerto Rico y de Puerto Rico a San Francisco es un boleto de ___.
3. Donde esperas el avión justo antes del vuelo
5. La persona que te trae bebidas y comida durante el vuelo
7. El documento necesario para pasar por la aduana
8. Las personas que viajan

¡TE TOCA A TI!

WB 9-2 | **Un viaje gratis** You've just won a free vacation and are consulting with the travel agent. Answer the agent's questions.

1. ¿Adónde quieres viajar? ¿Cuándo?

   _____

2. ¿Cuándo piensas viajar? ¿Deseas un boleto de ida y vuelta o solamente de ida?

   _____

3. ¿Con qué aerolíneas vuelas normalmente?

   _____

4. ¿Dónde prefieres sentarte en el avión?

   _____

5. Por lo general, ¿facturas las maletas cuando vuelas?

   _____

6. ¿Qué piensas hacer en esa destinación?

   _____

ESTRUCTURA I Simplifying expressions: indirect object pronouns

¡A PRACTICAR!

WB 9-3 | **¿Locos de amor?** Pablo and Inés are on their honeymoon and are discussing the souvenirs they are going to bring back. What souvenir did Pablo buy for Inés? To find out, complete their conversation with the appropriate indirect object pronouns.

PABLO: Inés, mi amor, ¿a mi mamá ya **1.** _____ mandamos una tarjeta postal?

INÉS: Pues, yo no **2.** _____ mandé nada, cielo. Y ahora no queda tiempo. A tus

padres **3.** _____ compramos un recuerdo; no necesitan tarjeta postal.

PABLO: Tienes razón, mi amor. Pero me siento mal porque ellos a nosotros ya

4. _____ mandaron dos cartas, ¡y ellos no están de vacaciones!

INÉS: Pero tus padres son así. ¡No te preocupes *(Don't worry)*! No van a estar enojados. Ahora, a

tu hermana, ¿qué 5. _____ compraste ayer en San Juan?

PABLO: Nada, mi amor, porque no sabía que quería algo de San Juan.

INÉS: Pues, Pablito (a ti), 6. _____ pidió una estatua de Lladró, que son muy caras

donde vive ella. ¿No lo recuerdas, cielo?

PABLO: No, no recuerdo nada. Creo que estoy demasiado enamorado de ti como para pensar en

otras personas.

INÉS: Ah, ¡qué mono eres! Pues, ayer cuando estabas de compras, (a mí) 7. _____

compraste algo?

PABLO: Claro que sí. ¡A ti 8. _____ compré mil años más conmigo!

INÉS: ¡Qué romántico! Pero, Pablo, entonces, ¿a quién 9. _____ vas a regalar este

equipo de buceo que tienes escondido *(hidden)* en el armario?

PABLO: Eh, eh, pues, mi amor, sabes cuánto me gusta bucear... y el año pasado a ti yo

10. _____ pedí un equipo de buceo y tú nunca 11. _____

regalaste el equipo que quería.... y pues el precio era muy bueno....

INÉS: ¡PABLO! Creo que tienes que volver a San Juan, «mi amor».

¿Qué recuerdo le regaló Pablo a Inés? ¿Le gustó?

_____

_____

WB 9-4 **¿Qué hiciste?** Your friend Teresa Enrollada always finds herself in difficult situations. As she tells you her latest troubles, ask her how she will solve each problem. Write out your questions using indirect object pronouns. Follow the model.

MODELO: La profesora está enojada y quiere hablar conmigo. (¿hablar?)
    ¿Le vas a hablar?
  o *¿Vas a hablarle?*

1. Mis amigos quieren copiar mi tarea. (¿enseñar / tarea?)

_____

2. Mi ex novio(a) necesita 300 dólares. (¿dar / dinero?)

_____

3. Tengo que hacerte una pregunta importante. (¿hacer / pregunta?)

_____

4. Mi nuevo amigo del Internet quería una foto mía. (¿ofrecer / foto?)

_____

5. Este amigo del Internet quiere mandarnos una foto a nosotros dos. (¿mandar / foto?)

_____

¡TE TOCA A TI!

WB 9-5 | **Expresiones de amor** Answer the following questions in complete sentences and make sure to use the indirect object pronouns. Follow the model.

MODELO: ¿A quién le vas a escribir esta semana?
Voy a escribirle a mi amigo Alberto.
o *Le voy a escribir a mi amigo Alberto.*

1. ¿A quién le escribes frecuentemente? ¿Quién te escribe a ti frecuentemente?

   _____

2. ¿A quiénes les das regalos durante el año? ¿Quiénes te dan regalos a ti durante el año?

   _____

3. ¿A quién le ofreces ayuda con frecuencia? ¿Quién te ofrece ayuda frecuentemente?

   _____

4. ¿A quién le pides dinero?

   _____

5. ¿A quiénes les hablas por teléfono regularmente? ¿Quién te habla a ti por teléfono con frecuencia?

   _____

ESTRUCTURA II Simplifying expressions: double object pronouns

¡A PRACTICAR!

WB 9-6 | **¡Feliz cumpleaños!** Carmen is telling her friend about Olga's birthday party last night. Complete her story by filling in the blanks with either a direct or an indirect object pronoun. **¡OJO!** You will only use one or the other pronoun, not both at the same time.

Ayer fue el cumpleaños de Olga y ella **1.** _____ pasó muy bien. Todos sus amigos

2. _____ dieron muchos regalos. **3.** _____ compraron en diferentes tien-

das especializadas del viejo San Juan. Por ejemplo, Paco **4.** _____ compró una blusa

de seda. A Olga le gustó mucho la blusa y ella **5.** _____ dio un beso a Paco.

Mateo, el novio de Olga, también **6.** _____ dio un regalo especial. A nosotros

Mateo **7.** _____ dijo que iba a ser algo increíble, y realmente fue increíble. Después de

que Olga abrió todos sus regalos, Mateo miró a Olga y **8.** _____ dijo, «Olga,

9. _____ quiero mucho, y tú **10.** _____ sabes. Y también creo que tú

11. _____ quieres a mí, ¿verdad? Pues, **12.** _____ compré este regalo,

¡ábre **13.** _____ ahora mismo!». Cuando Olga **14.** _____ abrió, empezó

a gritar. Era un anillo de diamantes. De repente ella **15.** _____ miró a nosotros y

16. _____ dijo, «¡Voy a casarme con Mateo!».

WB 9-7 | **Regalos para todos** Ernesto is asking Fernando questions about the presents he gave and received for Three Kings **(Reyes Magos)** Day. Select the correct answers to Ernesto's questions based on the drawings. Then circle the direct object and underline the indirect object of that sentence. Follow the model.

MODELO: ¿Quién te dio las maletas?

___√___ Tú (me) las diste.

_____ Uds. te las dieron.

_____ Nos las dieron Uds.

1   2   3   4

1. ¿A quién le regalaste el libro?

_____ Me lo regaló mi abuela.

_____ Me la regaló mi abuela.

_____ Se lo regalé a mi abuela.

2. ¿A quién le regalaste los discos compactos?

_____ Se las regalé a mis hermanas.

_____ Se los regalé a mis hermanas.

_____ Me las regaló mis hermanas.

3. ¿Quién les compró las bicicletas a ti y a tu hermano?

_____ Nos las compraron nuestros padres.

_____ Se las compramos a nuestros padres.

_____ Nos los compraron nuestros padres.

4. ¿A quién le mandaste dinero?

_____ Se los mandé a mis sobrinos.

_____ Nos los mandaron mis sobrinos.

_____ Se lo mandé a mis sobrinos.

¡Tienes que... ! On the last day of Alfonso and Javier's vacation, Alfonso gets sick and needs Javier to do several things for him. What does he ask Javier to do? Use the elements below to help him ask for things, and don't forget to use both direct and indirect object pronouns. Follow the model.

> MODELO: Tengo sed y necesito un vaso de agua. (traer / el vaso de agua / a mí)
> *Tienes que traérmelo, por favor.*
> o *Me lo tienes que traer, por favor.*

1. A mi novia todavía no le compré su regalo. (comprar / el regalo / a mi novia)

   _____

2. Tengo que preparar mis maletas, pero no puedo. (preparar / las maletas / a mí)

   _____

3. Tengo que mandar la tarjeta postal a mis padres, pero no puedo. (mandar / la tarjeta postal / a ellos)

   _____

4. Quiero comer fruta. (servir / fruta / a mí)

   _____

5. Necesito aspirina. (dar / la aspirina / a mí)

   _____

6. Necesitamos reconfirmar los vuelos. (reconfirmar / los vuelos / a nosotros)

   _____

¡TE TOCA A TI!

WB 9-9 **Cuando vas de viaje** Use direct and indirect object pronouns to answer the following questions about what you do while on vacation.

1. Cuando viajas, ¿quién te hace los planes (las reservaciones del avión, del hotel, etc.)?

   _____

   _____

2. ¿A quiénes les escribes cartas o tarjetas postales cuando estás de viaje?

   _____

3. ¿A quiénes les tienes que traer recuerdos cuando vuelves de viaje?

   _____

4. Cuando vuelves de viaje, ¿a quiénes les enseñas tus fotos?

   _____

Nombre _____ Fecha _____

VOCABULARIO El hotel

¡A PRACTICAR!

WB 9-10 **¿Un hotel de cuatro estrellas?** Mr. Vargas wants to stay in a four-star hotel when he goes to the Dominican Republic. Did he find one? Complete his conversation with the receptionist of Hotel Las Brisas with the appropriate words from the list to find out.

aire acondicionado	baño privado	cuarto	quejarse
llave	cuatro estrellas	ascensor	cómodos
camas sencillas	limpio	quedarse	cama doble

SEÑOR VARGAS: Buenos días. Quiero un **1.** _____ para dos personas, por favor.

RECEPCIONISTA: ¿Con una **2.** _____ o con dos **3.** _____, señor?

SEÑOR VARGAS: Una doble, por favor, con un **4.** _____.

RECEPCIONISTA: Bien. Tengo un cuarto en el sexto piso: número 606. ¿Está bien, señor?

SEÑOR VARGAS: Pues, el hotel tiene **5.** _____, ¿verdad?

RECEPCIONISTA: No, señor. Lo siento. Ése es el encanto del hotel. A nuestros clientes les ofrecemos un descanso de la modernidad.

SEÑOR VARGAS: Pues, hace mucho calor allí. ¿Tiene **6.** _____ el cuarto?

RECEPCIONISTA: No, señor, pero cada cuarto sí tiene abanico *(handheld fan)*. ¡No se preocupe, señor! Nuestros cuartos son muy **7.** _____. ¿Cuántas noches quiere **8.** _____?

SEÑOR VARGAS: Tres noches, pero no sé si puedo aguantar *(put up with)* el calor y las escaleras.

RECEPCIONISTA: No va a haber ningún problema, señor. A Ud. nuestro pequeño paraíso le va a gustar mucho. Éste no es un hotel de **9.** _____, pero todo está muy **10.** _____ y Ud. no va a **11.** _____ de nada.

SEÑOR VARGAS: Pues, no sé. ¿Puedo ver el cuarto antes de decidir?

RECEPCIONISTA: Sí, señor. Aquí está la **12.** _____.

¿Es el hotel Las Brisas un hotel de cuatro estrellas? ¿Por qué?

_____

_____

¡TE TOCA A TI!

WB 9-11 | **Hoteles** While visiting Puerto Rico, Lourdes stayed in two very different hotels. How were these hotels? Look at the two pictures below and describe each one using the vocabulary you learned in your text.

1. **Hotel El Lagarto**

_____

_____

_____

_____

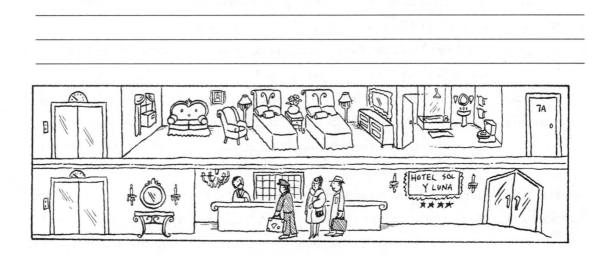

2. **Hotel Sol y Luna**

_____

_____

_____

_____

ASÍ SE DICE Giving directions: prepositions of location, adverbs, and relevant expressions

¡A PRACTICAR!

WB 9-12 | **En la ciudad** Read the following description of this city while you refer to the city map. Put a circle around the appropriate preposition in each sentence based on the layout of the city.

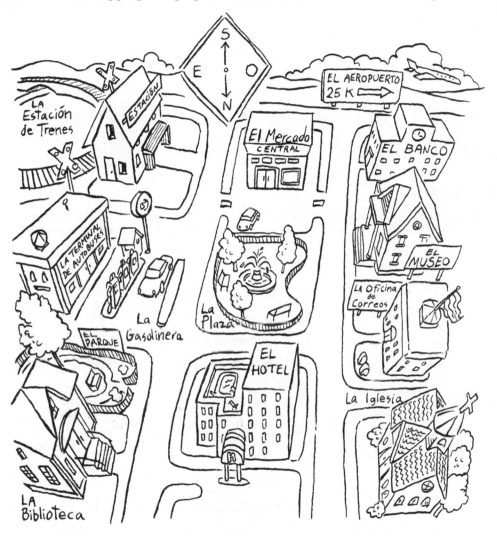

La plaza está en el centro de la ciudad. Allí hay un parque que está **1. (al lado de / detrás de / cerca de)** la biblioteca. Hay un museo **2. (entre el / a lado del / a la derecha del)** banco y la oficina de correos. **3. (Lejos del / Entre / Al lado del)** parque está la gasolinera. La gasolinera está **4. (a la derecha de / delante de / cerca de)** la terminal de autobuses. **5. (Cerca de / Lejos de / Detrás de)** la terminal está la estación de trenes, que está **6. (a la izquierda del / a la derecha del / lejos del)** mercado central. **7. (A la derecha del / En frente del / Detrás del)** hotel hay una iglesia. La iglesia está **8. (lejos de / entre / al lado de)** la oficina de correos. El aeropuerto está **9. (cerca de / lejos de / enfrente de)** la ciudad.

¡TE TOCA A TI!

WB 9-13 | **En tu ciudad** Julio Rojas, a new student on campus wants some tips on how to get around. Answer his questions by writing out the directions he requests. Also indicate the forms of transportation available for him to get there.

1. de la biblioteca de la universidad a la cafetería

   _____

   _____

2. de la universidad a tu restaurante favorito

   _____

   _____

ESTRUCTURA III Giving directions and expressing desires: formal and negative *tú* commands

¡A PRACTICAR!

WB 9-14 | **De compras** Gloria has just arrived in San Juan and needs to ask directions to find her way around the city. Complete the following conversations with formal commands of the verbs in parentheses.

En la calle:

GLORIA: Perdón, señor. ¿Sabe Ud. si hay un supermercado por aquí?

SEÑOR ORTEGA: Sí, señora. **1.** _____ (Seguir) Ud. derecho hasta la esquina. Luego,

2. _____ (doblar) a la derecha en la calle Unamuno y

3. _____ (pasar) dos cuadras más hasta la Sexta Avenida. Allí está

el supermercado.

GLORIA: Gracias, señor.

SEÑOR ORTEGA: De nada, señora.

En el supermercado:

EMPLEADO: Señora, **1.** _____ (decirme) qué quiere Ud.

GLORIA: **2.** _____ (Darme) medio kilo de esas naranjas, por favor. Y, ¿están

frescos los melones?

EMPLEADO: Sí, **3.** _____ (mirar) Ud. Están super frescos.

GLORIA: Muy bien. Y, ¿dónde puedo encontrar la sección de carnes?

EMPLEADO: Lo siento, señora. Aquí no vendemos carnes. **4.** _____ (Ir) a la

carnicería. Queda muy cerca de aquí.

GLORIA: Bien. Entonces, eso es todo. Gracias.

EMPLEADO: De nada. **5.** _____ (Tener) Ud. un buen día. ¡Y **6.** _____

(volver) pronto!

GLORIA: Gracias. ¡Adiós!

WB 9-15 **¡Despiértense!** Ernesto and his friends thought they were spending Spring Break at a beach resort in Puerto Rico, but their travel agent booked them into a weight loss spa by mistake. Now it is 6:00 a.m., and the weight loss coach is shouting orders at them. Write out these commands using the elements below. **¡OJO!** Pay attention to whether the command is directed at one person (informal, singular) or the group (formal/plural). Also, pronouns are connected to the end of affirmative commands, but go in front of negative commands. Follow the models.

MODELOS: **A todos:** levantarse
¡Levántense todos!

A Ernesto: no dormirte otra vez.
¡No te duermas otra vez!

1. **A todos:** vestirse rápidamente

   _____

2. **A Ernesto:** no ducharse

   _____

3. **A todos:** ponerse los zapatos de tenis

   _____

4. **A todos:** echarse a correr 10 millas

   _____

5. **A Ernesto:** no pararse para descansar

   _____

6. **A todos:** subirse la escalera

   _____

7. **A todos:** quitarse los zapatos y meterse en la piscina

   _____

¡TE TOCA A TI!

WB 9-16 **¡Qué alivio!** Your psychologist has determined that you suffer from too much stress because you never express your opinions. Your treatment is to tell people what you want them to do. Write one affirmative and one negative command for each person indicated. **¡OJO!** If it is more than one person, you will have to use the plural command.

1. tu profesor(a) de español

   _____

2. los autores de tu libro de español

   _____

3. tu jefe del trabajo

   _____

4. tus ex novios(as)

   _____

5. tus padres

   _____

SÍNTESIS

¡A LEER!

CUANDO ERA PUERTORRIQUEÑA: ESMERALDA SANTIAGO The following literary selection comes from the novel *Cuando era puertorriqueña*, written by Esmeralda Santiago. In the novel, Santiago, who has lived her life in both Puerto Rico and the continental U.S., tenderly tells of her memories of growing up in Puerto Rico. Written from a child's perspective, the novel explores many aspects of the tropical island culture. In this selection Santiago explains one of the many dilemmas she faced as a child: Was she a **jíbara** or not? What exactly is a **jíbara**? After you read this selection, try to guess what it is.

Strategy: Using format clues

Printed material often contains different kinds of cues that can help you skim, scan, and guess meaning. For example, some words and phrases appear in large, boldface, or italic print to attract the reader's attention; some words are repeated several times to persuade the reader; and other words appear together with a graphic design to help the reader remember a particular concept.

Paso 1: Look at the text and make a few notes about what you anticipate finding in this story.

_____

_____

_____

Paso 2: When reading a story about a particular place, a good strategy to facilitate reading is to recall what you know about that place. In this chapter you learned a good deal about Puerto Rico. Write a few sentences describing what you learned about Puerto Rico's geography, climate, people, etc.

_____

_____

_____

Paso 3: Having reflected on what you learned about Puerto Rico, read the first paragraph and note some of the words or ideas used by the author to set the scene of Puerto Rico.

_____

_____

_____

Paso 4: Now read the story twice and answer the following questions.

1. Santiago dice que cuando era niña escuchaba música jíbara. ¿Cómo era esta música?

_____

2. ¿Por qué decía la mamá de Santiago que ella no era jíbara?

_____

3. ¿Cuál era el dilema de Santiago con respecto a ser jíbara?

_____

4. ¿Por qué se burlaban (*made fun*) los puertorriqueños de los jíbaros?

_____

5. ¿Qué piensas que es un jíbaro?

_____

Mis hermanas y yo dormíamos en hamacas colgadas de las vigas[1] con nudos fuertes de que Mami o Papi hacían y deshacían todas las noches. Una cortina separaba nuestra parte de la casa del área donde Mami y Papi dormían en una cama de caoba[2] velada con mosquitero.[3] Los días de trabajo, Papi salía antes de la madrugada y decía que era él quien despertaba a los gallos que despertaban el barrio.

No lo veíamos hasta el anochecer,[4] cuando bajaba por el camino con su caja de herramientas[5] jalándole del brazo, haciéndole caminar ladeado. Cuando no salía a trabajar, él y Mami murmuraban detrás de la cortina, haciendo rechinar los muelles de su cama,[6] cuchicheando palabras que yo trataba de oír pero no podía.

Yo era madrugadora, pero no se me permitía salir afuera hasta que un rayito de sol se metiera por entre las grietas[7] de la pared al lado de la máquina de coser y barriera una franja dorada en el piso anaranjado.

Al otro día, salté de la hamaca y salí corriendo afuera tan pronto el sol se metió dentro de la casa. Mami y Papi tomaban su pocillo de café fuera del ranchón[8] que servía de cocina. Mis brazos y vientre estaban salpicados[9] de puntillos rojos. La noche anterior, Mami me había bañado en alcoholado, lo que alivió la picazón[10] y refrescó el ardor en mi piel.

—¡Ay, bendito! —exclamó Mami—. Pareces que tienes sarampión.[11] Ven acá, déjame ver —me hizo voltear, sobando las motas—. ¿Te pican?[12]

—No, ya no me pican.

—Quédate en la sombra hoy pa' que no se te marque la piel.

Papi vocalizaba con el cantante de la radio. Él no salía sin su radio de batería. Cuando trabajaba en casa, la colocaba sobre una piedra, o la colgaba de un palo, y la ponía en su estación favorita, la cual tocaba boleros, cha-cha-chás y un noticiero cada media hora. A él le encantaban las noticias de tierras lejanas como Rusia, Madagascar, Estambul. Cuando el locutor mencionaba un país con un nombre particularmente musical, Papi lo convertía en una cancioncita. «Pakistán. Sacristán. ¿Dónde están?» cantaba mientras mezclaba cemento o clavaba tablas,[13] su voz un eco contra la pared.

Todas las mañanas escuchábamos el programa «El club de los madrugadores», el cual presentaba música jíbara. Aunque las canciones y la poesía jíbara describían una vida dura y llena de sacrificios, decían que los jíbaros eran recompensados con una vida comtemplativa, independiente, vecina con la naturaleza, respetuosa de sus caprichos,[14] orgullosamente nacionalista. Yo quería ser una jíbara más que nada en el mundo, pero Mami dijo que eso era imposible ya que yo nací en Santurce, donde la gente se mofaba de[15] los jíbaros por sus costumbres de campo y su dialecto peculiar.

—¡No seas tan jíbara! —me regañaba,[16] dándome cocotazos[17] como para despertar la inteligencia que decía que yo tenía en mi casco.

Yo salía corriendo, casco ardiendo, y me escondía detrás de las matas[18] de orégano. Bajo su sombra aromática me preguntaba, ¿si no éramos jíbaros por qué vivíamos como ellos? Nuestra casa, un cajón sentado sobre zancos bajos,[19] parecía un bohío. Nuestro programa de radio favorito tocaba la música tradicional del campo y daba información acerca de la cosecha, la economía agrícola y el tiempo. Nuestra vecina, doña Lola, era jíbara, aunque Mami nos había advertido nunca llamarla eso. Poemas y cuentos relatando las privaciones y satisfacciones del jíbaro puertorriqueño era lectura obligatoria en cada grado de la escuela. Mis abuelos, a los cuales yo tenía que respetar tanto como querer, me parecían a mí jíbaros. Pero yo no podía serlo, ni podía llamar a nadie jíbaro, porque se ofenderían. Aún a la edad tierna, cuando todavía no sabía ni mi nombre cristiano, me dejaba perpleja la hipocresía de celebrar a una gente que todos despreciaban,[20] pero no había manera de resolver ese dilema, porque en aquellos tiempos, los adultos lo sabían todo.

Cuando era puertorriqueña, by Esmeralda Santiago. Reprinted by permission of Vintage Books, a division of the Random House, Inc.

[1]**vigas** *beams* [2]**caoba** *mahogany* [3]**mosquitero** *mosquito netting* [4]**anochecer** *dusk* [5]**herramientas** *tools* [6]**haciendo rechinar... cama** *making their bedsprings creak* [7]**grietas** *cracks* [8]**ranchón** *shed* [9]**salpicados** *pimpled* [10]**alivió la picazón** *soothed the itching* [11]**sarampión** *measles* [12]**¿Te pican?** *Does it itch?* [13]**mezclaba... tablas** *mixed cement or hammered nails* [14]**caprichos** *whims* [15]**se mofaba de** *mocked* [16]**me regañaba** *she would scold me* [17]**cocotazos** *head bangs* [18]**matas** *bushes* [19]**un cajón... bajos** *a box on low stilts* [20]**despreciaban** *looked down on*

¡A ESCRIBIR!

EXPLORANDO TU CIUDAD The Álvarez family is coming from Puerto Rico to visit your city for the first time. They want to know what they should do while there, where they should stay, and of course, where they should go for fun. Write a letter to Señor Álvarez describing your city and giving them directions to get to your favorite place in the city from the closest airport.

Strategy: Using commands to give directions

If you're traveling in a Spanish-speaking country or city, chances are you might need to ask for directions. In addition, you might even have to give directions! The most important element of explaining to someone how to get from one place to another is accuracy. If you explain your directions clearly and concisely, people will be able to follow them easily.

Here are six basic requirements for giving directions to a place.

1. Choose the easiest route.
2. Be very clear in your directions.
3. Give the directions in chronological order.
4. Use linking expressions such as **Primero..., Luego..., Después de eso..., Entonces..., Usted debe..., Después...,** and **Finalmente...**
5. Identify clearly visible landmarks such as:

   la avenida *avenue*   **el cruce de caminos** *intersection*

   el bulevar *boulevard*   **el edificio** *building*

   la calle *street*   **el letrero** *sign*

   el camino *road*   **el puente** *bridge*

   la colina *hill*   **el semáforo** *traffic light*

6. When possible, include a sketch of the route.

   MODELO: *Para llegar a mi casa desde el aeropuerto, siga estas indicaciones. Primero, siga la calle del aeropuerto hasta la salida. Doble a la derecha y siga por el bulevar Glenwood dos kilómetros hasta el primer semáforo, donde hay un cruce de caminos. Entonces, doble a la izquierda y siga por el camino Parkers Mill dos kilómetros (pasando debajo de un puente) hasta la calle Lane Allen. En esa calle, doble a la derecha y siga otros dos kilómetros hasta el segundo semáforo. Después, doble a la izquierda en el camino Beacon Hill y siga derecho medio kilómetro hasta el camino Normandy. Doble a la izquierda y vaya a la cuarta casa a la derecha. Allí vivo yo, y ¡allí tiene su casa!*

Paso 1: Using the strategy above, write out the directions from the airport to your favorite part of the city.

_____

_____

_____

_____

_____

_____

_____

Functions: Asking for and giving directions; Linking ideas; Expressing distance; Expressing location
Vocabulary: City; Directions and distance; Means of transportation; Metric systems and measurements
Grammar: Verbs: imperative: **usted(es)**, **ser** and **estar**, **tener** and **haber**

Paso 2: Using the directions you wrote in **Paso 1,** write out a first draft of the letter and include information about where the Álvarez family should stay and what they should do in your favorite part of the city.

Paso 3: After revising your first draft, write out your final draft below.

_____

_____

_____

_____

_____

_____

_____

_____

Autoprueba

VOCABULARIO

WB 9-17 **Viajes** Match the appropriate descriptions from the left-hand column with the words from the right-hand column.

_____ 1. maletas y mochilas

_____ 2. las horas de salida y llegada

_____ 3. las personas que viajan

_____ 4. donde hacen la inspección de las maletas

_____ 5. donde los turistas presentan los pasaportes

_____ 6. donde los turistas compran sus boletos de viaje

_____ 7. el documento oficial para entrar a otro país

a. la aduana

b. el horario

c. el equipaje

d. los pasajeros

e. el pasaporte

f. la inmigración

g. la agencia de viajes

WB 9-18 **En el hotel** Sr. Morales has to spend three nights in a hotel in San Juan and the hotel manager is telling him about the hotel. Complete his description using the appropriate words from the list.

aire acondicionado	cuartos	limpios	sencillas	ascensor
cuatro estrellas	privado	sucios	cómodo	dobles
recepción				

Éste es un hotel de lujo, es decir de **1.** _____. En este hotel todos los

2. _____ siempre están **3.** _____ y nunca están **4.** _____.

Según su preferencia, tenemos habitaciones con camas **5.** _____ o

6. _____. Todas tienen baño **7.** _____. Como esta zona es tropical y nor-

malmente hace mucho calor, todas las habitaciones también tienen **8.** _____. La mejor

habitación está en el octavo piso, pero no se preocupe, tenemos **9.** _____. Si durante

su visita necesita cualquier cosa, por favor, llame a la **10.** _____. Le pueden traer todo

lo que Ud. necesite. Creo que Ud. va a estar muy **11.** _____ en este hotel.

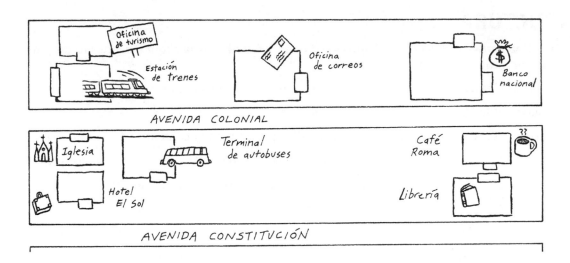

¿Dónde está todo? Look at the map and assume you are on **la avenida Constitución.** Complete the sentences with the appropriate prepositions from the list. Do not repeat a word.

a la derecha	a la izquierda	al lado	delante	detrás	enfrente	entre

1. La terminal de autobuses está _____ de la iglesia.

2. El Hotel El Sol está _____ de la iglesia.

3. La estación de trenes está _____ de la oficina de correos.

4. La oficina de correos está _____ la estación de trenes y el Banco Nacional.

5. El Banco Nacional está _____ de la oficina de correos.

6. Café Roma está _____ de la librería.

7. La oficina de turismo está _____ de la estación de trenes.

Indicaciones Ana Marie is lost on the streets of Santo Domingo and asks someone for help to get back to her hotel. Complete the directions she receives with the appropriate words.

cruce	doble	hacia	siga	suba

Para llegar a su hotel de aquí, **1.** _____ esta calle y **2.** _____ derecho dos cuadras más. **3.** _____ a la izquierda y luego **4.** _____ una cuadra por la calle Palacios. **5.** _____ derecho **6.** _____ el sur y el hotel estará a la derecha.

ESTRUCTURA

WB 9-21 **Una carta** Complete Juan Carlos's conversation with Gloria about his letter to his parents by using indirect object pronouns.

JUAN CARLOS: Celina, **1.** _____ escribí una carta a mis padres hoy.

GLORIA: ¿Qué **2.** _____ dijiste?

JUAN CARLOS: A mi mamá **3.** _____ dije que estoy muy contento aquí y a mi papá

4. _____ dije que necesito más dinero. Pero es interesante porque

cuando fui a enviar **5.** _____ la carta, encontré que ellos

6. _____ habían escrito (*had written*) una carta a mí.

GLORIA: ¡Qué coincidencia! ¿Qué **7.** _____ dijeron a ti?

JUAN CARLOS: Pues, **8.** _____ dijeron que están bien y que no **9.** _____

van a enviar más dinero. Al final, decidí no mandar **10.** _____ la carta.

WB 9-22 **Elena, la buena** Elena always does all the favors her friends ask of her. Write her responses to her friends' latest requests using direct and indirect object pronouns.

1. Elena, ¿me puedes prestar (*loan*) tu chaqueta azul?

_____

2. Elena, ¿nos preparas una cena especial?

_____

3. Elena, ¿nos puedes escribir el ensayo?

_____

4. Elena, ¿te podemos pasar nuestra tarea?

_____

5. Elena, ¿le puedes comprar un regalo a Rosa?

_____

WB 9-23 **Antes de salir del mercado** Complete the following conversation with formal commands of the verbs in parentheses. **¡OJO!** In some cases you will need to use the pronoun.

CLIENTE: **1.** _____ (Perdonar), señor. Por favor, **2.** _____ (darme) una

bolsa plástica para estos tomates.

VENDEDOR: Cómo no, señora. **3.** _____ (Tomar) Ud. esta bolsa limpia.

CLIENTE: Gracias. **4.** _____ (Decirme) una cosa, señor. ¿Sabe Ud. si hay un banco

cerca de aquí?

VENDEDOR: Pues, sí. **5.** _____ (Salir) del mercado y **6.** _____ (ir) dos

cuadras todo derecho. El banco está a la izquierda.

CLIENTE: ¡Muchas gracias! **7.** _____ (Tener) Ud. un buen día.

VENDEDOR: Y Ud., señora. **8.** _____ (Volver) pronto. Hasta luego.

Las relaciones sentimentales: Honduras y Nicaragua

0

VOCABULARIO Las relaciones sentimentales

¡A PRACTICAR!

WB 10-1 | **Buscapalabras** Read the clues and find the words of love and marriage that they describe. Then organize the boldfaced letters to find the hidden phrase.

A	N	O	V	I	A	Z	G	O	L	P	E
O	I	Ñ	I	**E**	R	O	**M**	P	L	E	F
P	E	I	N	E	R	**I**	E	E	A	L	A
E	L	R	A	M	O	R	I	S	O	O	**R**
ñ	E	A	C	E	Z	M	A	R	E	I	R
U	R	C	U	L	E	I	D	**A**	S	T	S
A	E	O	R	D	I	V	O	R	C	I	O
R	G	E	A	A	L	U	B	A	U	J	**I**
D	A	N	T	**R**	E	D	E	P	**T**	A	E
O	U	E	N	E	F	I	A	E	D	R	D
L	U	C	I	B	**C**	E	R	S	E	C	**A**

1. Otro nombre para el amor que demuestran los novios: _____.

2. El viaje que hacen los novios después de casarse: _____.

3. Lo opuesto al matrimonio: _____.

4. Lo que hacen los novios que no se llevan bien: _____.

5. Decoración utilizada en la ceremonia: _____.

6. Lo que lleva la novia durante la ceremonia: _____.

7. La fase de la relación amorosa justo antes del matrimonio: _____.

8. Nombre para la ceremonia que inicia el matrimonio: _____.

La frase escondida: (Es un momento memorable para los novios.)

___ ___ ___ ___ ___ ___ ___   ___ ___ ___ ___

¡TE TOCA A TI!

WB 10-2 | **Una boda típica** What is a "typical wedding" in your family? Use the wedding and reception vocabulary you have learned to describe this tradition in your family.

_____

_____

_____

_____

_____

_____

ESTRUCTURA I Describing recent actions, events, and conditions: the present perfect

¡A PRACTICAR!

WB 10-3 | **¡La he perdido!** Marta has lost something at the university. To find out what it is, complete the following conversation with the appropriate forms of the verb **haber.**

MARTA: Hola, soy Marta.

CATALINA: Hola, soy Catalina. ¿Qué te **1.** _____ pasado?

MARTA: **2.** _____ perdido mi bolsa con mi pasaporte. ¿La **3.** _____ visto tú por aquí?

CATALINA: Pues, no. Lo siento. No **4.** _____ visto ninguna bolsa. ¿De dónde eres?

MARTA: Soy de Managua. Mi hermana y yo **5.** _____ venido a la universidad para estudiar informática.

CATALINA: ¡Qué bueno! Uds. son nicaragüenses. ¿**6.** _____ llamado Uds. a la policía?

MARTA: No, nosotras no lo **7.** _____ hecho todavía. Lo vamos a hacer ahora mismo.

CATALINA: Bien. ¡Buena suerte!

WB 10-4 | **Los últimos detalles** Linda and her mother are discussing Linda's wedding plans. Complete their conversation with the present perfect tense of the verbs indicated. **¡OJO!** Remember that several verbs have irregular participles.

LINDA: Bueno, mamá, ¿qué más tenemos que hacer?

MAMÁ: ¿**1.** _____ _____ (comprar) las invitaciones?

LINDA: Sí, y ya les **2.** _____ _____ (mandar) invitaciones a todos los invitados.

MAMÁ: ¿**3.** _____ _____ (pagar) el vestido de boda?

LINDA: Ahhh. Se me olvidó. Y tampoco **4.** _____ _____ (hablar) con el sastre (_tailor_) sobre las alteraciones. Y mamá, ¿sabes si papá ya **5.** _____ _____ (reservar) su smoking (_tuxedo_)?

Nombre _____ Fecha _____

MAMÁ: Sí, Linda. ¡No te preocupes! Tu papá ya lo **6.** _____ _____ (hacer). ¿No **7.** _____ _____ (ver) el recibo?

LINDA: No, mamá. Papá todavía no me lo **8.** _____ _____ (traer). Se lo voy a pedir. Bueno, mamá, ¿algo más?

MAMÁ: No, Linda, creo que nosotras **9.** _____ _____ (recordar) todo. Ay, a lo mejor queda un detalle. Tu novio, ¿**10.** _____ _____ (decir) que quiere casarse contigo?

LINDA: ¡Mamá!

WB 10-5 | **Queridos abuelos** Newlyweds Miguel and Ana write the following letter to their grandparents to tell them how married life is treating them. Complete the letter by forming phrases in the present perfect. Follow the model.

MODELO: nosotros / pasarlo bien
Nosotros lo hemos pasado bien.

Queridos abuelos:

1. nosotros / volver / de la luna de miel
_____
_____

2. la vida de casados / ser / perfecto
_____
_____

3. todos los días / Miguel / decir / que me quiere mucho
_____
_____

4. nuestros amigos / escribirnos / muchas cartas
_____
_____

5. nosotros / abrir / una cuenta bancaria
_____
_____

6. Y, ¿saben qué?, ¡el conejo / morirse!
_____
_____

Con mucho cariño,

Ana y Miguel

¡TE TOCA A TI!

WB 10-6 | **Cita a ciegas** *(Blind date)* You are going on a blind date with a friend of your friend José, and he wants to know more about you. Answer his questions in complete sentences, using the present perfect where appropriate.

1. ¿Te gusta ir al cine? ¿Qué películas has visto en los últimos dos o tres meses?

   _____

   _____

   _____

2. ¿Tienes un buen sentido del humor? ¿De qué te has reído últimamente?

   _____

   _____

   _____

3. ¿Qué clases has tomado este año en la universidad?

   _____

   _____

4. ¿Qué tipo de cosas te gusta hacer con tus amigos? ¿Cuáles son varias de las actividades que tú y tus amigos han hecho este mes?

   _____

   _____

   _____

   _____

   _____

ASÍ SE DICE Describing reciprocal actions: reciprocal constructions with *se, nos,* and *os*

¡A PRACTICAR!

WB 10-7 | **La pareja famosa** All of Julio and Ana María's friends are fed up with their constant public displays of affection. Are they over the top? Look at these pictures of them and describe in complete sentences what the couple is doing in each one using reciprocal constructions. Choose from the list of verbs and follow the model.

> abrazarse / y mirarse / profundamente
> besarse / en público
> contarse secretos / en público
> escribirse cartas / durante la clase
> hablarse por teléfono / muy tarde

MODELO: *Se hablan por teléfono hasta muy tarde.*

1. _____
   _____

2. _____
   _____

3. _____
   _____

4. _____
   _____

Do you think Julio and Ana María are over the top? Explain in Spanish.

_____

_____

¡TE TOCA A TI!

WB 10-8 | **¡La guerra de las Rosas!** Claudia and Juan José Rosas are on the brink of a divorce and are explaining their situation to their counselor. To find out what they say is wrong with their relationship, form reciprocal phrases with the verbs below, or use others. Follow the model.

MODELOS: *Claudia y yo no nos vemos nunca; trabajamos demasiado.*
Juan José y yo ya no nos ayudamos en la casa...

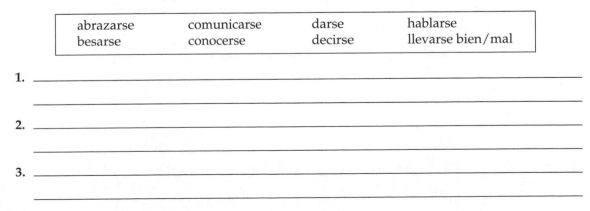

| abrazarse | comunicarse | darse | hablarse |
| besarse | conocerse | decirse | llevarse bien/mal |

1. _____
   _____

2. _____
   _____

3. _____
   _____

4. _____

_____

5. _____

_____

VOCABULARIO La recepción

¡A PRACTICAR!

WB 10-9 | **Así se hace** To find out how wedding receptions are in Maribel's country, complete her description with the following words. **¡OJO!** You have to conjugate the verbs.

agarrar   aplaudir   asistir   banquete   felicitar   orquesta   terminar

Después de la ceremonia todos los invitados **1.** _____ a una fiesta elegante para celebrar el matrimonio. Todo empieza con un brindis para los novios. Después los invitados toman su champán y **2.** _____ los recién casados.

Generalmente el **3.** _____ comienza a las 9:00 de la noche. Hay todo tipo de comida rica, y mientras comen los invitados, la **4.** _____ toca música moderna y tradicional.

Después de la cena, todos se divierten mucho bailando y charlando hasta muy tarde. Al final, la novia tira su ramo de flores y una chica lo **5.** _____. Eso significa que ella va a casarse pronto. La fiesta **6.** _____ cuando los novios se van. Todos **7.** _____ y los recién casados salen para su luna de miel.

¡TE TOCA A TI!

WB 10-10 | **En los Estados Unidos** Mariana is from Honduras, but is coming to the States for her cousin's wedding. She wants to know what typical weddings are like in the U.S. Answer her questions in Spanish.

1. Típicamente, ¿son elegantes las bodas? ¿Cómo se visten los invitados?

_____

_____

2. ¿Dónde tuvo lugar la última boda a que asististe?

_____

_____

3. ¿Bailaste mucho en la última boda a la que fuiste?

_____

_____

4. ¿Cómo son las recepciones? ¿Hay orquestas? ¿Qué tipo de música tocan?

_____

_____

Nombre _____ Fecha _____

5. ¿Cuáles son algunas de las costumbres que se siguen en las recepciones?

_____

_____

ASÍ SE DICE Qualifying actions: adverbial expressions of time and sequencing of events

¡A PRACTICAR!

WB 10-11 | **Don Juan** Berta has just met Esteban, the dorm "don Juan," and she is asking her friend, Cristina, about him. Write out Cristina's answers by changing the adjectives to adverbs. Follow the model.

MODELO: ¿Es paciente Esteban cuando conquista a las chicas?
Sí, conquista a las chicas pacientemente.

1. ¿Es fácil para Esteban conquistar a las chicas?

_____

2. ¿Es elocuente cuando habla con las chicas?

_____

3. ¿Les hace llamadas frecuentes a las chicas?

_____

4. ¿Les da besos apasionados?

_____

5. ¿Es rápido cuando corta con las chicas?

_____

WB 10-12 | **Las vacaciones de Pedro** Pedro wrote his pen pal a letter about his vacation. Finish the letter by choosing the appropriate adverbs or adverbial expressions from the list below.

| a veces   regularmente   nunca   siempre   solamente   probablemente |

1. _____ voy de vacaciones a las lindas playas de Nicaragua. Cuando era joven 2. _____ iba con mi familia, pero ahora que soy mayor, voy solo. De hecho, prefiero viajar solo; 3. _____ invito a nadie. Normalmente paso tres semanas, pero este año, 4. _____ voy a poder pasar una semana. Pero, ¡voy a aprovechar el tiempo! 5. _____ voy a bañarme en el mar y después voy a explorar la selva.

6. _____ me gusta pasar tiempo en Managua con algunos de mis amigos, pero este año con tan poco tiempo, creo que voy a quedarme cerca de la playa y la selva. ¡Sé que lo voy a pasar super bien!

¡TE TOCA A TI!

WB 10-13 **Tus hábitos** Describe how you do the following activities by writing sentences using adverbs. **¡OJO!** Choose a different adjective each time and change it to an adverb. Follow the model.

básico	frecuente	rápido	constante	inmediato	regular
contento	lento *(slow)*	tranquilo	cuidadoso	nervioso	

MODELO: ir al cine
Voy al cine frecuentemente.

1. estudiar para un examen

_____

2. prepararte para salir en una cita

_____

3. leer el periódico

_____

4. responder a tus llamadas telefónicas

_____

5. resolver un problema difícil

_____

WB 10-14 **¿Qué pasó?** Javier didn't attend his ex-girlfriend's wedding last week, but you did. However, he insists seeing your pictures and on knowing every detail of the day. Write a short description, based on your pictures below, and use some of the adverbs to sequence the events.

| después | finalmente | luego | por fin | primero |

_____

_____

_____

_____

_____

_____

_____

_____

_____

_____

_____

_____

ESTRUCTURA II Using the Spanish equivalents of *who, whom, that,* and *which:* relative pronouns

¡A PRACTICAR!

WB 10-15 **Chismes *(Gossip)*** Antonio is telling his friend the latest dorm gossip. To find out what he says, fill in the blanks with the appropriate forms of the following relative pronouns.

| lo que | que | quien |

1. Marta, la chica _____ vive en el tercer piso, está saliendo con Roberto.

2. La chica con _____ salía Roberto el mes pasado está saliendo ahora con el hermano de Roberto.

3. _____ sorprende a Roberto es que esa chica está saliendo también con el chico con _____ cortó hace dos meses.

4. Carlos dañó *(damaged)* la computadora _____ está en la habitación de Tomás.

5. Tomás cree que su compañero, a _____ le prestó *(loaned)* la computadora la dañó.

6. Carlos no le dijo a Tomás _____ pasó.

¡TE TOCA A TI!

¿Y tus chismes? Now Antonio wants you to gossip. Answer his questions in complete sentences using the relative pronouns listed below. Follow the models.

MODELOS: ¿Quién es la persona que más quieres?
Juan Carlos es la persona que más quiero.

¿Qué es lo que más te molesta?
La falta de cortesía es lo que más me molesta.

lo que	que	quien

1. ¿Quién es la chica que sale con tu mejor amigo?

   _____

2. ¿Cuál es la comida que más te gusta?

   _____

3. ¿Quién es la persona con quien sales ahora?

   _____

4. ¿Qué es lo que más te molesta?

   _____

SÍNTESIS

¡A LEER!

AMOR EN EL CIBERESPACIO The following article discusses the topic of finding love on the Internet.

Strategy: Summarizing a reading passage

Summarizing in English a reading passage that you have read in Spanish can help you synthesize its most important ideas. Some guidelines for writing this type of summary are as follows.

- Underline the main ideas in the reading passage.
- Circle the key words and phrases in the passage.
- Write the summary of the passage in your own words.
- Do not include your personal reactions in the summary.
- Avoid the following common errors in writing a summary:
  too long/short
  too many details
  main ideas not expressed
  key ideas not emphasized
  wrong key ideas

Paso 1: Read the article and underline the principal ideas of each paragraph.

Amor en el ciberespacio

Si el día de San Valentín te encuentra sin pareja, no importa. Desde la oficina o la casa se puede lanzar a la conquista amorosa con la ayuda del Internet. No hace falta ponerte ropa especial ni buscar el club más popular. Las posibilidades de cultivar el amor que ofrece la computadora no sólo son amplias sino que llegan hasta el asombro. Hay para todos los gustos.

Para establecer un romance primero hay que buscar pareja. Para eso te pueden ser útiles los miles de sitios de la World Wide Web dedicados a los asuntos del amor. Hoy día abundan sitios que mantienen bases de datos personales, y con un método de búsqueda refinado que rastrea[1] por sexo, rango de edad, estado civil, ciudad y gustos, es bastante fácil pescarte una pareja compatible. Cada vez que se da con alguna persona que interese, se podrán ver todos sus datos, su dirección de email y hasta su foto. A partir de ese momento, todo queda librado al gusto y la imaginación del navegante. Para explorar las posibilidades más, siempre se puede probar con el Chat, es decir, con las charlas por computadora.

Ahora, si el romanticismo llega hasta el extremo de invertir unos pesos, no viene mal invertir en un ramito de flores. No hace falta salir de casa o de la oficina. Y se las puede enviar a cualquier parte del mundo. Existen varias florerías internacionales y en cualquiera de estas tiendas virtuales se puede comprar un ramo con tarjeta de dedicatoria y todo. Eliges las flores y la tarjeta, escribes unas líneas y pagas, claro está, y dentro de poco tiempo el ramo parte hasta su destinación. Y para los bolsillos vacíos hay otras posibilidades. Se trata de mandar tarjetas, flores, regalos y hasta besos virtuales. O sea, imágenes de los mismos a las que se puede añadir alguna frase dulce.

De aquí si todo va viento en popa[2] y la relación tiene solidez, puedes empezar a sustituir los encuentros virtuales por algunos encuentros «reales», en algún café o restaurante. Pero, ¡no te preocupes! Si las cosas van hacia la otra dirección, el Internet también te puede ayudar. Hay sitios que ofrecen consejos y hasta te escriben cartas de ruptura que, por su contenido, aseguran una separación inmediata.

---

[1]**rastrea** *checks*   [2]**va viento en popa** *is successful*

Paso 2: Read the article again and this time circle the key words and phrases that relate to the main idea of each paragraph. When you are done, write the main ideas you have found.

_____

_____

_____

_____

_____

_____

_____

_____

Paso 3: Read the article once more and then write a short summary based on the main ideas you underlined and the key words and phrases you circled.

_____

_____

_____

_____

_____

_____

_____

_____

_____

Paso 4: Answer the following questions to see how much the summary facilitated your comprehension of the article.

1. Según el artículo, ¿cuál es la ventaja del email con respecto a las relaciones amorosas?

_____

2. ¿Qué tipo de información personal ofrecen las bases de datos personales del Internet?

_____

3. ¿Qué opción ofrece el Internet para los amantes que quieren quedar bien *(to impress)* con alguien, pero que no tienen dinero para gastar?

_____

4. ¿Qué servicio ofrece el Internet para las relaciones amorosas que fracasan *(fail)*?

_____

¡A ESCRIBIR!

LA FAMILIA DE MIS SUEÑOS Y YO In this section you will describe the activities you do with your "fantasy family."

Strategy: Writing a descriptive paragraph

Descriptive paragraphs occur in many contexts. They are often found in works of fiction such as novels and short stories, but they also appear in newspaper articles, advertising materials, educational publications, and personal letters. A descriptive paragraph contains sentences that describe people, places, things, and/or events. In this chapter we will focus on describing events. To express how often events take place or how often you or others do something, you can use adverbs of frequency such as the following.

a veces	*sometimes*
cada año	*each year*
dos veces a la semana	*twice a week*
muchas veces	*often*
nunca	*never*
raras veces	*rarely, infrequently*
siempre	*always*
todos los días	*every day*
una vez al mes	*once a month*

You can also modify these expressions to express a wide variety of time frames: **dos veces al mes, tres veces a la semana, cada mes,**
and so on.

Paso 1: Begin by assuming that all your dreams have come true. On a separate piece of paper make a list of all the activities you and your family do now that life is perfect.

Functions: Expressing time relationships; Linking ideas; Talking about habitual actions
Vocabulary: Family members; Leisure; Time expressions
Grammar: Adverbs; Adverb types

Paso 2: Now think about how frequently you do these activities. Next to each one write a phrase describing the frequency. Remember to use the adverbs you learned in your text.

Paso 3: Now write a well-developed paragraph to describe these activities, with whom you do them, and with what frequency. Revise the paragraph and write the final draft below.

_____

_____

_____

_____

_____

_____

_____

_____

Autoprueba

VOCABULARIO

WB 10-17 **El noviazgo** Gregorio and his girlfriend are discussing their relationship. Complete their conversation with the appropriate words from the list without repeating any. **¡OJO!** If you choose a verb you will have to conjugate it.

> amor   casados   enamorarse   matrimonio   cariño   enamorados   llevarse   noviazgo

GREGORIO: Mi amor, ¿no es cierto que nuestro **1.** _____ comenzó el día que nos

conocimos?

MARÍA: Sí, cariño, fue **2.** _____ a primera vista, ¿verdad?

GREGORIO: Claro porque **3.** _____ en un instante.

MARÍA: Tan grande era nuestro **4.** _____ desde el principio.

GREGORIO: Ay, cómo recuerdo nuestra primera cita. Me invitaste al cine y luego fuimos a un café.

MARÍA: Sí, y **5.** _____ tan bien juntos, estábamos **6.** _____. ¡Ay!

GREGORIO: Y al poco tiempo te hice una propuesta de **7.** _____.

MARÍA: Y cinco años después, ¡todavía estamos **8.** _____!

WB 10-18 **La boda** Complete Mónica's description of U.S. weddings by filling in the blanks with the words and phrases provided. **¡OJO!** If you choose a verb you may have to conjugate it.

agarrar	casarse	novios	recién casados	aplaudir
divorciarse	orquesta	separarse	banquete	felicitar
ramo de flores	tener lugar	besarse	luna de miel	recepción
tirar	brindis			

Muchas veces los **1.** _____ deciden **2.** _____ en una iglesia. Cuando

3. _____ delante del altar, ya están casados. Después de esa ceremonia, los

4. _____ salen de la iglesia y todos **5.** _____ y les **6.** _____ arroz.

Luego todos salen para la **7.** _____.

A veces estas fiestas **8.** _____ en un restaurante o también en un parque bonito.

Allí es típico tener un **9.** _____ elegante, pero antes de comer alguien le hace un

10. _____ a la pareja. Todos los invitados **11.** _____ a los novios y entonces

empiezan a comer. Después de comer, la **12.** _____ empieza a tocar música y

todos salen a bailar. Más tarde, la novia tira el **13.** _____ y una chica lo trata de

14. _____. Finalmente, los novios salen para la **15.** _____ y los otros

continúan la fiesta.

Con suerte, los novios no **16.** _____, pero típicamente, el 50 por ciento de los

novios **17.** _____ después de siete años de matrimonio.

Nombre _____ Fecha _____

ESTRUCTURA

WB 10-19 | **¿Qué han hecho?** Just back from a business trip, Lionel wants to know what his family members have been doing this week. Use the elements provided to form complete sentences.

1. Pablo / leer / tres libros

   _____

2. Teresa y Ángela / ver / una película nueva

   _____

3. mamá y yo / escribirle / cartas a la familia

   _____

4. yo / divertirse / con mis amigos

   _____

5. tú / volver / de un viaje largo

   _____

WB 10-20 | **El romance de Ken y Barbie** How did Ken and Barbie get together? Tell the story by forming reciprocal sentences with the elements below. **¡OJO!** Remember to conjugate the verbs in the preterite and to use the appropriate pronouns. Follow the model.

   MODELO: Ken y Barbie / presentarse / un día en la playa
   Ken y Barbie se presentaron un día en la playa.

1. Ken y Barbie / conocerse / en Malibú

   _____

2. ellos / mirarse / intensamente

   _____

3. ellos / abrazarse / fuertemente

   _____

4. ellos / enamorarse / inmediatamente

   _____

5. ellos / casarse / en junio de ese año

   _____

WB 10-21 | **Miguel lo hace así** How does Mike do things? Form complete sentences by combining elements from **Columna A** and **Columna B**. **¡OJO!** You have to change adjectives into adverbs.

Columna A		Columna B	
leer el periódico	comer	fácil	frecuente
hablar con las chicas	sacar buenas notas	rápido	nervioso
	ir a fiestas		detenido (*careful*)

1. _____
2. _____
3. _____
4. _____
5. _____

WB 10-22 La rutina Complete Arcelia's description of her daily routine by filling in the blanks with the appropriate adverbs from the list.

| a veces | muchas veces | nunca | siempre | solamente |
| una vez | todos los días | | | |

1. _____ me despierto a las 6:00 de la mañana porque tengo muchísimas cosas que hacer en un día típico. 2. _____ tengo ganas de volver a dormirme, pero no puedo, así que me levanto en seguida. 3. _____ los sábados y domingos puedo levantarme tarde, ya que son mis días de descanso. Cuando me levanto, me preparo rápidamente y en seguida me voy corriendo a la universidad.

4. _____ voy a un café para tomar un cafecito, pero normalmente no tengo tiempo porque mi primera clase empieza a las 7:30. 5. _____ pensé que tenía tiempo para el café, pero no lo tenía. Llegué tarde a la clase y el profesor me regañó enfrente de todos. ¡Qué vergüenza!

Después de la clase desayuno. 6. _____ pierdo el desayuno con mis amigos porque es casi la única oportunidad que tengo para descansar durante todo el día. Después de desayunar, voy a mis otras clases, y finalmente, a trabajar. Vuelvo a la casa a las 9:30 de la noche y 7. _____ estoy cansada.

WB 10-23 ¿Cómo lo hago? Jorge wants to send his girlfriend an email, but he doesn't know how. Help him by writing out the instructions using the adverbs of sequence below.

| después entonces finalmente luego primero |

_____ Te compras software para el email.

_____ Te consigues una cuenta electrónica de Internet.

_____ Le pides a tu novia su dirección electrónica.

_____ Le envías el mensaje.

_____ Puedes escribir el mensaje que quieres mandar.

_____

_____

_____

_____

_____

WB 10-24 ¿El nuevo novio de Valeria? Complete the sentences with the appropriate relative pronouns to find out some information about Valeria's new boyfriend.

1. Es el chico _____ vive con su hermano.

2. Tiene ese coche viejo _____ siempre hace tanto ruido.

3. Valeria está loca porque no sabe _____ dice todo el mundo de él.

4. Creo que el chico con _____ salía antes Valeria era mucho más guapo.

1 El mundo del trabajo: Panamá

VOCABULARIO Profesiones y oficios

¡A PRACTICAR!

WB 11-1 **Sopa de palabras** Put the letters in correct order to reveal the names of the careers you studied in your text, and then write a short sentence to describe the career. Follow the model.

> MODELO: feje: *jefe*
> *Supervisa a los empleados.*

1. dabaogo: _____

_____

2. iroiranetev: _____

_____

3. narquebo: _____

_____

4. ótagarfof: _____

_____

5. enioringe: _____

_____

6. urisaqita: _____

_____

7. ostepridia: _____

_____

8. dorcanot: _____

_____

¡TE TOCA A TI!

WB 11-2 **¿Qué materias?** Write the appropriate major to study for each of the following careers. **¡OJO!** You may wish to review the vocabulary for academic fields in **Capítulo 1** of your text.

1. contador: _____

2. siquiatra: _____

3. abogado: _____

4. veterinario: _____

5. programador: _____

ESTRUCTURA I Making statements about motives, intentions, and periods of time: *por* vs. *para*

WB 11-3 | *¿Por o para?* Read each sentence below and write the letter of the reason for the use of **por** or **para**.

a. in order to / for the purpose of

b. during

c. through

d. employment

e. opinion

f. on behalf of

g. duration of time

h. cost

i. destination

j. specific time

k. member of a group

_____ **1.** Alicia tiene que estudiar para el examen.

_____ **2.** Claudio gana $40,00 por hora.

_____ **3.** Antonio sale para el trabajo a las 6:00.

_____ **4.** Antonio trabaja para Telefónica.

_____ **5.** Para Carmela, ser dentista es muy agradable.

_____ **6.** Julia iba a trabajar por su amiga ayer.

_____ **7.** Juan Carlos trabajó por 30 años.

_____ **8.** Compró el CD para Julieta.

_____ **9.** Para extranjera, Teresita habla español muy bien.

_____ **10.** Nidia necesita el artículo para el martes que viene.

WB 11-4 | *¿Puedes ir?* Tita and Sara are making plans to go shopping, but Sara has to work. Complete their conversation with **por** or **para**.

SARA: ¿Aló?

TITA: Hola, Sara, habla Tita. Oye, ¿quieres ir de compras hoy **1.** _____ la tarde?

SARA: Sí, me encantaría, pero hoy tengo que trabajar **2.** _____ Amanda. Está enferma hoy y no puede trabajar.

TITA: ¡Otra vez! Ésta es la tercera vez este mes. **3.** _____ una chica tan joven, está enferma muchísimo.

SARA: Ya lo sé. **4.** _____ mí ya es demasiado, pero ¿qué puedo hacer? Es mi hermanita.

TITA: Bueno, ¿**5.** _____ cuántas horas tienes que trabajar hoy?

SARA: Sólo dos o tres. ¿**6.** _____ qué no pasas **7.** _____ mi casa a las 7:00 de la tarde?

TITA: A las 7:00 va a haber mucho tráfico así que voy a salir **8.** _____ tu casa a las

6:00. ¿Sabes qué? ¿Va a estar allí Mónica?

SARA: No lo sé. ¿Qué quieres con Mónica?

TITA: Pues, mi hermano, Carlos, le compró algo **9.** _____ su cumpleaños, pero le da

mucha vergüenza dárselo. Entonces, se lo voy a llevar yo.

SARA: ¡Ay, **10.** _____ Dios! ¡Esa Mónica tiene a todos los chicos pero locos de verdad!

¡TE TOCA A TI!

WB 11-5 | **Entrevista** You are applying for a position with Hewlett Packard at their division that works with Spanish-speaking countries. Part of the application requires that you answer the following questions in complete sentences. **¡OJO!** Pay attention to the use of **por** and **para.**

1. ¿Por cuántos años ha trabajado Ud.?

_____

_____

2. ¿Para qué compañías ha trabajado?

_____

_____

3. Para Ud., ¿cuál es el mejor lugar en el mundo hispano para trabajar y vivir? ¿Por qué?

_____

_____

4. ¿Cree Ud. que es difícil para un norteamericano vivir y trabajar en un país extranjero?

_____

_____

5. ¿Cuánto dinero piensa Ud. ganar al año?

_____

_____

¡A PRACTICAR!

WB 11-6 | **¡Un buen trabajo!** Carolina writes to her sister to tell her about what her son has been doing since graduation. Complete the letter with the appropriate words from the list. **¡OJO!** You have to conjugate some of the verbs in the preterite.

beneficios	currículum	llamar	reunirse	empresa
llenar	solicitud	contratar	sueldo	jubilarse
puesto	tiempo completo	pedir un aumento	entrevista	

Hola Tita:

Espero que estés bien de todo. Aquí te cuento que mi querido Jorgito acaba de graduarse de la universidad y ahora busca trabajo con una 1. _____ internacional. La semana pasada encontró un 2. _____ con AT&T en el campo de telecomunicaciones.

Ya que las telecomunicaciones son su especialidad, Jorge va a ser un buen candidato para el trabajo. Jorge los 3. _____ por teléfono y pidió una 4. _____. Se la mandaron inmediatamente y en seguida (right away) *él la 5. _____ y se la mandó de vuelta. Y, ¡ahora quieren hacerle una 6. _____!*

Es un trabajo de 7. _____, es decir, cinco días a la semana desde las 8:00 de la mañana hasta las 6:00 de la tarde. Tal vez va a ser difícil, pero la compañía ofrece muy buenos 8. _____. Le van a pagar los seguros médicos privados y le van a dar tres semanas de vacaciones durante el primer año. Además, el 9. _____ es relativamente alto para un principiante (beginner): *¡ofrecen 20.000 pesos al año! Jorge dice que después de su primer año, si todo va bien, él puede 10. _____. Jorge dice que la persona que antes hacía este trabajo acaba de 11. _____ y él, al final de su carrera de 20 años con la compañía, ganaba 60.000 pesos al año. La única desventaja del trabajo, para mí, es que Jorge va a tener que viajar mucho. Pero, bueno, en esta época de la tecnología, siempre puedo mandarle algún correo electrónico para estar en contacto con él.*

Jorge quiere prepararse bien, así que hoy va a 12. _____ con su consejero y él le va a ayudar a pulir (polish) *su 13. _____. Jorge quiere saber si ha incluido toda la información necesaria porque sabe que es una parte muy importante de la presentación. Jorge está super preocupado porque quiere este trabajo, pero yo sé que AT&T lo va a 14. _____. Claro, es mi hijo, así que ¡es perfecto! Bueno, Tita, ya te aviso si tengo alguna noticia del trabajo.*

Un abrazo fuerte y un besito,

Carolina

¡TE TOCA A TI!

WB 11-7 | **Solicitando trabajo** Javier is from Panamá and is interested in working in the U.S. He wants more information about careers and the way to find jobs here. Answer his questions.

1. ¿Cuál es la información más importante para incluir en el currículum?

   _____

   _____

2. ¿Cuáles son algunos de los beneficios que les ofrecen las grandes empresas a sus empleados?

   _____

   _____

3. ¿Cuáles son algunas de las preguntas que se hacen típicamente en las entrevistas?

   _____

   _____

4. ¿Qué recomendaciones tienes para conseguir un buen trabajo con una empresa grande en los Estados Unidos?

   _____

   _____

   _____

ESTRUCTURA II Expressing subjectivity and uncertainty: the subjunctive mood

¡A PRACTICAR!

WB 11-8 | **¡El amor en el trabajo!** Tomás found his coworker Laura's diary and learned a surprising secret. Read Laura's thoughts and circle the verbs in the subjunctive. Then, write the reason the subjunctive was used. Follow the model.

MODELO: Quiero que Tomás (limpie) la casa más. _Volition_

| volition   negation   doubt   emotion |

1. Dudo que la novia de Tomás lo quiera. _____

2. Siento que la novia de Tomás tenga otro novio. _____

3. Estoy muy contenta de que Tomás trabaje conmigo. _____

4. No hay otra mujer que conozca mejor a Tomás que yo. _____

5. Estoy muy triste que Tomás no sepa cómo es su novia. _____

6. El siquiatra recomienda que yo hable con Tomás sobre mis sentimientos. _____

7. Es imposible que yo le diga a Tomás cómo me siento. Tengo demasiado miedo. _____

¿Qué descubre Tomás al leer el diario de Laura?

_____

¡TE TOCA A TI!

WB 11-9 | **Los consejos** After finding out Laura's secret, Tomás asks his boss for advice. Read his advice and state whether you agree or disagree. Follow the model.

MODELO: Recomiendo que ya no hables con Laura en el trabajo.
Estoy de acuerdo.
o *No estoy de acuerdo.*

1. Es necesario que consultes con la jefe de Laura también.

_____

2. Es importante que ya no almuerces con Laura.

_____

3. Es probable que Laura cambie de trabajo.

_____

4. Recomiendo que dejes de leer su diario.

_____

VOCABULARIO Las finanzas personales

¡A PRACTICAR!

WB 11-10 | **Gemelos distintos** Juan and Juana are twins, but they are very different. To find out how they differ, look at the pictures and choose the words from the list that best complete the descriptions. You will need to conjugate the verbs.

a plazos	facturas	cajero automático	prestar	cuenta de ahorros
presupuesto	depositar	sacar	efectivo	tarjeta de crédito

JUANA

JUAN

1. Todos los días Juana _____

dinero en su _____ .

Todos los días Juan _____

dinero del _____ .

JUANA	JUAN

2. Juana compra poco y siempre paga en _____. Sólo gasta lo que le permite su _____.

Juan compra mucho y lo paga todo con su _____.

3. Juana siempre le _____ dinero a Juan porque él nunca lo tiene.

Juan no puede pagar sus _____ con todo el dinero a la vez. Siempre tiene que pagar _____.

¡TE TOCA A TI!

WB 11-11 **¿Juan o Juana?** Are you more like Juan or like Juana? Justify your answer by writing a short paragraph about your financial habits.

_____

_____

_____

_____

_____

_____

_____

ESTRUCTURA III Expressing desires and intentions: the present subjunctive and statements of volition

¡A PRACTICAR!

WB 11-12 | **Marimandona** Gloria is a very bossy boss. Luz is telling her friend about the orders that Gloria is always giving them. Write the orders she describes by forming complete sentences using the words below. Remember to use the subjunctive in the subordinate clause. Follow the model.

> MODELO: Gloria / querer / Juan Carlos y Antonio / traerle café / todas las mañanas
> *Gloria quiere que Juan Carlos y Antonio le traigan café todas las mañanas.*

1. Gloria / insistir en / todos los empleados / trabajar / 10 horas al día

   _____

   _____

2. Gloria / no permitir / Magaly y yo / usar / el correo electrónico

   _____

   _____

3. Gloria / prohibir / nosotros / hacerle / preguntas

   _____

   _____

4. Gloria / no querer / yo / divertirme / durante las horas de trabajo

   _____

   _____

5. Gloria / mandar / Alejandro / servirle / el almuerzo / todos los días

   _____

   _____

WB 11-13 | **Tertulia** Cecilia and her friends are in a café talking about the world and how they want it to be. What do they say? Form sentences by combining words from each column. **¡OJO!** You have to use the subjunctive in the subordinate clause. Follow the model.

> MODELO: *Alicia espera que los sueldos suban.*

yo	insistir en	nosotros	ser más justa
tú	desear	tú	saber más de las necesidades de la gente
Felipe	esperar	la policía	haber más trabajos para todos
Cecilia	recomendar	tú	subir
nosotros	preferir	el presidente	no tener que trabajar tanto
Felipe y Cecilia	querer	la gente	ser felices por toda la vida
ellos	desear	los sueldos	no dormirse mientras hablamos
Alicia	esperar		

1. _____
2. _____
3. _____
4. _____
5. _____
6. _____
7. _____

WB 11-14 **¡Qué horror!** Tere is watching her mischievous nephew while his mom works the night-shift. Out of desperation she sends her the following email to get advice on what to do. Complete the email with the appropriate form of the verbs. You will have to choose between the infinitive and the subjunctive.

Hola, Lupe:

Te cuento que ahora quiero **1.** _____ (matar) a tu hijo. Manuel insiste en no

2. _____ (acostarse) y no sé qué hacer. Deseo que Manuel

3. _____ (dejar) de jugar con sus juguetes porque ya es demasiado tarde, pero

prefiere que nosotros **4.** _____ (jugar) más. De hecho, insiste en que nosotros

5. _____ (seguir) jugando. No deseo **6.** _____ (ser) antipática,

pero te juro que ¡este niño me tiene loca! Espero que tú **7.** _____ (poder)

ayudarme. Me interesa saber qué recomiendas que yo **8.** _____ (hacer) con

este niño travieso. Por favor, ¡contéstame pronto!

Tere

¡TE TOCA A TI!

WB 11-15 **¿Qué le recomiendas?** Imagine that you are Lupe's secretary and have received Tere's email. Lupe is too busy to answer, so you must do it for her. Write an email to Tere and give her at least four recommendations.

Hola, Tere:

_____
_____
_____
_____
_____
_____
_____
_____
_____
_____
_____

Situaciones What advice do you give to your friends in the following situations? For each situation write at least two recommendations. Try to use different verbs of volition.

1. Un amigo tuyo quiere estudiar en Costa Rica el próximo año. El problema es que no ha ahorrado suficiente dinero y necesita 1.000 dólares más. ¿Qué sugieres que haga?

   _____

   _____

   _____

   _____

   _____

2. Una amiga tuya acaba de cortar con tu mejor amigo. Dice que piensa en él todo el día y no sabe qué hacer. ¿Qué le recomiendas?

   _____

   _____

   _____

   _____

   _____

3. Dos amigos tuyos necesitan un lugar donde vivir porque acaban de botarlos (kick them out) de su propio apartamento y ahora quieren vivir contigo. No quieres ofenderlos, pero no quieres que vivan en tu casa. ¿Qué les recomiendas?

   _____

   _____

   _____

   _____

   _____

SÍNTESIS

¡A LEER!

EL CURRÍCULUM VITAE: CONSEJOS PRÁCTICOS The following article offers advice on writing a curriculum vitae.

Strategy: Guessing unfamiliar words and phrases

When you read a passage in English and come to an unfamiliar word or phrase, you probably try to guess its meaning from context, or skip over it and continue reading. When learners of Spanish as a foreign language read literature in Spanish, they will likely encounter a number of unfamiliar vocabulary items. However, if you can guess word meaning from context in Spanish, your reading comprehension will increase significantly, as will your reading speed.

Paso 1: The following article offers advice on writing a curriculum vitae. Read the title and look at the accompanying picture. Write a list of ideas or words that you expect to find in the article.

_____

_____

_____

Paso 2: Read the entire text without looking up any words in the dictionary. If you do not understand a word or phrase, underline it and keep reading. After reading the entire text one time, look for the following words in the text. Using the context in which they appear, try to guess their meaning.

____	**1.** reclutador	**a.**	absolutamente necesario
____	**2.** rechazar	**b.**	apoyar; aportar evidencia que demuestre algún punto
____	**3.** imprescindible	**c.**	persona que busca candidatos para puestos de trabajo
____	**4.** respaldar	**d.**	no seleccionar

Paso 3: Read the entire article again. This time, thinking about the context of the article, try to guess the meaning of the words and phrases you underlined during your first reading. Then, answer the following questions.

1. Según el artículo, ¿cuáles son dos datos necesarios para incluir en cualquier currículum?

_____

2. Según el artículo, ¿es siempre buena idea incluir información sobre los premios que has ganado?

_____

3. ¿Por qué no debes mencionar información personal en el currículum?

_____

4. Imagina que tu amigo(a) solicita trabajo y quiere que tú le des algunas sugerencias para escribir su currículum bien. Pensando en el artículo que acabas de leer, ¿qué le vas a aconsejar? Escribe dos recomendaciones, usando un mandato informal o una frase con el subjuntivo.

_____

_____

EL CURRÍCULUM VITAE: CONSEJOS PRÁCTICOS

Tu currículum es uno de los instrumentos más importantes a la hora de solicitar trabajo. Cuando las empresas tratan de llenar un puesto, hay ocasiones en las que los reclutadores reciben más de 200 currículum vitae y, claro está, sólo pueden escoger los que más se asemejen a[1] las características de la posición. Para evitar que tu solicitud sea rechazada, es imprescindible tener un currículum con un contenido bien organizado, conciso y, sobre todo, fácil de leer.

El contenido de un currículum vitae

El contenido de tu currículum es lo que te vende al empleador. Es por medio de este documento que el empleador decide si quiere comprar tus servicios y hacerte parte de su equipo de trabajo. Por eso, al considerar el contenido que vas a incluir, piensa en todos los logros[2] que hayas alcanzado en tus anteriores empleos. Por ejemplo, si en algún trabajo anterior contribuiste un método nuevo para realizar más ventas, no dudes en mencionarlo. Sin embargo, sé modesto y no exageres tu potencial. Es mejor escribir el contenido de tu información de tal manera que la puedas respaldar con tu experiencia profesional.

A la hora de la entrevista no quieres que el empleador descubra que has mentido. Junto con tu experiencia profesional, es necesario incluir los datos sobre tu formación académica.

Incluye el nombre de tu universidad o instituto, el grado que obtuviste (por ejemplo, bachillerato o posgrado) y las fechas del período que estuviste allí.

Si ganaste algún premio durante tus años universitarios, es preciso mencionarlo sólo si es relevante para el puesto que solicitas.

Recuerda que entre más concisa y corta sea tu información, las posibilidades de que los reclutadores la lean son mucho mejores. Esto implica que no debes incluir información innecesaria. No incluyas, por ejemplo, datos personales como el número de tu permiso de manejar, tu fecha de nacimiento o cualquier otro documento de identidad.

Tampoco menciones tu estado civil, tus preferencias religiosas ni tu estado de salud.

Enfócate en lo que estás vendiendo y no en lo que podrían utilizar los empleadores para rechazarte.

El formato del currículum

Un gerente tiene aproximadamente de 28 a 45 segundos para hojear rápidamente un currículum y decidir si le interesa o no. Por esto es importante que sigas un formato estándar para mantener tu currículum conciso y fácil de leer. Limita tu contenido a una hoja solamente, dos hojas como máximo.

Aconsejamos que utilices hojas de tamaño carta (8½ X 11) y de buena calidad que tengan peso y alguna textura.

No te olvides que la primera impresión de tu currículum puede ser un factor definitorio en la decisión de ofrecerte una entrevista o para rechazarte.

Por eso, es imprescindible que el documento tenga un alto nivel de organización y que no tenga ningún error. Revisa el documento varias veces y muéstraselo a por lo menos cuatro personas antes de mandarlo con una solicitud de trabajo. Un solo error de ortografía puede costarte una oportunidad de empleo.

Con estos consejos estás listo para prepararte tu propio currículum. Explota todos los recursos disponibles para escribir un currículum que se destaque[3] entre los demás. ¡Buena suerte!

[1]**se asemejen a** *resemble*   [2]**logros** *achievements*   [3]**se destaque** *stands out*

¡A ESCRIBIR!

EL EMPLEADO IDEAL In this section, you will write a paragraph about the personal qualities that make you an ideal employee.

Strategy: Writing from an idea map

An idea map is a tool for organizing your ideas before you begin developing them in a composition. In this section, you are going to use an idea map to write a paragraph about the personal qualities that make you an ideal employee. Using an idea map will help you organize your thoughts about this topic before you write about it.

Paso 1: Spend ten minutes thinking about the personal qualities that make you a good employee. Write each of these qualities down on a piece of paper. Do not worry about grammar or spelling at this point. Just get your ideas on separate piece of paper.

Functions: Expressing hopes and aspirations; Expressing intention
Vocabulary: Professions, trades, working conditions
Grammar: Verbs: present; Verbs: subjunctive

Paso 2: Try to categorize the ideas you have just written. For example, did you mention information about your character? about your professional experience? about your academic history? These categories can help you to organize your paragraph.

Paso 3: For each of your qualities, draw a line to a space on the paper where you can write an example that demonstrates this quality. For example, if you mentioned that you have studied in one of the best universities in the country, write the name of the university in the space. These examples will help form the content of your paragraph.

Paso 4: Look at the map you have drawn and write a sentence that summarizes all the information you have included. This will be the topic sentence of your paragraph. An example might be:

Tanto mi experiencia profesional como mi preparación académica me hacen el (la) empleado(a) ideal.

Paso 5: On a separate piece of paper write your paragraph following the organization of your map. Then, review the grammar, vocabulary, and spelling, and finally write the final draft below.

_____

_____

_____

_____

_____

_____

_____

_____

_____

_____

_____

_____

_____

_____

Autoprueba

VOCABULARIO

WB 11-17 **¿Qué debe hacer?** Ernesto is considering his career options and is trying to find a career that matches his hobbies, skills, and, interests. Write the name of the career that would best match each of these.

1. Me gusta dibujar y diseñar edificios.

   _____

2. Me gusta cortar pelo.

   _____

3. Me encantan los animales.

   _____

4. Quiero escribir artículos interesantes.

   _____

5. Me interesa escribir programas de software.

   _____

6. Quiero enseñar en una escuela.

   _____

7. Me encantan las lenguas.

   _____

8. Quiero proteger a la gente.

   _____

9. Me interesa analizar los problemas de la gente.

   _____

10. Me fascinan los dientes.

   _____

WB 11-18 **Solicitando trabajo** Juan Antonio is a career counselor who is helping Ana María to find a good job. To find out what he says, fill in each blank with the appropriate word or phrase from the list.

beneficios	entrevista	proyectos	computadora	fotocopias	solicitar
impresora	solicitud	currículum	imprimir	sueldo	jubilarte
tiempo completo	empleados	llamar	tiempo parcial	contratar	despedir

Si vas a **1.** _____ un puesto, lo primero que tienes que hacer es actualizar *(to update)* tu

2. _____. Tienes que escribirlo en la **3.** _____ e **4.** _____ el docu-

mento en un papel muy fino. Recomiendo una **5.** _____ laser. Después, tienes que

hacer muchas **6.** _____ porque lo vas a mandar a muchas compañías.

Si encuentras un trabajo que te interesa, tienes que pedir una **7.** _____ de la com-

pañía. Creo que debes **8.** _____ por teléfono para pedirla. Así vas a tener tu primera oportunidad de impresionar a los empleados de la compañía. Si les caes bien, pueden ofrecerte

una **9.** _____ inmediatamente.

Si te invitan a la compañía, vístete bien. Llévate un traje azul o negro. Ese día te van a

explicar mejor el puesto y los **10.** _____ que vas a tener que llevar a cabo.

También te van a describir los **11.** _____ que les ofrecen a los **12.** _____.

Ése no es el momento de hablar del **13.** _____. Si la compañía decide que te quiere

14. _____, te lo va a decir y entonces puedes hablar de dinero.

Antes de aceptar el trabajo, tienes que establecer si es un puesto de **15.** _____ o de

16. _____. También vas a querer hablar más de los beneficios. Vas a querer saber cuál

es la edad para **17.** _____, y vas a querer saber qué seguros ofrecen si te tienen que

18. _____.

WB 11-19 **Consejos financieros** You are going to buy a new car and your parents give you advice. To find out what they say, complete the following paragraphs with the appropriate words or phrases. If you choose a verb you must decide whether to use the infinitive or the subjunctive.

| a plazos | cuenta de ahorros | prestar | ahorrar | depositar | presupuesto |
| cajero automático | en efectivo | cheques | facturas | tarjeta de crédito | |

Primero, tienes que **1.** _____ mucho dinero. Para hacerlo, recomendamos que

2. _____ dinero en tu **3.** _____ todas las semanas. También, recomendamos

que no saques dinero del **4.** _____ todos los días. Es mejor escribirte un

5. _____ y sólo gastar el dinero que sabes que puedes gastar.

Claro, esperamos que no uses tu **6.** _____. Debes pagar todo con tus

7. _____ porque así al fin del mes no vas a recibir **8.** _____ que te espanten

(*frighten you*). Para comprar el coche, nosotros te queremos **9.** _____ el dinero. Así

puedes pagar **10.** _____ y no vas a tener que pagar **11.** _____ y perder

dinero en interés.

ESTRUCTURA

WB 11-20 **De vacaciones** Marta is returning to her office after her vacation. Complete her conversation with Elena with **por** or **para**.

MARTA: ¿Sabes qué, Elena? La semana pasada estuve en un crucero y pasamos

1. _____ el canal de Panamá. ¡Fue fantástico! Regresé ayer **2.** _____

la tarde.

ELENA: ¡Qué bueno, Marta! ¿**3.** _____ cuánto tiempo estuviste en el crucero?

MARTA: Fue un crucero de catorce días. No te diste cuenta de que yo no estaba aquí.

ELENA: Ay, Marta, lo siento, pero no. Tuve que preparar un informe **4.** _____ el jefe

y él lo quería **5.** _____ hoy. No noté nada porque estaba trabajando como loca.

MARTA: Ay, sí, Hector, el jefe horrible. **6.** _____ padre de dos hijos tan simpáticos, es

un hombre demasiado antipático. Pues, dime, ¿lo terminaste?

ELENA: Sí, casi. Sólo hace falta sacar una fotocopia, pero la máquina está descompuesta. ¿No hay otra **7.** _____ aquí?

MARTA: Sí, en la oficina de Juan. Pero antes de irte, compré este regalito **8.** _____ ti. Si no te gusta, selecciona otro. Compré un montón de cosas en el Caribe **9.** _____ muy poco dinero.

ELENA: Bueno, gracias. Pues, ahora, ¿qué vas a hacer?

MARTA: Me siento un poco cansada todavía. Creo que me voy **10.** _____ la casa a descansar. No le digas nada a Hector.

ELENA: No, no le digo nada. ¡Adiós!

MARTA: Chao.

WB 11-21 | **El amor y los negocios** While working on your colleague's computer you find an email he wrote to a woman who works for your rival company. Finish the email by selecting the appropriate verbs from the list and conjugating them in the present subjunctive.

divertirse   enamorarse   escribir   ir   llamar   mandar   mirar   pensar   perder   tener

Mi amor:

Gracias por tu mensaje. También he pensado mucho en ti. Quiero que me 1. _____ más cartas y que me 2. _____ por teléfono a veces. Espero que 3. _____ un buen día hoy, y que no te 4. _____ ningún otro hombre. También prefiero que tú no 5. _____ en otros hombres. ¡Sabes que soy muy celoso!

*   Sabes que te quiero mucho y espero con todo el corazón que tú 6. _____ de mí. Sé que tu jefe no quiere que sus empleados 7. _____ mucho tiempo con los emails, pero te pido que me 8. _____ por lo menos uno al día y así voy a saber que estás pensando en mí.*

*   Quiero invitarte a salir el viernes que viene. Quiero que nosotros 9. _____ al nuevo restaurante caribeño y que 10. _____ mucho. Espero verte muy pronto.*

Con todo mi cariño,
Paulino

WB 11-22 | **Entre amigos** Complete the following conversation between two work colleagues. ¡OJO! You have to decide whether the verb should be in the infinitive or the present subjunctive.

LUIS: Tengo ganas de descansar un poco, Jorge. Quiero **1.** _____ (salir) a tomar algo. ¿Quieres **2.** _____ (ir) conmigo al Coyote Pub?

JORGE: No, prefiero que nosotros **3.** _____ (seguir) trabajando un poco más. Sólo nos queda una hora más.

LUIS: Tienes razón, pero quiero que **4.** _____ (trabajar) rápidamente para así terminar temprano.

JORGE: Bueno, pero después de terminar no quiero **5.** _____ (ir) al Coyote. Mi esposa insiste en que yo siempre **6.** _____ (volver) a casa después del trabajo. Así prefiero que tú me **7.** _____ (acompañar) a mi casa para tomar algo. ¿Qué te parece?

LUIS: Pues, está bien. Entonces te acompaño.

---

2 El medio ambiente: Costa Rica

VOCABULARIO La geografía rural y urbana

¡A PRACTICAR!

WB 12-1 **Crucigrama** Read the clues on page 192 and solve the following crossword puzzle about rural and urban geography.

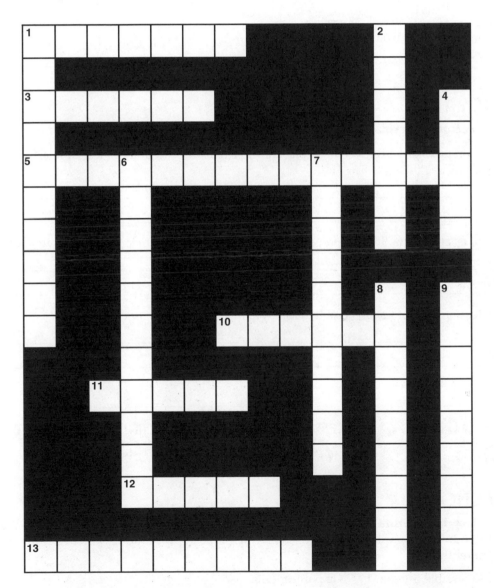

Horizontal

1. La causa de mucho ruido urbano
3. Río
5. Demasiada gente concentrada en una metrópolis
10. Lo que ya no se usa y se tira
11. Echar agua a las plantas
12. La _____ del Amazonas
13. Sin problemas o complicaciones

Vertical

1. Autobuses, metros y trenes son formas de _____ público.
2. Lugar donde se producen varios productos
4. Lugar donde se cultivan plantas
6. Edificios altísimos
7. La persona que cultiva la tierra
8. La persona que trabaja en el campo
9. Destinación popular para una luna de miel

¡TE TOCA A TI!

WB 12-2 | **¿Cómo es tu vida?** Answer the following questions about your life and your city.

1. ¿Vives en una zona urbana o una zona rural? ¿Cuáles son algunas de las características de este lugar?

_____

_____

2. ¿Cómo es el sistema de transporte público donde vives? ¿Es eficiente? ¿Es conveniente?

_____

_____

3. ¿Cuáles son algunos de los problemas ambientales actuales en tu ciudad?

_____

_____

ESTRUCTURA I Expressing emotion and opinions: subjunctive following verbs of emotion, impersonal expressions, and *ojalá*

¡A PRACTICAR!

WB 12-3 | **La primera visita a Costa Rica** What do Luis and Ana think of Costa Rica after their first day in the country? Complete their conversation with the appropriate subjunctive form of the verbs in parentheses.

ANA: ¡Es increíble este país! ¿No te parece, Luis?

LUIS: Sí, Ana. ¡Qué bueno que nosotros **1.** _____ (estar) aquí y no en Atlanta!

ANA: Me alegro de que el lugar **2.** _____ (ser) tan bonito y tranquilo.

LUIS: Tranquilo, sí. Es increíble que acá en San José, la capital, no **3.** _____ (haber) mucho tráfico ni mucho ruido.

ANA: Es cierto. Me sorprende a mí que en un lugar tan grande, la ciudad no **4.** _____ (tener) problemas de sobrepoblación, como la contaminación, el tráfico, la basura, etcétera.

LUIS: De acuerdo. Es muy interesante eso porque vivimos en una ciudad más pequeña pero nos quejamos siempre de que la gente no **5.** _____ (respetar) el medio ambiente. Es una lástima que todo el mundo no **6.** _____ (poder) ser como Costa Rica.

ANA: Bueno, Luis, es imposible que todo el mundo **7.** _____ (ajustarse) *(to adjust itself)* al modelo de Costa Rica. Pero de todas formas, sería *(it would be)* una situación ideal.

LUIS: Pues, sí. Oye, mañana es necesario que nosotros **8.** _____ (hacer) el tour por el bosque nuboso Monteverde. ¿Está bien?

ANA: Sí, pero, ¿por qué es necesario hacerlo mañana?

LUIS: Pues, mañana es viernes, y si no lo hacemos mañana es posible que el sábado no **9.** _____ (ir) a poder hacerlo porque va a haber mucha gente.

ANA: Tienes razón, pero entonces es importante que tú **10.** _____ (llamar) ahora para hacer la reserva.

LUIS: Bueno, la voy a hacer ahora mismo.

WB 12-4 | **Una reunión de Greenpeace** You are at a Greenpeace meeting, and the members are expressing their opinions about important topics. Form complete sentences by matching verb phrases from the first column with subordinate clauses from the second. **¡OJO!** Remember that only the subordinate clause verb will be in the subjunctive. Follow the model.

MODELO: *Yo siento que algunas de nuestras actividades sean radicales.*

COLUMNA A
Yo sentir que
Nosotros tener miedo de que
Es necesario que
Ojalá que
Es una lástima que
Es ridículo que
Nosotros sentir que

COLUMNA B
nuestro grupo conservar el medio ambiente
la gente tener miedo de nosotros
el gobierno nos apoyar
las grandes compañías no hacer más inversiones «verdes»
mucha gente no entender los objetivos de Greenpeace
nuestros esfuerzos no tener éxito en este caso
algunas de nuestras acciones ser radicales

1. _____

2. _____

3. _____

4. _____

5. _____

6. _____

¡TE TOCA A TI!

WB 12-5 | **Tus opiniones** What opinion do you have on the following topics? Express it using an expression of emotion and the present subjunctive. Follow the model and use a different expression each time.

> MODELOS: vivir en una finca
> *Ojalá que viva en una finca algún día.*
>
> los sueldos de los trabajadores de las fábricas
> *Me molesta que los sueldos de los trabajadores de las fábricas sean tan bajos.*

1. algunas organizaciones activistas ser radicales

   _____

2. basura en tu ciudad

   _____

3. el sistema de transporte público de tu ciudad

   _____

4. el gobierno construir menos carreteras

   _____

5. la gente destruir los bosques tropicales

   _____

6. vivir una vida tranquila

   _____

7. vivir una vida acelerada

   _____

VOCABULARIO La conservación y la explotación

¡A PRACTICAR!

WB 12-6 | **Una clase de ecología** Jorge's ecology class is changing his life. To find out how, complete the following paragraph with the appropriate words from the list.

capa de ozono	escasez	reciclar	conservar	medio ambiente	recursos naturales
resolver	naturaleza	energía solar	contaminación	proteger	

Antes de tomar la clase de ecología yo nunca pensaba en la **1.** _____. Nunca me

preocupaban los problemas del **2.** _____ como la **3.** _____ de petróleo o

la destrucción de la **4.** _____. Sin embargo, en la clase aprendí que cada persona tiene

que **5.** _____ sus **6.** _____ y tiene que **7.** _____ el aire y la

tierra. Ahora sé que tengo que hacer mi parte para **8.** _____ nuestros problemas am-

bientales. Voy a **9.** _____ todos los productos de plástico y de papel que uso en mi

casa para evitar el desperdicio. También, voy a tratar de usar **10.** _____ para calentar mi piscina. Finalmente, siempre que sea posible, voy a tomar el autobús o cualquier otra forma de transporte público para así no contribuir a la **11.** _____ del aire. Sé que yo solo no puedo cambiar el mundo, pero en la clase aprendí que puedo hacer mi parte.

¡TE TOCA A TI!

WB 12-7 **Leyendo las noticias** You are browsing the headlines of the latest edition of *La naturaleza*, an ecological magazine. What is your opinion about the headlines? Write your reactions in complete sentences using phrases of emotion. Follow the model.

MODELO: *Me alegro de que Costa Rica desarrolle más programas de reciclaje.*

Greenpeace batalla por las energías limpias

El gobierno colombiano consigue la suspensión de exploración petrolera

Los incendios destruyen la vegetación natural de Asturias

Muchos de los huracanes son productos de la destrucción de la capa de ozono

Costa Rica desarrolla más programas de reforestación de reciclaje

1. _____

2. _____

3. _____

4. _____

5. _____

¡A PRACTICAR!

WB 12-8 **¿Qué hacemos ahora?** Luis and Ana are still in Costa Rica and are planning how to spend the next days of their vacation. Complete their conversation with the appropriate form of the verbs in parentheses. You must decide whether the verbs should be in the indicative or the subjunctive.

LUIS: Ana, mañana creo que nosotros **1.** _____ (deber) ir al Parque Nacional Volcán Poás. Tomás y María también van mañana. ¿Qué te parece?

ANA: Bueno, no pienso que ellos **2.** _____ (ir) mañana. Me dijeron que iban a otro lugar. Pienso que **3.** _____ (ser) mejor ir a Puntarenas mañana. Allí es donde está el Parque Nacional Palo Verde.

LUIS: No creo que **4.** _____ (estar) allí el Palo Verde. En Puntarenas pienso que **5.** _____ (poder) visitar las playas y tal vez el Parque de Manuel Antonio.

ANA: Ay, Manuel Antonio. Sí, lo quiero ver. No creo que **6.** _____ (quedar) muy lejos del Hotel La Mariposa, ¿verdad?

LUIS: Es cierto que La Mariposa **7.** _____ (estar) al lado del parque. Pero, bueno... ¿Qué hacemos, entonces?

ANA: Mañana es lunes y es dudoso que **8.** _____ (haber) mucha gente en cualquier lugar, así que todo depende de ti.

LUIS: Como no estamos seguros que Tomás y María **9.** _____ (visitar) el Volcán Poás mañana, ¿por qué no los llamamos y así averiguamos? Si van mañana, los podemos acompañar.

ANA: Pienso que **10.** _____ (ser) una buena idea.

WB 12-9 **¡Qué preciosidad!** Luis and Ana decide to go to Manuel Antonio National Park, and they are discussing the trip. Complete their conversation forming sentences with the following words. Determine whether the phrases require the present indicative or the present subjunctive. Follow the model.

MODELO: LUIS: ¿tú / estar seguro / Catalina ir al parque hoy?
ANA: sí / yo / no tener duda / Catalina ir al parque hoy
LUIS: *¿Estás segura que Catalina vaya al parque hoy?*
ANA: *Sí, no tengo duda que Catalina va al parque hoy.*

1. LUIS: yo / no poder creer / el viaje a Quepos pasar tan rápidamente

ANA: yo / creer / nosotros haber tardado demasiado tiempo en llegar

LUIS: _____

_____

ANA: _____

_____

2. LUIS: María y Tomás / pensar / los titís (*squirrel monkeys*) venir a jugar en la playa de Manuel Antonio

ANA: yo / dudar / los titís venir a jugar en la playa

LUIS: _____

_____

ANA: _____

_____

3. LUIS: yo / creer / haber más de 600 tipos de aves en el Parque de Manuel Antonio

ANA: no ser cierto / haber tantas aves en ese lugar

LUIS: _____

_____

ANA: _____

_____

4. LUIS: yo / no estar seguro / el parque estar abierto toda la noche

ANA: ser imposible / el parque cerrarse temprano

LUIS: _____

_____

ANA: _____

_____

WB 12-10 **Más planes** Now Ana and Luis are planning a trip to the Poás volcano and discussing the arrangements. Form complete sentences by matching phrases from the first column with the adjectival phrases from the second.

Tenemos que buscar el autobús	que puede hacer el viaje de San José a Poás
Queremos un autobús	que es muy barato
Es mejor alquilar un coche	que va a Poás
Tomás tiene un coche	que dure por lo menos tres horas
Podemos tomar ese servicio de taxi	que vaya directamente a Poás
En el hotel no conocen ningún servicio de taxi	que dura cuatro horas
Necesitamos buscar un tour del parque	que pueda hacer el viaje de San José a Poás
Tomás conoce un tour muy bueno	que sea muy barato

1. _____

2. _____

3. _____

4. _____

5. _____

6. _____

7. _____

8. _____

¡TE TOCA A TI!

WB 12-11 **Lo que quieras** Imagine that someone is going to give you the following things. How would you want them to be? Write complete sentences using the subjunctive in an adjective clause. Follow the model.

MODELO: una ciudad
Quiero una ciudad que no tenga contaminación.

1. una casa

   _____

2. compañeros de cuarto

   _____

3. un coche

   _____

4. un trabajo

   _____

5. una clase

   _____

VOCABULARIO Los animales y el refugio natural

¡A PRACTICAR!

WB 12-12 **En el zoo** You are in the zoo and see the following animals. What are they? Follow the model.

MODELO: *Es un elefante.*

6

7

8

1. _____   5. _____
2. _____   6. _____
3. _____   7. _____
4. _____   8. _____

¡TE TOCA A TI!

WB 12-13 **¿Dónde se ven?** Describe the ecological environment in which each of the following animals is most commonly found. Follow the model.

MODELO: el oso
        El oso vive en el bosque.

1. el elefante

_____

2. la culebra

_____

3. el gorila

_____

4. el ave

_____

SÍNTESIS

¡A LEER!

CARTA DE UN CIUDADANO The following is a letter of a citizen on environmental issues in Costa Rica.

Strategy: Understanding the writer's perspective

In many cases, you can use information you know about the author, his/her background, or his/her previous work to give you some perspective on the reading. Often this information can be useful in interpreting themes or messages that the author is attempting to convey via literature. Many literary works (novels, collections of short stories, collections of poems, etc.) contain an introduction that gives at least some biographical information about the author, and in many cases provides some insight into the nature of the author's literary production. For those texts where we do not have biographical information about the author, the reader can rely on other clues to the author's perspective, such as the type of text, or genre of the reading, and where it was published. The following text is a letter written by a citizen directed to the President and Congress of Costa Rica. Given this, we can assume that the topic might be of a political nature or treat some salient civic concern. Moreover, since the letter is from Costa Rica, we can guess that the issue might be of an ecological nature.

Paso 1: Knowing what you have learned about Costa Rica, make a short list of two or three environmental issues that a citizen might want the President and Congress to consider.

_____

_____

_____

Paso 2: Since this is a letter, it is likely that the author's opinion will be expressed in the first paragraph. Read just the first paragraph and then answer the following questions.

1. ¿Cuál es el tema de la carta? ¿Parece ser diferente de lo que esperabas?

   _____

   _____

   _____

2. ¿Encontraste algunas palabras o frases que demuestren la opinión del autor sobre este tema? ¿Cuáles son?

   _____

   _____

   _____

Paso 3: Now read the letter and then answer the comprehension questions that follow.

Estimados congresistas de la Asamblea Legislativa de Costa Rica.
Estimado señor presidente de la república de Costa Rica.

Les escribo como ciudadano del Planeta Tierra, muy preocupado por la grave situación ambiental que enfrentan los jaguares en todo Latinoamérica, pero en particular, en Costa Rica. El jaguar es el más importante depredador[1] terrestre de los ecosistemas tropicales y es el tercero en tamaño entre todos los felinos del mundo. Debido a la cacería[2] ilegal y la destrucción de sus hábitats, es una de las especies en extinción más amenazadas.

La presencia del jaguar en el bosque es un síntoma inequívoco de que el ecosistema está bien de salud, ya que mantienen el equilibrio de otras poblaciones de animales. El jaguar se alimenta de caimanes, monos, cocodrilos, tortugas de agua y tierra y peces, y así regula las poblaciones de esas especies. Sin embargo, una de las consecuencias directas de la acción devastadora del hombre, como la cacería ilegal y la deforestación, ha provocado severas disminuciones[3] de estos animales. De la extinción de especies como el jaguar se derivan extinciones secundarias, y ese proceso se refleja en la transformación de la estructura y composición de los bosques.

Ya que ustedes son la voz del pueblo costarricense y tienen el poder de salvar de la extinción a estas especies, les pido con toda seriedad y respeto que tomen las siguientes medidas para proteger el jaguar y nuestro medio ambiente. Al tomar estas medidas, no pondrán en riesgo al ecoturismo, que es el futuro económico de Costa Rica. Les ruego que:

- *establezcan un área privada, lo más extensa posible, de hábitats naturales que sirvan de sustento a las poblaciones de jaguares y de sus presas[4] naturales.*
- *desarrollen un modelo de cooperación entre propietarios de tierras con el objetivo común de conservar la población de jaguares de la región y sus hábitats.*
- *promuevan el desarrollo de actividades turísticas y artesanales que tengan al jaguar como principal foco de atracción.*
- *declaren ilegal la cacería deportiva en Costa Rica.*

La protección de la naturaleza debe de ser un objetivo común para todos los pobladores del globo indiferentemente del sector en el cual se desenvuelvan, pues de la «buena salud» de la madre tierra depende la nuestra.

Atentamente,

Lic. Gerardo Gómez Villaverde

[1]**depredador** *predator*   [2]**cacería** *hunting*   [3]**disminuciones** *reductions*   [4]**presas** *prey*

Comprehension questions

1. ¿Cuáles son las palabras relacionadas con el medio ambiente o la ecología que usa el autor?

_____

_____

2. ¿Cuál es el tema ecológico de esta carta? Describe en detalle.

_____

_____

3. ¿Cuál es la perspectiva del autor de la carta acerca de este problema ecológico? ¿Cuáles son algunas de las palabras que usa el autor para expresar su opinión?

_____

_____

4. ¿Qué soluciones al problema les propone el autor al presidente y a la Asamblea?

_____

_____

5. ¿Piensas que son buenas soluciones? ¿Por qué sí o por qué no? ¿Tienes otra recomendación?

_____

_____

¡A ESCRIBIR!

MI OPINIÓN In this section you are going to express your opinion about one of the topics you will select.

Strategy: Making your writing persuasive

Writers often try to convince readers to understand or adopt particular points of view. Persuasive writing is used by writers of editorials, by political figures, and often by professionals such as attorneys, medical personnel, educators, and reviewers or critics. In this section you will write an essay in which you try to convince your reader of your point of view regarding a particular environmental issue. The following words and phrases will allow you to connect your ideas in this type of composition.

To express opinions . . .

creo que	*I believe*
pienso que	*I think*
en mi opinión	*in my opinion*

To support opinions . . .

primero	*first*
una razón	*one reason*
por ejemplo	*for example*

To show contrast . . .

pero	*but*
aunque	*although*
por otro lado	*on the other hand*

To summarize . . .

por eso	*therefore*
finalmente	*finally*
en conclusión	*in conclusion*

Nombre _____ Fecha _____

Paso 1: Form your opinion about one of the following topics (one that you didn't select in your textbook).

- El problema global más grande
- La mejor manera de resolver los problemas del mundo
- Si es justo mantener los animales en los zoológicos
- Si el gobierno debe permitir la manipulación genética

Functions: Persuading; Expressing an opinion; Agreeing and disagreeing; Comparing and contrasting
Vocabulary: Animals; Automobile; Geography; Means of transportation
Grammar: Verbs: present; Verbs: subjunctive

Paso 2: On a separate sheet of paper write a sentence that demonstrates your opinion about the topic you select. Then, write two to three reasons that support your opinion. Finally, write your essay. Remember that the essay must include:

- Introduction—statement of your opinion
- The reasons in favor of your opinion along with specific examples where possible
- Conclusion—a summary of your opinion

Paso 3: After writing the first draft, revise the content and check the vocabulary and grammar. Try to incorporate several of the expressions you learned in this chapter to express your opinion. If you use these phrases, decide whether they require the indicative or the subjunctive. When you are finished, write your final draft below.

_____

_____

_____

_____

_____

_____

_____

_____

_____

_____

_____

_____

_____

Autoprueba

VOCABULARIO

| WB 12-14 | **La geografía rural y urbana** Complete the following paragraphs with the appropriate words from the list.

| acelerado | recogen | basura | ruido | contaminación |
| tráfico | metrópolis | medio ambiente | sobrepoblación | |

1. La Ciudad de Nueva York es una de las _____ más conocidas en todo el mundo. Como en cualquier otra ciudad grande, el ritmo de la vida es muy _____ en Nueva York y allí es común encontrar problemas asociados con la _____. Estos problemas incluyen el _____, el _____ y la _____ del aire. Sin embargo, la ciudad tiene un sistema de transporte público que facilita el movimiento de gente y también protege el _____. Para ser una ciudad tan grande, no está demasiado sucia. La gente no arroja mucha _____ a las calles y hay muchas personas que la _____ cuando alguien lo hace. A pesar de ser grande, es una ciudad bella.

| arroyos   regar   campesinos   tranquila   cultivar   colinas |

2. A diferencia de la vida urbana, la vida rural es bastante _____, pero es todavía bastante dura. Los _____ trabajan desde muy temprano de la mañana. Sus trabajos incluyen _____ la tierra, _____ las plantas y atender a los animales. Sin embargo, las zonas rurales pueden ser muy pintorescas. Las _____ y los _____ ayudan a crear un ambiente bastante agradable para trabajar, vivir y jugar.

| capa de ozono | explotar | desarrollar | petróleo | desperdicio | reciclar |
| recursos naturales | destrucción | energía solar | reforestar | escasez | resolver |

3. Tanto en las zonas urbanas como en las zonas rurales hay problemas ecológicos que hay que _____ para proteger el medio ambiente. Si no hacemos algo rápidamente, vamos a acabar todos los _____, como el _____. Algunas soluciones incluyen _____ los bosques, preservar la _____ y _____ programas para limpiar el aire. También es importante _____ otras formas de energía como la _____. Cada individuo puede hacer su parte para evitar el _____ y la _____ de la naturaleza. Por ejemplo, todos pueden _____ botellas, latas y papeles que usan en la casa. Si todos hacen su parte, no vamos a tener que hablar de la _____ de los recursos importantes.

Nombre _____ Fecha _____

WB 12-15 | **Trivia animal** Write the name of the animal that each sentence describes.

1. Vive en los árboles de la selva y come bananas. _____

2. Asociamos este animal con la tentación. _____

3. Es otro nombre para pájaro. _____

4. Es muy grande y come cacahuetes. _____

5. Vive en los bosques de África y se parece a los seres humanos. _____

6. Es el rey de la selva. _____

7. Este animal se parece al perro. _____

8. Este animal vive en los bosques y le gusta comer miel. _____

9. Este animal es de la familia felina y vive en la China. _____

ESTRUCTURA

WB 12-16 | **Entre amigos** Complete the following conversation using the infinitive or the subjunctive of the verbs in parentheses.

JORGE: Me alegro de que nosotros **1.** _____ (estar) en Costa Rica otra vez. Me gusta

2. _____ (poder) explorar las selvas y ver todas las especies de animales.

LUIS: Sí, creo que es bueno **3.** _____ (venir) a Costa Rica todos los años, pero siento

que Moni y Alicia no **4.** _____ (estar) aquí con nosotros.

JORGE: ¿Cómo? ¡Es ridículo que tú **5.** _____ (decir) eso! Es mejor que las novias no

nos **6.** _____ (acompañar) en estos viajes.

LUIS: ¡Jorge! Me sorprende que **7.** _____ (pensar) así. Creo que es una lástima que

Moni y Alicia no **8.** _____ (ir) a poder disfrutar de la belleza de Costa Rica.

JORGE: Bueno, Luis, cálmate. Quiero mucho a mi novia. Pero también creo que es importante que

los hombres **9.** _____ (tener) su tiempo libre, ¿no? Y otra cosa: ojalá que esta

conversación **10.** _____ (ser) secreto nuestro, ¿eh?

WB 12-17 | **Hablando del viaje** Carmen and Tere are talking about their trip to Costa Rica. Form sentences using the following words. You have to determine whether the verbs should be in the present indicative or subjunctive.

1. TERE: yo / creer / estas vacaciones / ser / excelentes

CARMEN: sí, pero yo / dudar / David / querer venir / este año

TERE: _____

_____

CARMEN: _____

_____

2. TERE: Gabriela / no estar segura / el hotel / ser / bueno

CARMEN: yo / estar segura / todos los hoteles / ir a ser / muy buenos

TERE: _____

_____

CARMEN: _____

_____

3.   TERE: en San José nosotros / tener que buscar / un restaurante / servir / gallo pinto (*a Costa Rican dish of rice, beans, and cilantro*)

CARMEN: yo / conocer / un buen hotel / servir / gallo pinto

TERE: _____

_____

CARMEN: _____

_____

4.   TERE: yo / querer visitar / una reserva biológica / tener muchas especies exóticas

CARMEN: Manuel Antonio / ser una reserva preciosa / tener todo tipo de animales exóticos

TERE: _____

_____

CARMEN: _____

_____

El mundo del espectáculo: Perú y Ecuador

3

VOCABULARIO Programas y películas

¡A PRACTICAR!

| WB 13-1 | **Teleprogramas** Read each program description from a TV guide and identify what type of program or show it is. Follow the model.

> MODELO: La periodista Carmen Rico Godoy preparará en el estudio cocina algunas de sus recetas preferidas.
> *un programa educativo*

1. En un futuro próximo, la gran astronave comercial «Nostromo» se dirige a la Tierra tras una larga ausencia, transportando un cargamento de minerales extraterrestres.

   _____

2. Desde llegar a convertirse en la estrella de un circo, hasta dedicarse a gondolero en Venecia, el oso Yogui y sus amigos, Bu-Bu y Cindy, viven sus aventuras en el parque Jellystone.

   _____

3. La misma noche en que se encuentra una nueva víctima de Jack, el Destripador, un hombre alquila una habitación en casa de los señores Burton.

   _____

4. Transmisión de un partido de fútbol entre la selección joven peruana, actual subcampeona del mundo y su homóloga danesa.

   _____

5. Comprueba científicamente que el hombre alcanza la plenitud física a los 20 años, que se mantiene en buena forma durante una década y que a los 30 años comienza el declive físico.

   _____

6. El meteorólogo José Antonio Maldonado ofrece la predicción del tiempo para las próximas horas, tanto en nuestro país, como en el resto de Europa.

   _____

7. El coronel Thursday llega a Fort Apache para hacerse cargo del mando. Fort Apache es un puesto avanzado en la frontera de Arizona, cuyos oficiales y soldados han luchado mucho contra los indios.

   _____

¡TE TOCA A TI!

WB 13-2 | **Programas y películas interesantes** Based on your own opinion, complete the following sentences with an appropriate title.

1. El documental «＿＿＿＿＿＿＿＿＿＿＿＿＿» es muy interesante.

2. Creo que los dibujos animados «＿＿＿＿＿＿＿＿＿＿＿» son muy cómicos.

3. He visto un drama maravilloso que se titula «＿＿＿＿＿＿＿＿＿＿＿».

4. He visto una comedia excelente; se titula «＿＿＿＿＿＿＿＿＿＿＿».

5. Una película de intriga que me gusta mucho es «＿＿＿＿＿＿＿＿＿＿＿».

6. A veces, veo «＿＿＿＿＿＿＿＿＿＿＿», que es un programa de entrevistas.

ESTRUCTURA I Talking about anticipated actions: subjunctive with purpose and time clauses

¡A PRACTICAR!

WB 13-3 | **¿Vamos o no?** Ana and Julia are discussing whether they will go to the movies with Tomás or not. To find out what they are saying, circle the most logical conjunction.

ANA: Julia, Antonio nos invitó al cine, pero no sé si quiero ir. ¿Quieres ir?

JULIA: Bueno, Ana, voy **1. (con tal de que / para que / a menos que)** vaya también David, el hermano de Antonio. ¿Sabes que me gusta mucho? Si él no va, yo no voy.

ANA: Julia, ¡no seas tan difícil! **2. (Cuando / Aunque / Después de que)** no vaya David, te vas a divertir mucho con Antonio y conmigo. También nos va a acompañar Tomás.

JULIA: ¿Tomás? Ay, no, por favor. Ese tipo me molesta demasiado. No voy entonces. **3. (Para que / Cuando / Hasta que)** veas a Antonio y Tomás, diles que estoy muy enferma y por eso no pude acompañarte. A propósito *(By the way)*, ¿qué película van a ver?

ANA: No te lo voy a decir **4. (tan pronto como / cuando / a menos que)** nos acompañes. Si no vas, ¿qué te importa qué película vemos?

JULIA: Ay, chica, **5. (antes de que / en caso de que / después de que)** te enojes conmigo, te voy a decir que sí los voy a acompañar... ¡**6. (Para que / Tan pronto como / Hasta que)** invites a David! ¡Por favor!

ANA: Julia, David no puede ir al cine esta tarde; tiene que trabajar. Pero, mira, **7. (sin que / en caso de que / después de que)** salgamos del cine, vamos a visitar a David en su trabajo. ¿Qué te parece?

JULIA: Me parece muy bien. Pero no voy a salir de la casa **8. (sin que / para que / aunque)** me digas el título de la película que vamos a ver. ¡Espero que sea la nueva película de Almodóvar!

ANA: Sí, Julia, es la nueva de Almodóvar.

WB 13-4 | **La telenovela del momento** Several students are discussing today's and future episodes of the new hot soap opera, "**Decepciones.**" To find out what they say, follow the model and form complete sentences using the following words. You will have to put the verbs in the subordinate clause in the subjunctive.

> MODELO: Gerardo ir a casarse con Juanita / aunque / Juanita estar enamorada de otro hombre
> *Gerardo va a casarse con Juanita aunque Juanita esté enamorada de otro hombre.*

1. Javier no ir a volver a Lima / hasta que / la policía encontrar al asesino

_____

_____

2. Elena tomar tratamientos médicos / para que / ella y Omar poder tener un bebé

_____

_____

3. Manuel nunca firmar su nombre en las cartas que escribe a Analisa / en caso de que / su esposo las leer

_____

_____

4. Alberto y Claudia ir a divorciarse / a menos que / Alberto conseguir trabajo

_____

_____

5. Santi ir a estar mejor / tan pronto como / los médicos lo operar

_____

_____

WB 13-5 **¿Qué hacemos esta noche?** Daniel wants to do something fun tonight and he sends this email to his friend Carlos. Write the correct form of the verbs in parentheses. You have to decide whether the verbs should be in the present indicative or the subjunctive.

Hola, Carlos,

Esta noche no sé qué vayamos a hacer. La verdad es que no me importa mucho exactamente qué hagamos, con tal de que nosotros **1.** _____ (hacer) algo divertido. Hoy es el cumpleaños de Amalia y su novio le va a hacer una fiesta. Aunque **2.** _____ (ser) fiesta de cumpleaños, creo que lo van a pasar bien allí. Otra opción es ir al cine del centro para ver una película. Me gusta ese cine porque tan pronto como **3.** _____ (salir) las películas nuevas, las pasan allí, y no cobran demasiado dinero. Prefiero ver una película de intriga a menos que tú **4.** _____ (querer) ver algo diferente.

Mira, Carlos, cuando tú **5.** _____ (recibir) este mensaje, llámame y podemos decidir qué hacemos. En caso de que yo no **6.** _____ (estar) en casa, llámame en casa de Elvia —ella va a ayudarme con mi tarea de matemáticas. No te preocupes, ¡no voy a salir con Elvia esta noche! De hecho *(In fact)*, no voy a hacer planes para esta noche hasta que tú me **7.** _____ (llamar).

¡TE TOCA A TI!

WB 13-6 | **Y tú, ¿qué planes tienes?** Write a paragraph about the plans you have for after you graduate from college. You can use the following phrases to begin your paragraph.

Cuando yo me gradúe de la universidad, pienso _____ con tal de que _____. Después de que mis padres _____, yo _____. A menos que _____, yo...

_____

_____

_____

_____

_____

VOCABULARIO Las artes

¡A PRACTICAR!

WB 13-7 | **En el Museo de Arte de Lima** To promote interest in art, the Art Museum of Lima offers several workshops about different types of art. Look at their brochure and write the name of each type of art for which there will be a workshop.

1. _____
2. _____
3. _____
4. _____
5. _____
6. _____
7. _____
8. _____
9. _____
10. _____

¡TE TOCA A TI!

WB 13-8 | **Taller de arte** The Art Museum of Lima offers one of its workshops via the Internet, and you decide to take it. To enroll, you must complete the following survey about your interests and taste in art. Answer the questions in complete sentences.

Museo de Arte de Lima
Taller artístico del Internet

Fecha: _____

Nombre: _____

Por favor, conteste las siguientes preguntas sobre sus intereses en los diferentes tipos de arte.

1. ¿Cuáles son los tres tipos de arte que más le gustan?

   _____

2. ¿Quiénes son sus artistas preferidos de cada tipo de arte que Ud. acaba de mencionar?

   _____

   _____

   _____

3. ¿Cuántas obras de teatro ha visto Ud.? ¿Cómo se titulan?

   _____

   _____

4. ¿A cuántos conciertos ha asistido Ud.? ¿Quiénes fueron los cantantes o grupos musicales?

   _____

   _____

5. ¿Cuántas veces al año va Ud. a algún museo?

   _____

ESTRUCTURA II Talking about unplanned or accidental occurrences: no-fault *se* construction

¡A PRACTICAR!

WB 13-9 | **¡No tenemos la culpa!** During the two weeks that Gilberto and his two brothers have been working at the Museum of Art they have had several costly "accidents." Every time the boss accuses Gilberto of one of these accidents, he responds implying that it wasn't his fault. Write out his responses using the no-fault **se.** Follow the model.

> MODELO: Gilberto, has perdido tres cuadros valiosos.
> *Bueno, se me perdieron los cuadros.*

1. Gilberto, tus hermanos dejaron caer *(dropped)* dos floreros muy caros.

   _____

2. Gilberto, tú y tus hermanos rompieron una escultura muy valiosa anoche.

   _____

3. Gilberto, tú no recordaste limpiar la sala de arte clásico.

   _____

4. Gilberto, tu hermano perdió a dos clientes en el tour de museo ayer.

   _____

5. Gilberto, tú y tus hermanos dejaron escapar a tres ladrones la semana pasada.

   _____

¡TE TOCA A TI!

WB 13-10 | **¿Y tú?** What do you do in the following situations? Follow the model and answer in complete sentences.

> MODELO: ¿Qué haces cuando se te pierde algo valioso?
> *Cuando se me pierde algo valioso, pongo un anuncio en el periódico.*

1. ¿Qué haces cuando se te acaba el dinero?

   _____

   _____

2. ¿Qué haces cuando se te escapan las ideas o las palabras?

   _____

   _____

3. ¿Qué haces cuando se te rompe algo valioso que no sea tuyo?

   _____

   _____

4. ¿Qué haces cuando se te va un(a) novio(a)?

   _____

   _____

5. ¿Qué haces cuando se te olvida hacer la tarea de español?

_____

_____

ASÍ SE DICE Describing completed actions and resulting conditions: use of the past participle as adjective

¡A PRACTICAR!

WB 13-11 | **Una oportunidad más para Gilberto** Gilberto's boss is going to give him another chance to do a good job at the museum. Gilberto is being very efficient, and each time his boss asks him to do something, he responds that it is already done. Write Gilberto's responses using an adjective with the verb **estar** to indicate what Gilberto has already done. Follow the model.

MODELO: Gilberto, abre la puerta principal.
La puerta ya está abierta.

1. Gilberto, cubre los cuadros de Picasso con la tela.

_____

2. Gilberto, cierra las puertas de la sala de arte folklórico.

_____

3. Gilberto, pon los anuncios para la nueva exhibición en las paredes.

_____

4. Gilberto, invita a los patrocinadores del museo a la cena especial.

_____

5. Gilberto, lava las esculturas de esa sala.

_____

6. Gilberto, resuelve el problema que tienen los otros trabajadores.

_____

WB 13-12 | **Cultura peruana** Tomás has to write a review of Peruvian sculpture and film history. Help him to write the review by changing the following sentences using the verb **ser** + the past participle. Follow the model.

MODELO: Armando Robles Godoy dirigió la película peruana *La muralla verde*.
La película peruana La muralla verde *fue dirigida por Armando Robles Godoy.*

1. Los españoles introdujeron los patrones occidentales a la escultura peruana.

_____

_____

2. En el siglo XX establecieron la Escuela de Artes y Oficios en Perú.

_____

_____

3. También en el siglo XX formaron un grupo de escultores peruanos.

_____

_____

4. Iniciaron el cine peruano en 1897.

_____

_____

5. En 1929 presentaron la primera película con sonido en Perú.

_____

_____

6. En 1934 filmaron _Resaca_, la primera película peruana con sonido.

_____

_____

¡TE TOCA A TI!

WB 13-13 | **Dime de tu vida** Describe the following things or people in the situations indicated. You can use the verbs listed or your own. Follow the model.

MODELO: tú antes de tomar un examen difícil
Estoy preocupada antes de tomar un examen difícil.

aburrir	despertar	organizar	cansar	dormir
desorganizar	hacer	preparar	pagar	

1. las facturas al final del mes

_____

2. las tareas el día que tienes que entregarlas

_____

3. tu cuarto normalmente

_____

4. los estudiantes cuando el (la) profesor(a) pasa una película histórica en la clase

_____

_____

5. tú después de tomar cuatro tazas de café

_____

SÍNTESIS

¡A LEER!

UNA LEYENDA DE LA SELVA PERUANA You will now read an indigenous myth from the jungle of Peru called, "**La noche del Tatú**." For the **aymarás**, an indigenous group that lives in parts of Bolivia, Chile and Peru, the **tatú** is an armadillo.

Strategy: Following a chronology

Diaries, travel logs, anecdotes, and short stories usually contain a series of interrelated actions and events, including the writer's opinions. These kinds of narrative descriptions require the reader to follow a chronology. The central questions implicit in most narrations are:

• What happened?
• Where, when, and how did it happen?
• To whom did it occur, why, and for how long?
• What else was going on at the same time?

Paso 1: Read the myth one time to familiarize yourself with the context and content. Don't look up any words in the dictionary. You won't understand every word, but you just want to get some basic ideas of the story in this reading.

Paso 2: After you have read the myth once, write a brief summary of what you have understood from the story, using the guiding questions from the reading strategy to help you.

_____
_____
_____
_____
_____

Paso 3: Read the myth one more time. Don't look up words in the dictionary this time either. Underline what you think are the most important events of the story. That is, underline only what you believe to be the most essential information without which the story would not make sense.

Paso 4: Go back to your underlined phrases and, in your own words, write a brief summary of the narration. Don't worry about small details of the story, just the main events.

_____
_____
_____
_____
_____

Paso 5: Read the myth one more time. This time, if it is absolutely necessary, you may look up words you don't know. Write their definition above the words in the text. When you are done, answer the following questions.

1. ¿Cuál es el tema principal del mito?

_____

2. ¿Quién consiguió la noche perfecta? ¿Piensas que este hecho tiene alguna importancia?

_____

_____

3. ¿Por qué, según los aymarás, no duerme el Tatú?

_____

_____

La noche del Tatú

Los indios tejieron[1] techos de paja[2] y colgaron debajo de ellos sus hamacas. Pero no pudieron dormir. El Padre Primero aún no había creado la noche y el sol alumbraba todo el tiempo. El brillo y el calor caían sobre las criaturas de la tierra sin descanso. Los hombres se quejaban y decían: —¿Para qué no sirven estas hamacas? Sin una noche nunca vamos a poder dormirnos.

A lo que las mujeres les reclamaban: —Como no hay noche los hombres y los niños quieren comer todo el día y nosotras tenemos que cocinar sin descanso.

Un día Cochipil, uno de los niños del pueblo, jugaba cerca de la entrada de la cueva del ratón y descubrió que allí el ratón guardaba una pequeña noche. El niño se quedó asombrado al ver cuán tranquilo dormía el ratón con su propia noche. Cochipil decidió pedirle prestada la noche al ratón así que al día siguiente guardó los pedacitos de carne que le sobraba[3] de la cena y se los trajo al ratón.

—Si me prestas tu noche —le dijo Cochipil al ratón—, te daré esta carne y te traeré más.

Al ratón le brillaron los ojos negros y aceptó. Cuando el ratón acabó los pedacitos de carne, salió de sus ojos y de sus orejas un aire negro que subió al cielo y empezó a cubrir rápidamente la luz del sol. Y el sol, huyendo[4] de la noche del ratón, bajó por el cielo y se escondió en el horizonte. Y así fue la primera noche en la selva peruana.

Los indios vieron desaparecer el sol y se alegraron. Luego, todos corrieron rápidamente a sus hamacas para disfrutar la dulzura de la oscuridad. Pero el descanso les duró poco tiempo.

Casi de inmediato empezó a amanecer y el cielo se llenó otra vez de una luz fuerte que les quitó las ganas de dormir.

—¿Qué pasó? —exclamó Nahua, uno de los hombres del pueblo.

—Ésa fue la noche del ratón, se la pedí prestada. ¿No les gustó? —le preguntó Cochipil.

—Sí, nos gustó, nos hacía falta una noche, pero tenemos que buscarnos una noche más larga para así dormir a gusto —contestó Nahua.

Ese día varios de los hombres cazadores[5] del pueblo encontraron en medio de la selva un tapir que comía hojas tiernas. Se enteraron que el tapir también tenía su propia noche y los hombres se la pidieron prestada. El tapir accedió[6] y, casi de inmediato, de su cuerpo grande y gordo, de sus orejas y de su pequeña trompa empezó a salir una noche espesa que cubrió rápidamente el cielo. El sol se cayó del cielo como una estrella fugaz[7] y así fue la segunda noche en la selva peruana.

Los indios corrieron felices al pueblo, mirando las estrellas con orgullo por el trabajo bien hecho. Al llegar, todos celebraron y luego se acostaron. Los indios del pueblo durmieron horas y horas y soñaron mil sueños. La noche del tapir fue muy larga. Tan larga que cuando por fin los indios se despertaron descubrieron que las malezas[8] del monte habían cubierto sus sembrados y sus casas y las enredaderas[9] habían trepado hasta sus hamacas. Decidieron que la noche del tapir era demasiado larga. Niva, una de las mujeres del pueblo anunció:

—Cochipil, como niño, encontró una noche muy corta; los cazadores, como hombres, otra demasiado larga. Yo, como mujer, buscaré la noche que conviene.

Y así fue Niva por las montañas hasta que encontró al Peludo, un armadillo, en su madriguera[10] y vio que él también guardaba su propia noche.

—Tatú, ¡despiértate! —gritó Niva—. Préstame tu noche.

El Peludo, protegido por su armadura, ni se movió.

—Si me prestas tu noche, te daré las sobras de la comida —le suplicó Niva.

Cuando el Peludo oyó lo de la comida, se despertó rápidamente y le dijo que sí, pero que sólo le prestaría una noche. Niva aceptó felizmente y volvió al pueblo.

Un poco más tarde, del fondo de la madriguera del Peludo, salió lentamente su noche. El sol bajó por el cielo poco a poco y los hombres tuvieron tiempo de terminar sus trabajos y las mujeres de preparar una buena comida antes de que oscureciera. Por todo el pueblo los indios comieron bien y charlaron un buen rato después. Cuando se acostaron en sus hamacas la dulzura de la noche del Tatú les cerró los ojos y así llegó la tercera noche en la selva peruana.

Amaneció a las pocas horas, luego de un buen sueño. Los indios estuvieron de acuerdo en que la noche del Tatú era la más conveniente. Por eso los hombres no quisieron devolvérsela nunca más y ésta es la razón por la que el Tatú duerme durante el día y corretea sin descanso en la oscuridad, porque no tiene noche.

[1]tejieron *wove* [2]paja *straw* [3]que le sobraba *that was left over* [4]huyendo *fleeing* [5]cazadores *hunters* [6]accedió aceptó [7]estrella fugaz *shooting star* [8]malezas *weeds* [9]enredaderas *vines from climbing plants* [10]madriguera *den*

¡A ESCRIBIR!

UN ENSAYO CRÍTICO In this section you will write a critical essay about a topic of interest to you.

Strategy: Identifying elements of a critical essay

Every day we evaluate many conditions, situations, and people. Sometimes, for personal or professional reasons, we write down our comments and opinions about them. Critical essays often appear in newspapers, magazines, and other similar publications and frequently deal with topics discussed in this chapter such as art, literature, film, and television. When beginning to write a critical essay, the following guidelines will help you get started.

1. Choose a subject or topic that interests you.

2. Write a brief introduction about the subject you choose.

3. List three or four things that you like about your subject.

4. Think of one or two things that could be done realistically to improve your subject and write these ideas down.

5. Come to a conclusion about your subject.

Paso 1: Recall the steps for writing this type of essay.

1. Selecciona el tema.

2. Escribe una breve introducción sobre el tema.

3. Haz una lista de tres o cuatro cosas que te gusten del tema.

4. Piensa en una o dos cosas que puedas hacer para mejorar el contenido de tu tema.

5. Escribe una conclusión sobre este tema.

Functions: Writing an essay; Writing an introduction; Writing a conclusion; Expressing an opinion
Vocabulary: Arts; Poetry; Prose; Musical instruments
Grammar: Verbs: subjunctive

Paso 2: Now it's time to select your topic. Write your essay about one of these topics.

• una película nueva
• un concierto
• un programa de televisión
• un disco compacto
• una novela que te guste

Paso 3: Write a first draft on a separate piece of paper. Once you have that draft, think about whether you can include more details to better explain the point you wish to make about your topic. Think also whether you need to delete some details for not being very relevant to explaining your point of view. Afterwards, review the grammar and make any necessary changes. Pay special attention to your spelling, use of accents, use of the verb **gustar,** and use of the subjunctive.

Paso 4: Write your final draft below.

_____

_____

_____

_____

_____

_____

_____

_____

_____

_____

_____

Autoprueba

VOCABULARIO

WB 13-14 | **Las películas y los programas** Match the names of the people with the types of programs or movies normally associated with them.

____ 1. Mia Hamm   **a.** un drama

____ 2. Dan Rather   **b.** una comedia

____ 3. Bugs Bunny   **c.** las noticias

____ 4. John Wayne   **d.** dibujos animados

____ 5. Al Roker   **e.** un programa deportivo

____ 6. Adam Sandler   **f.** una película del oeste

____ 7. Vanna White   **g.** pronóstico del tiempo

____ 8. David Letterman   **h.** un programa de concursos

____ 9. Steven Spielberg   **i.** un programa de entrevistas

____ 10. Andy García   **j.** una película de ciencia ficción

WB 13-15 | **El mundo de las bellas artes** Complete the following sentences with the appropriate words from the list.

| actriz | concierto | dramaturgo | arquitectura | cuadro | fotografía | bailarín |
| danza | fotógrafo | cantante | director | literatura | compositor | |

1. La _____ incluye tanto la poesía como el guión de una película.

2. El pianista va a dar un _____ mañana en el parque.

3. El arte de sacar fotos se llama _____ y quien lo practica es el _____.

4. El que dirige una película o una obra de teatro es _____.

5. Una mujer que interpreta un papel en una obra de teatro es _____.

6. El arte de diseñar edificios se llama la _____.

7. Lo que pinta el pintor se llama un _____.

8. El que escribe el guión de una obra de teatro es _____.

9. Un hombre que practica baile es _____.

10. El tango es una _____ de Argentina.

11. El que escribe música es _____.

12. El que canta es _____.

ESTRUCTURA

WB 13-16 **Consejos para la cita** Carlos is giving his friend Pablo advice for his big date tonight with Silvia. To find out what he says, fill in the blanks with the correct form of the verb in parentheses. You have to read the conversation and understand its context to be able to decide between the present indicative and the subjunctive.

CARLOS: Hola, Paulo, ¿qué me cuentas? ¿Cómo estás?

PAULO: ¡Estoy super bien! Sabes que Silvia por fin viene a visitarme, bueno, con tal de que 1. _____ (limpiar) la casa antes de que ella 2. _____ (venir).

CARLOS: ¿Silvia? ¿Te va a visitar a ti? Pero tu casa es un desastre. ¿Qué vas a hacer para que Silvia no 3. _____ (asustarse) cuando 4. _____ (llegar)?

PAULO: Mira, Carlos, aunque mi casa sí 5. _____ (estar) un poco sucia, no es un desastre. La puedo limpiar.

CARLOS: Pues, suponiendo que sí puedes limpiar la casa, ¿qué van a hacer Uds.?

PAULO: No lo sé. Creo que voy a alquilar un video de Jackie Chan. Creo que a Silvia le va a gustar. Pero, en caso de que no le 6. _____ (gustar), también voy a alquilar mi película favorita, *Smokey and the Bandit*. Sé que con una de ésas no puedo perder.

CARLOS: ¡Paulo, Paulo! ¿Cuándo 7. _____ (ir) a aprender? ¿Cuántas veces te lo tengo que decir? Cuando 8. _____ (invitar) a tu casa a una chica como Silvia, tienes que enfocarte en ella. Tienes que preguntarle a ella qué quiere ver. Esta noche, pregúntale a Silvia qué quiere ver y entonces, cuando ella te 9. _____ (decir) el título de la película, Uds. dos pueden ir juntos a la tienda para alquilarlo.

PAULO: Entonces, ¿no crees que una película de Jackie Chan le vaya a gustar?

CARLOS: Paulo, aunque le 10. _____ (gustar), tienes que esperar hasta que ella 11. _____ (decidir) qué es lo que prefiere ver. ¡Qué cabezota *(stubborn person)* eres!

WB 13-17 | **Pero ¡NO FUE CULPA NUESTRA!** You and your friend had a horrible day yesterday: all kinds of things accidentally happened to you. To describe what happened, follow the model and form sentences using no-fault **se.**

MODELO: Tú rompiste dos vasos de cristal.
Se me rompieron dos vasos de cristal.

1. Tú y tu amiga dejaron caer una escultura en la casa de otra amiga.

   _____

   _____

2. Tu amiga dejó escapar a los niños que cuidaba.

   _____

   _____

3. Tú no recordaste una cita con tu novio(a).

   _____

   _____

4. Tú y tu amiga acabaron todo el dinero que tenían para el mes.

   _____

   _____

5. Tú perdiste la llave de tu coche.

   _____

   _____

WB 13-18 | **¿Ya está hecho?** You're in charge of a committee to plan the university's biggest party of the year. Go over the list of things your committee has to do and indicate those things that are already done (**estar** + **el participio**) and who did them (**ser** + **el participio pasado**). Follow the model.

MODELO: escribir las invitaciones / Teresa
Las invitaciones ya están escritas.
Fueron escritas por Teresa.

1. invitar a los estudiantes / Jaime y Juan

   _____

   _____

   _____

   _____

2. confirmar el entretenimiento / Analisa

   _____

   _____

   _____

   _____

3. organizar la lista de música / Rosa y Eva

_____

_____

_____

_____

4. preparar la comida / Marta y Esteban

_____

_____

_____

_____

5. colgar las decoraciones / Julio

_____

_____

_____

_____

4 La vida pública: Chile

VOCABULARIO La política y el voto

¡A PRACTICAR!

WB 14-1 **Crucigrama** Read the clues on page 224 and solve this crossword puzzle.

Horizontal

1. Fidel Castro
3. Partido político
6. Acción de nombrar por elección
8. Regla
11. Líder de un gobierno democrático
12. Lo opuesto a liberal

Vertical

1. Discusión pública entre candidatos
2. Sinónimo de «proteger»
4. Parte del gobierno estadounidense que funciona conjuntamente con el senado
5. La persona que hace campaña para ganar algún puesto político
7. Lo que se ejecuta como innovación o mejora en el gobierno
9. El que pertenece a cierta ciudad o cierto país
10. Cuerpo militar

¡TE TOCA A TI!

WB 14-2 | **Hablando de política** Your pen pal wants to know your opinion about the current political situation in the U.S. Answer his questions according to your own beliefs and opinions.

1. ¿Participa mucha gente joven en las elecciones políticas?

_____

2. ¿Son liberales o conservadores los estudiantes de tu universidad? Justifica tu respuesta.

_____

_____

3. ¿Cuál es el partido político que tiene más apoyo público en los Estados Unidos actualmente?

_____

4. ¿Cuáles son dos de los temas políticos que más se discuten actualmente?

_____

_____

5. ¿Crees que los ciudadanos tienen el deber de votar en las elecciones políticas? ¿Por qué sí o por qué no?

_____

_____

Nombre _____ Fecha _____

ESTRUCTURA I Talking about future events: the future tense

¡A PRACTICAR!

WB 14-3 **Las predicciones de Óscar** Óscar thinks about his future and that of his friends. Use the future tense to write what he is thinking.

> MODELO: Yo... trabajar para una organización política el año que viene
> *Yo trabajaré para una organización política el año que viene.*

1. Yo... ir a Ecuador para encontrarse con Marina / estudiar filosofía con Marina / enamorarme de Marina / y / olvidarme de mi novia en Chile

_____

_____

_____

2. Marina... conocerme mejor / asistir a una clase de política contemporánea / querer cambiar de especialidad / decirme que me quiere

_____

_____

_____

3. El novio de Marina... saber que Marina ya no lo quiere / escribirle muchas cartas de amor / hacer muchos esfuerzos para no perderla / tener que buscar una nueva novia

_____

_____

_____

4. Marina y yo... irnos de Ecuador / volver a Chile / casarnos / tener cuatro hijos

_____

_____

_____

WB 14-4 **Querido diario** Marina is thinking about Óscar and writes out some of her predictions for the future. Complete the paragraphs using the appropriate verbs from each list.

1. tener / volver / ahorrar / venir / ir

Sé que algún día _____ a Chile. Esta vez mi mejor amiga, Carmen,

_____ conmigo. Creo que (yo) _____ más dinero que ahora porque

Carmen y yo lo _____ todas las semanas.

2. divertirse / visitar / escribir / alegrarse

Antes de salir para Chile, yo les _____ a mis otros amigos chilenos para decirles

que yo los _____. Estoy segura de que ellos _____ de verme y de

que nosotros _____ mucho.

3. saber / hacer / tomar / poder / haber / estar

Carmen y yo _____ el viaje en la primavera. En esa temporada

_____ menos visitantes que ahora y los precios de los boletos

_____ más baratos. Yo _____ más de la política contemporánea

porque _____ más clases. Así _____ hablar con Óscar sobre los

asuntos políticos de Chile.

¡TE TOCA A TI!

WB 14-5 **Una consulta con Walter Mercado** You have consulted the famous Latin psychic, Walter Mercado, to read your future. He asks what you will do or what you think your friends will do when his predictions occur. For each situation write a complete sentence using the future. Follow the model.

MODELO: Tu mejor amigo no tiene dinero y quiere vivir contigo hasta que gane más dinero.
Yo le daré dinero y le diré que no tengo suficiente espacio en mi apartamento.

1. El (La) novio(a) de tu mejor amigo(a) te dirá que quiere salir contigo.

Tu mejor amigo(a) _____

_____.

2. El rector *(president)* de tu universidad dejará su puesto el mes que viene.

Los estudiantes de la universidad _____

_____.

3. El dueño de la casa donde vives te dirá que tienes que mudarte inmediatamente.

Yo _____.

4. Tus padres se ganarán la lotería.

Nosotros _____.

5. Tú trabajarás en la Casa Blanca con el presidente de los Estados Unidos.

Yo_____.

VOCABULARIO Las preocupaciones cívicas y los medios de comunicación

¡A PRACTICAR!

WB 14-6 **Las últimas noticias** This morning Juanita found the following newspaper article reporting about a campus protest against the latest fee hike. Complete the article with the appropriate words from the list. **¡OJO!** Conjugate the verbs if necessary.

prensa	reportaje	desigualdad	protesta
huelga	derechos civiles	noticiero	corrupción
informar	inflación	reducir	eliminar

Mañana cientos de estudiantes universitarios realizarán una 1. _____
en contra del aumento de la matrícula, la cual subirá más del 200 por ciento el año que
viene. Según 2. _____ la administración de la universidad, el au-
mento es necesario debido a la 3. _____ general que ha causado la
subida de precios en todos los sectores de la economía. Sin embargo, los estudiantes
creen que si el gobierno estatal *(state)* 4. _____ la
5. _____ que ha plagado *(plagued)* la administración en los últimos
años, podrán hasta 6. _____ el costo de la educación para todos.

　　Los estudiantes señalan que el aumento de la matrícula constituirá una violación de
los 7. _____ de los estudiantes y sólo creará más
8. _____ entre los ciudadanos.

　　Parece que los profesores apoyan a los estudiantes. Hernán González, portavoz de la
Asociación de Profesores Universitarios (APU), dice que los profesores están dispuestos a
montar una 9. _____ y a no volver a trabajar hasta que el gobierno
haga algo para evitar el aumento de la matrícula. La manifestación será mañana a las
10:00 de la mañana y Lola Sebastián, representante de la 10. _____
universitaria, hará un 11. _____ en vivo para el
12. _____ de las 6:00 de la tarde.

¡TE TOCA A TI!

WB 14-7 **¿Qué dices?** Your friend Mario wants to know more about a student's perspective. Answer his questions in complete sentences.

1. ¿Qué debe hacer el gobierno estadounidense para controlar los actos de terrorismo cometidos por los jóvenes en las escuelas?

_____

_____

2. ¿En tu universidad hay problemas con la drogadicción? ¿Qué hace la universidad para prevenir o solucionar este problema?

_____

_____

3. En tu universidad o ciudad, ¿se cometen muchos crímenes contra mujeres? ¿Qué tipo de crímenes hay? ¿Qué hace la universidad para mejorar la situación? ¿Qué debe hacer?

_____

_____

_____

_____

¡A PRACTICAR!

WB 14-8 | **Si pudiera...** Lidia is talking to her friend Pedro about how university life would be if she made all the important decisions about how the university was run. Use the words below to form sentences. Follow the model.

MODELO: los estudiantes / no pagar / ninguna matrícula
Los estudiantes no pagarían ninguna matrícula.

1. los estudiantes / poder / obtener becas (*scholarships*) más fácilmente

_____

2. nosotros / no tener que / asistir a clases por la mañana

_____

3. el rector de la universidad / salir / de la universidad

_____

4. los profesores / no darles / notas a los estudiantes

_____

5. todos los estudiantes / querer / asistir a esta universidad

_____

WB 14-9 | **Paqui la periodista** Paqui will interview candidates for the governor's race in California and needs help writing the questions she will ask. Help her by filling in the blanks with the appropriate conditional form of the verbs in parentheses. **¡OJO!** Paqui will use the **usted** form when addressing the candidates directly.

1. ¿_____ (Tener) Ud. algún problema en hablar abiertamente conmigo sobre su campaña?

2. ¿_____ (Decir) Ud. que la inmigración ilegal es un problema en el estado de California?

3. ¿_____ (Querer) Ud. aprobar una ley para hacer el inglés la lengua oficial del estado?

4. ¿Le _____ (gustar) hacer ilegal el aborto en este estado?

5. ¿_____ (Saber) Ud. si el otro candidato tiene más experiencia política que Ud.?

¡TE TOCA A TI!

WB 14-10 | **Situaciones difíciles** Read each of the following situations and write several things that you would do in each one. Follow the model.

MODELO: Estás en el centro de tu ciudad y ves un crimen que está pasando (*in progress*). Un hombre le está robando el bolso a una mujer.

¿Qué harías?

Llamaría al policía y les diría todo lo que vi. Les daría una descripción del ladrón.

Situación 1: Imagina que estás de vacaciones en Chile con un(a) amigo(a) de habla española. Uds. iban a hacer muchas actividades durante su viaje, pero anoche tu amigo(a) conoció a una persona de quien se enamoró. Ahora ya no quiere salir contigo y no piensa volver a los Estados Unidos.

¿Qué harías?

_____

_____

_____

_____

Situación 2: Descubres que tu compañero(a) de cuarto comete actos de terrorismo contra la universidad por medio del Internet.

¿Qué harías?

_____

_____

_____

_____

Situación 3: Descubres que tu mejor amiga está embarazada y considera el aborto.

¿Qué harías? ¿Qué le dirías?

_____

_____

_____

_____

Situación 4: Descubres que alguien te ha robado el número de seguridad social y se ha sacado tarjetas de crédito en tu nombre.

¿Qué harías?

_____

_____

_____

_____

Situación 5: Ganas dos millones de dólares en la lotería.

¿Cómo los gastarías?

_____

_____

_____

_____

ESTRUCTURA III Making references to the present: the present perfect subjunctive

¡A PRACTICAR!

WB 14-11 | **El día después de las elecciones** While in a café the day after the national elections, María hears a lot of different opinions. Complete the sentences with the appropriate form of the verbs in the present perfect subjunctive to find out what these opinions are.

1. Me alegro de que mi candidato favorito _____ (ganar).

2. No puedo creer que los perdedores _____ (montar) una manifestación tan rápidamente.

3. ¡Nidia! ¡Es imposible que tú _____ (votar) por ese candidato! Es horrible.

4. Es dudoso que los candidatos _____ (ser) totalmente honestos con nosotros.

5. ¡Qué bueno que _____ (haber) tanta propaganda acerca de las elecciones! Así la gente reconoce la importancia de los asuntos políticos.

6. Es interesante que nosotros siempre _____ (tener) ideas políticas tan diferentes y que sigamos siendo amigos.

WB 14-12 | **Foro abierto** Kati Homedes has invited the public to an open forum to discuss key issues for her candidacy. What is her opinion on the topics? Form complete sentences with the following words, conjugating the verbs in the present perfect. **¡OJO!** Use the subjunctive when it is necessary.

MODELO: no pensar / los impuestos / subir / mucho durante los últimos años
No pienso que los impuestos hayan subido mucho durante los últimos años.

1. dudar que / los ciudadanos / estar / suficientemente activos en la política hasta ahora

_____

_____

2. estar segura de que / la inmigración ilegal / no causar / problemas graves para el estado

_____

_____

3. estar contenta de que / el presidente / preocuparse / tanto por las violaciones de los derechos humanos

_____

_____

4. creer que / el gobierno / hacer / todo lo posible para eliminar el terrorismo nacional

_____

_____

5. no estar contenta de que / el público / decir / que no soy una buena candidata

_____

_____

¡TE TOCA A TI!

WB 14-13 **¿De verdad?** Through Internet chat Mario asks you about some things he has heard about the U.S. lately. Write your reaction, using complete sentences with the present perfect and the expressions in the box. **¡OJO!** When necessary, use the subjunctive.

Creo que	No es cierto que	Quiero que
No es posible	No es dudoso que	Insisto en que
Estoy seguro(a) de que	Me alegro de que	Es importante que
Es cierto que	Dudo que	

1. Los ciudadanos de Estados Unidos han votado por una ley para hacer el inglés la lengua oficial del país.

   _____

   _____

2. Los estudiantes universitarios de tu estado han estado de huelga durante tres semanas.

   _____

   _____

3. El presidente de los Estados Unidos ha eliminado el ejército.

   _____

   _____

4. El gobierno ha investigado soluciones posibles al problema de la drogadicción.

   _____

   _____

5. Los actos de terrorismo dentro del país han aumentado durante los últimos diez años.

   _____

   _____

SÍNTESIS

¡A LEER!

LA LIBERTAD DE LA EXPRESIÓN The reading in this section presents current opinions of Chileans about Pinochet, the former Chilean ruler.

Strategy: Reading complex sentences

Determining what is essential and what is nonessential in complex sentences will help you read Spanish more efficiently and effectively. As you have learned in previous reading strategies, it is not essential to understand the meaning of every single word you come across when reading in Spanish; in fact, as a learner of Spanish as a foreign language, such an expectation would be unrealistic. Instead, you should try to focus on understanding the overall meaning of sentences, which should lead you to a general understanding of the passage as a whole. When dealing with a complex sentence, the core of its meaning will come from its subject and its main verb.

Paso 1: The reading below presents current opinions of Chilenas about Pinochet. Briefly write down what you know about the former Chilean ruler. If you do not know anything, do some research on the web and then write down what you learned.

_____

_____

_____

Paso 2: Read only the first paragraph of the reading and underline the subject and the main verb in each sentence. This will help you get an idea about the main point(s) of the article before you attempt to read the entire thing. When you are done, write several of the details that are associated with Pinochet. Are these some of the same details you noted in **Paso 1**?

_____

_____

_____

Paso 3: Now read the entire article without using your dictionary. As you read try to identify the main subject and main verb of each sentence you come across. After reading the article once, write a short summary of what you understood to be the topic and several of the main points.

_____

_____

La libertad de la expresión en la sociedad del nuevo milenio

Como en cualquier otra sociedad demócrata, en Chile reina la libertad de expresión. Los ciudadanos tienen el derecho de opinar públicamente sobre los temas de más importancia y relevancia. Uno de los temas más debatidos al inicio del nuevo milenio en Chile ha sido el futuro del ex dictador Augusto Pinochet. Como leíste en tu libro de texto, después de haber sido detenido en la Gran Bretaña, Pinochet volvió a Chile, donde debido a su mal estado de salud, no fue demandado por sus crímenes y violaciones de derechos humanos. ¿Qué opina la gente de Chile de esta situación? Lee cómo respondieron varios chilenos a la siguiente pregunta:

PINOCHET: ¿EL EX GENERAL ESTÁ EN CONDICIONES DE ENFRENTAR UN JUICIO?

Javier Blasco:
La edad de una persona no puede constituir una excusa para que no se le juzgue. El criminal lleva ya mucho tiempo impune.[1] Debe pagar sus crímenes, debe pagar por las atrocidades por las que es responsable, sin importar su edad o su estado de salud. En Europa, todavía se procesa a criminales nazi que tienen más de ochenta años. Pinochet es un criminal tal como los nazis. Seamos consecuentes y juzguémoslos, el país necesita justicia, algo que los pinochetistas desconocen totalmente.

Diego Castellanos:
Sería irracional que Pinochet fuera juzgado en Chile; primero que nada, porque las personas que lo acusan de hechos relacionados a violaciones de los derechos humanos, son en su mayoría, terroristas. Ellos mismos fueron los que propiciaron[2] la grave crisis del «gobierno» del señor irónicamente llamado Salvador. Es por eso que no creo que el poder judicial chileno sea tan iluso de considerar estas acusaciones. Y en caso que estuvieran obligados a hacerlo, tampoco tendría efecto, dado su actual estado de salud. Los que tienen que ser enjuiciados son terroristas.

Francisco Lagunas:
Ojalá alguno de los fanáticos de Pinochet se disculpara por lo sucedido... Hasta la iglesia lo hizo con los eventos pasados. ¿Cómo no puede disculparse un viejito que está a punto de morir y cómo cuesta tanto admitir que hubo atrocidades por parte de ese gobierno? Y de una vez por todas, dejen de pensar que el que está en contra de Pinochet es terrorista... por favor, ¡que estrechez de mente! ¿Cómo resultará el juicio —ojalá se le juzgue— a ver si así, los ciegos de este país admiten las atrocidades cometidas y de una vez por todas pedimos perdón y perdonamos?

David Ponce:
El problema es que Chile no está en condiciones de juzgar a Pinochet, debido a que los plutócratas[3] de la derecha lo tiene aun como bandera de lucha.

[1]**impune** *unpunished* [2]**propiciaron** *paved the way for* [3]**plutócratas** *la clase rica que típicamente predomina en el gobierno de cierto país*

Paso 4: Read the article through once more. Do not use the dictionary this time either. If there are sentences or phrases you do not understand, try to identify the main verb and its subject to aid in your comprehension. Once you understand the basic part of the sentence or phrase, try to guess at the meaning of the rest. When you have finished reading, decide if you need to change anything in the summary that you wrote in **Paso 3,** and do so here.

_____

_____

_____

_____

_____

Paso 5: Read the article a third time. If you still are unsure of the meaning of key words and phrases, look them up now. When you finish, answer the comprehension questions.

1. Se ve que hay cierta diferencia de opinión con respecto a Pinochet. ¿Cuáles son las dos opiniones representadas aquí?

_____

_____

2. ¿Cuáles son algunas de las palabras usadas en las opiniones presentadas que caracterizan los dos puntos de vista? Por ejemplo, plutócrata, etc.

_____

_____

3. ¿Qué piensas que significa *pinochetistas?*

_____

_____

4. ¿Quién es «el señor irónicamente llamado Salvador» al que se refiere Diego Castaño? Por qué dice el término «irónicamente»?

_____

_____

5. ¿Crees tú que la edad o la condición física de Pinochet debe afectar la decisión de acusarlo *(indict)* y castigarlo?

_____

_____

6. ¿Cuáles han sido algunos de los sucesos más recientes en el caso de Pinochet? Si no lo sabes, puedes buscar más información en Internet.

_____

_____

¡A ESCRIBIR!

Strategy: Writing from diagrams

In your textbook you learned to write a paragraph about a current event or topic, based on information presented in charts, graphs, and diagrams, which offer specific information that can be readily understood and remembered. Written reports prepared by individuals in business, industry, government, and education often include diagrams, etc., and it is therefore important to learn to interpret them and to express the information they contain in a succinct and clear fashion.

Paso 1: Now, choose one topic and survey friends your age to find out their responses.

Paso 2: Organize the results you obtain from your survey in the form of a chart or table that can easily display the answer to the question.

Functions: Comparing and contrasting; Comparing and distinguishing
Vocabulary: Computers
Grammar: Comparisons

Paso 3: Now, on a separate piece of paper write a paragraph based on the results of the survey that you conducted. Write a sentence that indicates the result of the survey (i.e., what the majority of people said). Then mention the details of your survey. Explain why people responded the way they did. Finally, conclude your paragraph with a short statement that summarizes your results.

Paso 4: Finally, read your paragraph again and revise it accordingly. Write your final draft below.

_____

_____

_____

_____

_____

_____

_____

_____

_____

_____

_____

_____

_____

_____

_____

Autoprueba

VOCABULARIO

WB 14-14 **Políticamente hablando** Emma tells her cousin about how elections are in the U.S. Is what she says correct? To find out, complete her description with the appropriate words from the list. Conjugate verbs when necessary.

campaña	conservadores	elegir	debates	republicanos	votar
ciudadanos	deber	dictadura	liberales	democracia	paz
ejército	partidos políticos	candidatos	defender		

1. Hay varios _____ en los Estados Unidos, pero los dos más populares son

   el demócrata y el _____. Los primeros tienden a ser

   _____ y los últimos normalmente son más _____.

2. Cuando los _____ hacen su _____, normalmente

   tienen muchos _____ para discutir los temas importantes para los

   _____.

3. Ya que nuestro sistema de gobierno no es una _____, sino una

   _____, nosotros _____ a nuestro presidente. Todas las

   personas tienen el _____ de _____ en las elecciones.

4. Aparte de su trabajo como líder del país, el presidente también es el líder del

   _____. Así que el presidente también tiene que tratar de mantener la

   _____ y _____ el país.

WB 14-15 **Las preocupaciones cívicas** Match each phrase with its description.

_____ 1. la defensa

_____ 2. el noticiero

_____ 3. la drogadicción

_____ 4. la inflación

_____ 5. los impuestos

_____ 6. el reportaje

_____ 7. la inmigración

_____ 8. el terrorismo

_____ 9. la manifestación

_____ 10. la libertad de la prensa

_____ 11. la revista

_____ 12. el desempleo

_____ 13. la huelga

_____ 14. el analfabetismo

_____ 15. el aborto

Nombre _____ Fecha _____

a. el dinero que la gente tiene que pagarle al gobierno federal y estatal

b. la terminación de un embarazo

c. un informe periodístico

d. la falta de censura en cuanto a las publicaciones periodísticas

e. el aumento de precios y la reducción del valor del dinero

f. la protección

g. la falta de instrucción elemental / no saber leer ni escribir

h. la acción de entrar a un país la gente de otro país

i. la presentación de las últimas noticias, normalmente por medio de la radio o la televisión

j. la publicación periódica sobre diferentes temas o sobre un tema específico

k. la dependencia de una sustancia química

l. los actos violentos que tienen como objetivo crear miedo o inseguridad

m. la falta de trabajo

n. una reunión de la gente para expresar públicamente alguna opinión

o. la acción de dejar de trabajar voluntariamente para lograr alguna meta

ESTRUCTURA

WB 14-16 | **El primer día** Lorena Magaña was just elected student body president, and her secretary has left her the following message about her schedule on her first day in office. Complete the message with the appropriate future tense form of the verbs in parentheses.

Hola, Lorena:

Hoy tú **1.** _____ (tener) muchas cosas que hacer. Tu primera reunión **2.** _____ (comenzar) a las 10:00 y **3.** _____ (ser) en la oficina del rector de la universidad. Tu vicepresidente y otros miembros del senado **4.** _____ (venir) a buscarte a las 9:30 para acompañarte a la reunión. Ellos no **5.** _____ (saber) que el rector **6.** _____ (querer) planear el agenda para todo el año, pero no importa, tú se lo **7.** _____ (decir) cuando los acompañes a la reunión. A la 1:00 **8.** _____ (haber) otra reunión, pero esta vez es con los estudiantes. Ésta no **9.** _____ (durar) mucho tiempo.

A las 3:00 de la tarde yo te **10.** _____ (ver) aquí en la oficina. Tenemos que hablar de tu fiesta de inauguración y creo que **11.** _____ (poder) hacerlo a esa hora. ¡No te preocupes! Yo **12.** _____ (hacer) todos los planes, pero sólo necesito saber de ti algunos detalles importantes.

Bueno, sé que **13.** _____ (ser) una presidente excelente y que en tu primer día te **14.** _____ (ir) super bien.

Suerte,

Ana María

WB 14-17 **Puros sueños** David and Magali just bought lottery tickets and are talking about what they will do if they win. Complete their conversation with the appropriate conditional form of the verbs in parentheses.

DAVID: ¿Qué **1.** _____ (hacer) tú con tanto dinero, Magali?

MAGALI: Yo **2.** _____ (viajar) a todos los países del mundo.

DAVID: Me **3.** _____ (gustar) acompañarte. ¿**4.** _____ (Poder) ir yo?

MAGALI: ¡Cómo no! Nosotros **5.** _____ (salir) inmediatamente después de ganar.

DAVID: ¡Qué bueno! ¿Adónde **6.** _____ (ir) nosotros primero?

MAGALI: Pues mira, esto lo he pensado bastante. Primero **7.** _____ (tomar) el avión desde acá hasta Santiago de Chile. **8.** _____ (Pasar) unas semanas viajando por Chile y ya que también **9.** _____ (querer) pasar unas semanas en Argentina, después **10.** _____ (volar) a Buenos Aires.

DAVID: Y después de eso, nosotros **11.** _____ (tener) que ir a Europa, ¿no?

MAGALI: ¡Claro que sí! ¡Espero que ganemos!

WB 14-18 **No lo creo** Roberto never believes half of what Raúl says because he exaggerates a lot. Complete their latest conversation by writing Roberto's reaction to Raúl's news. Form sentences with the present perfect, using its subjunctive form where necessary.

1. ser imposible que / tú quedarse / en hoteles de cuatro estrellas

   _____

   _____

2. no creer que / tú y tu novia / conocer / al presidente de los Estados Unidos

   _____

   _____

3. estar seguro de que / tu novia / pasarlo bien / en Washington

   _____

   _____

4. no dudar que / tú / participar / en tres manifestaciones políticas

   _____

   _____

5. no pensar que / tu novia / decirte / que no quiere volver a Chile

   _____

   _____

Nombre _____ Fecha _____

15 Los avances tecnológicos: Uruguay

VOCABULARIO Los avances tecnológicos

¡A PRACTICAR!

WB 15-1 | **¡Qué desastre!** Alicia is complaining about her roommate, who is an electronics addict. Complete her conversation by choosing the appropriate words from the list.

antena parabólica	desconectar	grabar	teléfono celular
encendido	prender	control remoto	caseta de video
funcionar	satélite	videocasetera	contestador

ALICIA: Te juro, Leo, Marga es un desastre. Nunca sale de la casa porque siempre está pegada a la televisión. Desde que compramos la **1.** _____ para recibir los canales de **2.** _____, la pobre casi no se ha levantado de su sillón.

LEO: Pues, ¿qué hace? ¿Se duerme en el sillón?

ALICIA: No, por lo menos no se duerme allí. Pero todo comienza a las 10:00 de la mañana. **3.** _____ la televisión e inmediatamente después, le mete una **4.** _____ a la **5.** _____ para ver los programas que perdió durante la noche anterior cuando dormía.

LEO: ¿Cómo?

ALICIA: ¡Ah! ¿No te lo dije? Sí, Marga **6.** _____ en video casi todas las telenovelas. Claro, no las puede ver todas a la vez. Y bueno, cuando termina eso, empieza a cambiar canales como loca con el **7.** _____. Nunca puedo ver nada en la tele, porque está ella allí a toda hora *(all the time)*.

LEO: ¡Qué lata!

ALICIA: Pero, eso no es lo que más me molesta. Marga, como está tan ocupada durante el día, nunca contesta el teléfono. Siempre deja que el **8.** _____ conteste, o simplemente **9.** _____ el teléfono porque no quiere que nadie la moleste. ¿Te imaginas? Entonces nadie me puede dejar un mensaje.

LEO: Chica, yo en tu lugar, la botaría de la casa. Pero, una solución más inmediata sería comprarte un **10.** _____ y dejarlo **11.** _____ todo el día por si te llaman tus amigos. ¿Qué te parece?

ALICIA: Ya tengo uno, el problema es que no me **12.** _____ bien. Creo que necesito cambiarle las pilas *(batteries)*.

LEO: ¡Anda! ¡Ponte las pilas! *(Get with it!)*

WB 15-2 **Encuesta de seguridad** The energy company sent out the following pamphlet with safety recommendations, and yours arrived in Spanish. Since you read Spanish, read the pamphlet and fill out the survey.

Departamento de Energía

Con nuestra creciente dependencia de los aparatos electrónicos, se hace cada vez más importante tomar precauciones para evitar incendios y otros peligros que éstos presentan. Nos gustaría darles varias recomendaciones de seguridad para el uso de los aparatos electrónicos que Ud. tenga en la casa. Por favor, tome Ud. unos momentos para leer y hacer la siguiente encuesta.

1. ¿Qué aparatos electrónicos tiene Ud. en su casa? Para cada aparato, escriba dónde lo tiene puesto en la casa. Por ejemplo, encima de un escritorio o al lado del televisor, etcétera.

    _____   _____

    _____   _____

    _____   _____

2. ¿Cuántos de estos aparatos están enchufados ahora mismo?

    _____

Lea ahora nuestras recomendaciones para estos aparatos.

*   **Recomendaciones de seguridad para el uso de aparatos electrónicos:**
    Ponga televisores, equipos de audio, videograbadoras y computadoras en lugares con circulación de aire para evitar el recalentamiento de los mismos. Si un aparato electrónico larga humo *(smoke)* o despide olor *(odor)*, no lo utilice ni lo toque ni trate de desenchufarlo.
*   **Desconecte el equipo para llevarlo a reparar.**
    Evite poner recipientes con líquidos sobre el equipo electrónico. Su derrame *(spill)* puede generar cortos circuitos y/o incendios. Apague y desenchufe televisores, radios, computadoras y demás aparatos electrónicos durante tormentas eléctricas. Utilice protector de sobretensión en computadoras, televisores y videograbadoras. Limite el número de equipos enchufados en una misma toma.

3. Según la información, ¿tiene Ud. algún aparato mal colocado en su casa? ¿Cuál?

    _____

4. En algún lugar de su casa, ¿tiene Ud. más de un equipo enchufado? ¿Cuáles son estos equipos? ¿Necesitará Ud. un protector de sobretensión?

    _____

    _____

5. ¿Cree Ud. que sus aparatos electrónicos están seguros en su casa? ¿Por qué?

    _____

    _____

¡Gracias por haber hecho esta encuesta!

ESTRUCTURA I Making statements in the past: past (imperfect) subjunctive

¡A PRACTICAR!

WB 15-3   **Una carta al gerente** Javier had a bad experience buying a stereo today and now he is writing a letter to the store manager to complain. Help him complete the letter by filling in the blanks with the appropriate past subjunctive form of the verbs in parentheses.

Estimado señor Gangas:

1. _____ (Querer) informarle sobre una mala experiencia que tuve hoy cuando estaba en su tienda con mi novia. Lo que quería yo era muy simple. Buscaba algún estéreo que

2. _____ (tener) radio, que 3. _____ (tocar) discos compactos y que

4. _____ (ser) barato. Punto. Pero su dependiente, Jorge Demalaleche, tenía otra idea. Él recomendaba que yo 5. _____ (mirar) las computadoras. Dijo que era necesario que yo 6. _____ (comprar) un nuevo PC para que así mi novia y yo 7. _____ (poder) escuchar la radio en el Internet y no 8. _____ (necesitar) discos compactos. ¡Le dije que yo compraría el PC con tal de que él me lo 9. _____ (dar) al precio del estéreo barato que yo buscaba!

Pues, al señor Demalaleche, no le gustó para nada que yo le 10. _____ (decir) eso y me dijo que aunque las nuevas computadoras 11. _____ (venderse) al mismo precio que los estéreos, ¡no me vendería una! En ese momento le dije que antes de que (él)

12. _____ (abrir) la boca una vez más, que era importante que 13. _____ (hacer) un esfuerzo para ser más cortés con nosotros. Entonces mi novia le dijo que podríamos ir a cualquier otra tienda para comprar lo que buscábamos. El señor Demalaleche se puso más enojado y le dijo a mi novia que no tenía miedo de que nosotros 14. _____ (irse) a otro lugar.

Señor Gangas, yo sé que el señor Demalaleche esperaba que nosotros 15. _____ (gastar) mucho dinero en su tienda, pero ésa no fue la manera de lograrlo. Quizás él

16. _____ (deber) tomar un curso de cortesía. Yo, por mi parte, no volveré a su tienda.

Cordialmente,
Javier Begaña

WB 15-4 **¡Qué buen día!** What do Luis and Leticia remember about their friends' wedding? To find out, form sentences in the past subjunctive with the words below. Follow the model and use preterite or imperfect as indicated in the first part of the sentence.

MODELO: JORGE: yo / querer (imp. indicativo) que tú / sacar más fotos, Leticia
Yo quería que tú sacaras más fotos, Leticia.

1. LUIS: los novios tener (imp. indicativo) miedo de que / Uds. llegar tarde

_____

2. LETICIA: pues, nosotros no creer (imp. indicativo) que / el cura dejarnos sacar fotos dentro de la iglesia

_____

_____

3. JOSÉ: sí, y nosotros sólo querer (imp. indicativo) buscar un lugar que / ser bueno para sacar las fotos

_____

_____

4. LETICIA: ser (pret.) bueno que / la boda no empezar a tiempo

_____

5. LUIS: ser (pret.) una lástima que / el padre de Anita no estar allí

_____

_____

6. LETICIA: sí, pero yo alegrarse (pret.) de que / tú servir de compañero para Anita, Luis

_____

_____

7. LUIS: a mí gustarme (pret.) que / todo el mundo divertirse

_____

_____

8. JOSÉ: no haber (pret.) nadie que / irse antes de las 3:00 de la mañana

_____

_____

¡TE TOCA A TI!

WB 15-5   **En el pasado** What was your life like living with your parents? Complete each sentence by conjugating the verb in the past subjunctive. Be creative!

1. Mis padres nunca creían que yo _____.

2. Era importante que mis amigos y yo _____.

3. Mi madre quería que yo buscara un(a) novio(a) que _____.

4. Mi familia iba de vacaciones a menos que _____.

5. Mi padre nunca permitía que yo _____.

WB 15-6 **La primera cita** What was your first date like? Write a paragraph to describe the experience. Follow the model.

MODELO: *Cuando salí por primera vez con un(a) chico(a), esperaba que él (ella)...*
Me alegré de que nosotros... porque me preocupaba que... Para mí, era importante que...
El (La) chico(a) quería que yo... y le dije que... Me molestó que él (ella)... Por eso, le sugerí
que... Más tarde, yo sentí que... Pero así es la vida, ¿verdad?

_____

_____

_____

_____

_____

_____

VOCABULARIO La computadora

¡A PRACTICAR!

WB 15-7 **De compras en Compuventa** While web surfing you found the following deal on a computer. Look at the ad and identify each of the items in it.

1. _____

2. _____

3. _____

4. _____

5. _____

6. _____

7. _____

8. _____

¡TE TOCA A TI!

WB 15-8 **¿Y tú?** Answer the following questions.

1. ¿Tienes tu propia computadora? ¿De qué tipo es?

   _____

2. ¿Cómo te conectas al Internet?

   _____

3. ¿Cuál es tu dirección de correo electrónico?

   _____

4. ¿Cuántas horas al día pasas en el Internet?

   _____

5. ¿Has comprado algunas cosas por el Internet? ¿Qué has comprado?

   _____

6. ¿Usas los salones de charla? ¿Has conocido a alguien en estos salones de charla?

   _____

7. ¿Saldrías en cita con alguien que conocieras en un salón de charla? ¿Por qué sí o por qué no?

   _____

ESTRUCTURA II Talking about hypothetical situations: *if*-clauses

¡A PRACTICAR!

WB 15-9 | **Viajes** Anita's and Teresa's boyfriends are away on a trip, and they are discussing what they think might be happening. To find out what they say, fill in the blanks with the appropriate verb forms. Use the past subjunctive and the conditional, as appropriate.

1. Si ellos no _____ (hablar) español, no _____ (poder) comunicarse

   bien con la gente que conozcan allí, ni _____ (gozar) mucho de su viaje.

2. Si estos dos chicos _____ (tener) más tiempo, _____ (quedarse) allí

   dos semanas más y _____ (conocer) más las culturas indígenas.

3. Ellos dijeron que si _____ (llover) todos los días, _____ (volver)

   temprano.

4. Nacho me dijo que si _____ (estar) cerca de Argentina, _____ (ir) a

   visitar a Hernán.

5. Si nosotras no les _____ (escribir) cartas, ellos _____ (estar) enojados

   con nosotras y _____ (pensar) que nos hemos olvidado de ellos.

WB 15-10 | **¿Qué harían?** Carlos and his friends are thinking of setting up a virtual business and are talking hypothetically about their plans. Following the model, form complete sentences with the following words.

MODELO: CARLOS Y TONI: si nosotros / tener dinero / montar una tienda virtual
Si tuviéramos dinero, montaríamos una tienda virtual.

1. FERNANDO: si yo / saber más sobre diseño / poder ofrecer un servicio para diseñar páginas web

   _____

2. NIDIA Y LINDA: si nosotras / poder ir a Francia frecuentemente / establecer una tienda de perfume francés

   _____

3. CARLOS: si Juan / estudiar negocios / poder ser nuestro gerente

   _____

4. JUAN: Carlos, si tú / estar más al tanto con los negocios web / poder ser millonario

   _____

5. CARLOS: Si todos Uds. / no gastar tanto tiempo soñando / hacer algo más productivo

   _____

¡TE TOCA A TI!

WB 15-11 | **¿Cuándo lo harás y cuándo lo harías?** Under what conditions would you do the following things, hypothetically speaking? Write complete sentences. Follow the model.

MODELO: montar un negocio virtual con tus amigos
Si me gano la lotería, voy a montar un negocio virtual con mis amigos.
Si yo pudiera ganar tanto dinero como Bill Gates, montaría un negocio virtual con mis amigos.

1. salir en cita con alguien que conociste en un salón de charla

   _____

   _____

2. montar tu propia página web con una videograbadora para que otras personas te vean las 24 horas al día

   _____

   _____

3. comprar una casa por el Internet

   _____

   _____

4. tirar a la basura tu computadora

   _____

   _____

5. leer el correo electrónico de tu novio(a) sin su permiso

   _____

   _____

Nombre _____ Fecha _____

SÍNTESIS

¡A LEER!
¿ADICTOS AL INTERNET? In this section, you will read an article about the extreme use of Internet services.

Strategy: Integrating your reading strategies
In previous lessons, you have learned many strategies for becoming a more proficient reader of Spanish. In this section you will practice integrating several of these reading strategies.

Paso 1: Try to figure out as much background information as possible about the reading on the next page. Look at the title and the format of the text. Think about the following questions.

1. What kind of text does it appear to be? a newspaper or magazine article? an essay? a story? a poem?

2. What does the title suggest to you about the content of the reading? What do you already know about that topic?

Paso 2: First reading: Understanding the general idea of the text.

1. Read the text quickly to get the gist of the content. Use the cognates, prefixes, and suffixes to help you understand the meaning of the words you don't know.

2. Underline the principle ideas of the text.

Paso 3: Second reading: Finding specific information in the text

Read the text quickly a second time and circle the details that explain or support the main ideas that you have underlined.

Paso 4: Third reading: Check your comprehension of the reading by answering the following questions.

1. Según el artículo, ¿cómo son dos tipos básicos de «adictos» al Internet?

   _____

   _____

2. ¿Cómo sabe uno si es adicto al Internet?

   _____

3. ¿Están todos de acuerdo que el alto uso del Internet constituye una verdadera adicción?

   _____

4. ¿Qué tratamientos hay para los «adictos» al Internet?

   _____

5. ¿Eres adicto(a) al Internet?

   _____

¿Adictos al Internet?

En los últimos meses se ha convertido en noticia el posible síndrome de dependencia del Internet. Ya no es necesario ser un enamorado de la programación o un genio del hardware para engancharse en el ciberespacio, y es por eso que el rango de personas que usan o abusan de las computadoras y el Internet es ahora más amplio que nunca.

¿Cómo sabe uno si es adicto al Internet?

Hasta la fecha no existe un perfil bien definido del usuario adicto al Internet, pero en general hay dos modelos básicos. El primero de ellos se trata de aquellos sujetos muy aficionados e interesados por sus computadoras que utilizan la Red para recoger información, jugar solitarios, obtener nuevos programas, etcétera, pero sin establecer ningún tipo de contacto interpersonal, más que lo necesario para lograr sus propósitos.

El segundo tipo se trata de aquellos grupos que frecuentan los Chats, MOOs y listas de correo. Todos tienen en común la búsqueda de estimulación social. Las necesidades de filiación, ser reconocido, poderoso o amado subyacen a este tipo en la Red. En esta categoría de usuario compulsivo entran los que utilizan el Internet para alimentar su adicción a las compras y hasta los que utilizan el Internet para acceder a sitios pornográficos y participar en el sexo cibernético. Ahora bien, el uso del Internet en sí no es problemático, pero cuando uno pasa mucho tiempo conectado a la Red y ello interfiere de un modo significativo con las actividades habituales de la vida privada, hay un problema.

Cuando el problema crece, uno puede llegar a ser víctima de una adicción. Según los estudios, un 6% de los internautas es adicto al Internet, unos 11 millones de los 200 que hay en todo el mundo.

Pero muchos especialistas sostienen que el Internet no es el culpable de la adicción. Éstos creen que es sólo a través del Internet que se manifiesta una patología preexistente. Y no todos los especialistas están de acuerdo de tacharlo de adicción. Varios psicólogos creen que es todavía un problema poco entendido, y para poder analizarlo y entenderlo más a fondo, se tendrá que observar lo que hay detrás del comportamiento de dichos «adictos».

Sea problema o sea adicción, lo cierto es que durante los últimos años han proliferado las páginas en la Red ofreciendo asistencia en línea a los internautas «enfermos». Una de las propuestas curativas es la ciberterapia, que consiste en expresar públicamente en la Red cómo se vive con el problema.

En estos salones electrónicos se pueden leer mensajes desesperados tales como «Yo creo que soy adicto(a) al Internet» y «No tengo amigos reales, sólo ficticios, que duran el rato que "chateo" con ellos. ¿Hay algo para que uno pueda alejarse de esta adicción?» Quizás, en vez de hablar de adicción al Internet, es más razonable postular la existencia de un trastorno de características difusas caracterizado por el uso abusivo de la alta tecnología. ¿Quién no conoce a sujetos que realizan casi toda su actividad con un ordenador, que viven rodeados de dispositivos electrónicos, para quienes el teléfono móvil y el correo electrónico forman parte de su identidad y que igualan el ocio al uso de videojuegos, canales digitales de televisión, que apuestan a través del Internet y mucho más?

¿Figura Ud. aquí?

¡A ESCRIBIR!

UNA VIDA SIN COMPUTADORAS In this section you will project about what life without computers will be like.

Strategy: Speculating and hypothesizing

In this section, you are going to use what you have learned to write about a hypothetical situation and make a projection about what might occur under particular circumstances. You will then outline some of the positive and/or negative consequences of this situation. This will involve speculating about the future and imagining possible outcomes that may arise from the hypothetical situation you select. Individuals in many professions prepare projections based on hypothetical situations. For example, marketing and advertising managers speculate about the success of their products and individuals in government make projections about the effects of projects and programs.

Consider the situation of a university student.

> *Ojalá yo tuviera una computadora portátil. De momento, no poseo ninguna computadora, y estoy harto de hacer cola (stand in line) en los laboratorios de computadoras de la universidad. Si tuviera mi propia computadora portátil, podría navegar la red o mirar mi correo electrónico en cualquier momento. Tendría más tiempo para estudiar o pasarlo con mis amigos porque no tendría que hacer cola en la universidad para usar una computadora. No importaría si estuviera en casa, en la universidad o en la casa de un amigo —siempre la tendría a mi lado. Sería mucho más fácil conectarme al Internet. También la podría llevar conmigo cuando esté de vacaciones en casa de mis padres o en otro sitio.*

Paso 1: Think about how the world would be if there were no computers. Think about the following questions.

- In what ways would your life be easier?
- In what ways would your life be more difficult?
- Would people be different? How?
- How would the scientific world be different?
- What would international relations be like without the modes of communication that computers provide us?

Functions: Expressing a wish or desire; Expressing conditions; Hypothesizing
Vocabulary: Dreams & aspirations; Health: diseases & illnesses; Means of transportation; Working conditions
Grammar: Verbs: *If*-clauses

Paso 2: Organize your ideas under a general topic and write a first draft of your essay.

Paso 3: Revise your first draft, checking the vocabulary and grammar. Make sure you have used the imperfect subjunctive and conditional with *if*-clauses correctly. When you have finished, write your second draft below.

_____

_____

_____

_____

_____

_____

_____

_____

_____

Autoprueba

VOCABULARIO

WB 15-12 **Los domingueros modernos** Juan and Delma never leave home without their electronics equipment. Complete their conversation about an upcoming trip, choosing the appropriate words from the list.

antena parabólica	equipo	videocámara	cámara	estéreo
caseta de video	desconectar	satélite	videocasetera	enchufado
teléfono celular				

DELMA: Juan, ¿tienes todo preparado para el viaje?

JUAN: Creo que sí, Delma. Déjame pensar... Sé que vamos a sacar muchas fotos así que ya em-

paqué la **1.** _____ . Y para grabar en vivo lo que hacemos, empaqué también

la **2.** _____ .

DELMA: Muy bien. Y empaqué el **3.** _____ por si nos llaman los vecinos que vienen a

cuidar la casa. ¿No te parece buena idea?

JUAN: Es una idea excelente. Sabes, no quiero perder el partido de fútbol este domingo así que

voy a meter una **4.** _____ a la **5.** _____ y ponerla a grabar el

partido.

DELMA: ¡Juan! ¡Eres imposible! Y no te olvides que el hotel adonde vamos tiene una

6. _____ y recibe todos los canales por **7.** _____ . Ahora,

dime, ¿vas a **8.** _____ la computadora y el **9.** _____ de

10. _____ ?

JUAN: Había pensado dejarlo **11.** _____ por si los vecinos, cuando vengan a cuidar

la casa, quieren escuchar música. ¿Qué piensas?

DELMA: Está bien, pero si se nos quema la casa va a ser tu culpa.

WB 15-13 **¿Estás al tanto?** Are you computer savvy? To find out, match each word with its definition.

- **a.** el teclado
- **b.** el disco duro
- **c.** el ratón
- **d.** los altavoces
- **e.** el escáner
- **f.** la impresora
- **g.** el correo electrónico
- **h.** el salón de charla
- **i.** la pantalla

_____ **1.** Lo pulsas para seleccionar diferentes opciones de un programa.

_____ **2.** Es el lugar donde guardas tus archivos en la computadora.

_____ **3.** Es un lugar en el ciberespacio donde te comunicas por la computadora con otras personas.

_____ **4.** Los usas para escuchar sonido emitido por la computadora.

_____ 5. Es donde ves las imágenes en la computadora.

_____ 6. Es un mensaje que se manda por la computadora.

_____ 7. Lo usas para escribir con la computadora.

_____ 8. La usas para imprimir imágenes de la computadora.

_____ 9. Lo usas para pasar una foto o un documento a un formato electrónico.

WB 15-14 | **Las instrucciones** Help Jaime figure out the instructions that came with his new computer. Choose the appropriate words from the list.

| abrir el programa | disquete | navegar | pantalla |
| hacer click | página web | quitar | archivar |

Para **1.** _____, es necesario **2.** _____ sobre el ícono que aparece en su

3. _____. Cuando el programa se abra, Ud. puede empezar a trabajar en sus docu-

mentos. Antes de **4.** _____ el programa, se le recomienda **5.** _____ los

documentos directamente al disco duro. También se le recomienda siempre guardar una copia

en un **6.** _____. Si Ud. necesita más instrucciones, las puede encontrar en nuestra

7. _____. De allí Ud. puede **8.** _____ a la sección que necesite.

ESTRUCTURA

WB 15-15 | **Buenas amigas** Carmen has just received an email from an old friend from Uruguay with whom she has not been in touch for a long time. Complete the email by filling the blanks with the appropriate past subjunctive form of the verbs provided.

Querida Carmen:

Cuando recibí tu carta me alegré mucho de que tú **1.** _____ (recordarme).

Yo esperaba que nosotras **2.** _____ (ponerse) en contacto en algún momento

porque éramos tan buenas amigas en la secundaria. Déjame contarte un poco de lo que he he-

cho en los últimos seis años. Me casé con Adolfo. ¿Te acuerdas de él? Cuando nos graduamos,

mis padres no querían que nosotros **3.** _____ (casarse), ¿te acuerdas?, pero eso

fue porque deseaban que nosotros **4.** _____ (ir) a la universidad antes de que

5. _____ (meterse) en una situación tan seria. No iba a casarme sin que mis padres

me **6.** _____ (dar) su permiso, así que esperé y me casé después de graduarme.

Saqué mi título universitario y conseguí un trabajo inmediatamente. Tenía que ganar mucho

dinero para que Adolfo **7.** _____ (poder) seguir sus estudios de informática.

Al principio fue difícil, pero después de poco tiempo estaba super contenta de que él

8. _____ (estudiar) porque sabía que iba a poder encontrar un buen trabajo cuando

9. _____ (graduarse). ¡Y lo hizo! Ahora es el jefe de una compañía de computadoras.

Bueno, Carmen, ahora que me has localizado, escríbeme más y dime más de tu vida.

Un beso,

Belén

¿Qué harían? What would Juan and his friends do in the following situations? Form complete sentences with the past subjunctive and the conditional using the following words.

1. si / Juan no tener que trabajar, / pasar todo su tiempo en la computadora

   _____

2. si / Carlos y Marga comprar una mejor computadora, / poder usar el Internet

   _____

3. si / Tomás no ser tan tímido, / poder conocer a más chicas en los salones de charla

   _____

4. si / Nancy graduarse con un título en informática, / ganar mucho dinero

   _____

5. si / Óscar ofrecerme un trabajo con su compañía, / yo cambiar de carrera

   _____

Lab Manual

Nombre _____ Fecha _____

¡Mucho gusto!

VOCABULARIO Saludos y despedidas

1, track 2] **LM P-1** **Saludos y despedidas** You will hear five brief dialogs. After listening to each one, identify the correct speakers and situations by writing the number of the dialog in the appropriate space below.

_____ **a.** Two students meeting each other for the first time.

_____ **b.** Two close friends saying "good-bye."

_____ **c.** A student addressing her professor.

_____ **d.** Two people of the same age saying "hello."

_____ **e.** A patient greeting his doctor.

1, track 3] **LM P-2** **¿Qué dices?** *(What do you say?)* Respond to each statement you hear by choosing between the two replies that immediately follow it. Indicate your choice by circling **a** or **b**.

1. a   b   **2.** a   b   **3.** a   b   **4.** a   b   **5.** a   b

1, track 4] **LM P-3** **¿Informal o formal?** Listen to the following greetings. Decide if the speaker is addressing people in a formal or an informal manner by circling **I** (informal) or **F** (formal).

1. I   F   **2.** I   F   **3.** I   F   **4.** I   F

ESTRUCTURA I Talking about yourself and others: subject pronouns and the present tense of the verb *ser*

1, track 5] **LM P-4** **El verbo *ser*** You will hear sentences containing forms of the verb **ser**. Decide which subject pronoun corresponds to each sentence. Write the appropriate letter of the sentence next to each pronoun.

_____ **1.** yo   _____ **4.** nosotros

_____ **2.** tú   _____ **5.** ella

_____ **3.** Ud.

1, track 6] **LM P-5** **Yo...** Now orally introduce yourself. Then write down what you said.

Yo... _____

_____

[CD 1, track 7] **LM P-6**   **Identificación** Match the statement you hear with its corresponding illustration. **¡OJO!** Pay close attention to the **hay** form.

1. _____

2. _____

3. _____

4. _____

5. _____

[CD 1, track 8] **LM P-7**   **Los números** Listen carefully to the following numbers. After repeating them aloud, write them in the spaces below as numerals and then spelled out.

1. _____ _____
2. _____ _____
3. _____ _____
4. _____ _____
5. _____ _____

6. _____ _____
7. _____ _____
8. _____ _____
9. _____ _____
10. _____ _____

Nombre _____ Fecha _____

VOCABULARIO Palabras interrogativas

[CD 1, track 9] **LM P-8** **Interrogaciones** Listen carefully to the partial questions and choose the right interrrogative word from the list. Identify your choice with the number of the question. **¡OJO!** Some interrogative words can be used in several questions.

_____ **a.** ¿Cómo?
_____ **b.** ¿Cuál?
_____ **c.** ¿Cuándo?
_____ **d.** ¿Cuántos?
_____ **e.** ¿De dónde?

_____ **f.** ¿Por qué?
_____ **g.** ¿Qué?
_____ **h.** ¿Quién?

[CD 1, track 10] **LM P-9** **¿Quién es Ud.?** Answer the following questions posed by Detective Austin, **«el poderoso»** *(the powerful).* **¡OJO!** Make sure you spell out the numbers!

1. _____
2. _____
3. _____
4. _____
5. _____

ESTRUCTURA II Telling age: the present tense of the verb *tener*

[CD 1, track 11] **LM P-10** **¿Cuántos años tienen?** Listen to the questions and give each person's age using the verb **tener.** Follow the model.

MODELO: ¿Cuántos años tiene tu hermano(a)?
Tiene veinte años.

1. _____
2. _____
3. _____

PRONUNCIACIÓN I El alfabeto en español

All letters in the Spanish alphabet are feminine: **la a, la be, la ce,** etc. As opposed to the English alphabet, there are four more letters: **ch, ll, ñ,** and **rr.** In all Spanish dictionaries published prior to 1995, you will find separate sections for words beginning with **ch** and **ll** (**ñ** has always had its own section; **rr** is never found at the beginning of a word). Most Spanish dictionaries published after 1995 do not treat **ch** and **ll** separately. The letters **k** and **w** are not common and appear only in words of foreign origin, such as **karate** and **whiski.**

[CD 1, track 12] **LM P-11** **¡A repetir!** Repeat each letter after you hear it.

a	a	amor		**ñ**	eñe	ñandú
b	be	bueno		**o**	o	océano
c	ce	casa, circo		**p**	pe	pelota
ch	che	choza		**q**	cu	queso
d	de	dorado		**r**	ere	rico
e	e	estudiante		**rr**	erre	arriba
f	efe	fantástico		**s**	ese	selva
g	ge	gato, gente		**t**	te	tomate
h	hache	hola		**u**	u	uva
i	i (i latina)	indio		**v**	ve (ve chica,	
j	jota	jinete			ve corta, uve)	Venus
k	ka	kilo		**w**	doble ve (doble uve)	whiski
l	ele	lápiz		**x**	equis	xilófono
ll	elle	llama		**y**	i griega	yo
m	eme	madre		**z**	zeta	zorro
n	ene	novio				

PRONUNCIACIÓN II Las vocales *(Vowels)*

The Spanish vowel system consists of five clear, short, distinct sounds with minimal variation in their pronunciation. Each one is pronounced as follows: **a,** close to the *a* in *father,* although a bit more open; **e,** like the *e* in *egg;* **i,** like the *ee* in *see;* **o,** like the *o* in *born;* and **u,** like the *oo* in *moon.*

[CD 1, track 13] **LM P-12** **¡A repetir!** Repeat each word after you hear it.

a: casa	madre	mañana	alto
e: especial	éxito	mete	té
i: libro	típico	sí	Irma
o: como	rosa	bono	olmo
u: luna	Ud.	cucú	unidos

SÍNTESIS

[CD 1, track 14] **LM P-13** **Una conversación con el señor Martínez** Listen carefully to the narration in order to complete activity **LM P-14.**

[CD 1, track 15] **LM P-14** **¿Recuerdas?** *(Do you remember?)* You will hear some statements related to the narration you just heard. Indicate if they are true or false by writing **C** for **cierto** or **F** for **falso.**

1. _____   2. _____   3. _____   4. _____

En una clase de español: Los Estados Unidos

VOCABULARIO En la clase

1, track 16] **LM 1-1** **¿Qué? ¿Quién?** You will hear the names of objects and people typically found at a university. Write each one under its appropriate category below.

Objetos *(Things)*   **Personas** *(People)*

1. _____   _____

2. _____   _____

3. _____   _____

4. _____   _____

5. _____   _____

6. _____   _____

7. _____   _____

8. _____   _____

9. _____   _____

10. _____   _____

1, track 17] **LM 1-2** **¿Es posible?** *(Is it possible?)* Mari is going to tell you who and what can be found either in a classroom or in a backpack. As you know, she sometimes exaggerates. Listen to what she says and circle **Es posible.** or **Es imposible.** according to the statement she makes. Follow the model.

MODELO: En la clase: la pizarra

(Es posible.)   Es imposible.

1. Es posible.   Es imposible.   6. Es posible.   Es imposible.

2. Es posible   Es imposible.   7. Es posible.   Es imposible.

3. Es posible.   Es imposible.   8. Es posible.   Es imposible.

4. Es posible.   Es imposible.   9. Es posible.   Es imposible.

5. Es posible.   Es imposible.   10. Es posible.   Es imposible.

[CD 1, track 18] | **LM 1-3** | **La clase de español de la profesora Muñoz** You will hear pairs of sentences based on the illustration that appears below. After repeating each sentence aloud, select the one that best describes the illustration and circle its corresponding letter.

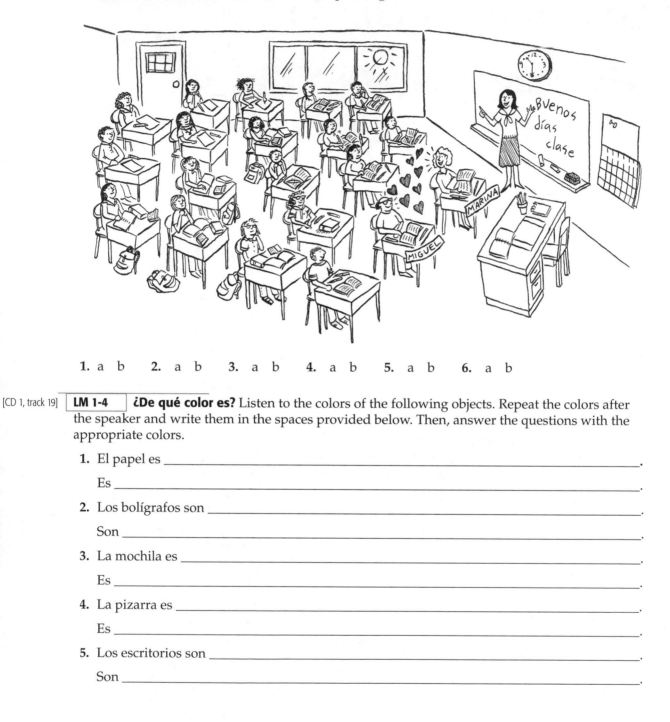

1. a b **2.** a b **3.** a b **4.** a b **5.** a b **6.** a b

[CD 1, track 19] | **LM 1-4** | **¿De qué color es?** Listen to the colors of the following objects. Repeat the colors after the speaker and write them in the spaces provided below. Then, answer the questions with the appropriate colors.

1. El papel es _____.

Es _____.

2. Los bolígrafos son _____.

Son _____.

3. La mochila es _____.

Es _____.

4. La pizarra es _____.

Es _____.

5. Los escritorios son _____.

Son _____.

ESTRUCTURA I Talking about people, things, and concepts: definite and indefinite articles and how to make nouns plural

[CD 1, track 20] **LM 1-5** **¿Definido o indefinido?** You will hear pairs of sentences. Choose the correct sentence from each set by circling **a** or **b**. ¡OJO! Pay close attention to the use of definite and indefinite articles.

1. a b   **2.** a b   **3.** a b   **4.** a b   **5.** a b

[CD 1, track 21] **LM 1-6** **¡En plural!** You will hear words from the vocabulary in the singular form. Write their plural form in the spaces provided below.

1. _____   **5.** _____

2. _____   **6.** _____

3. _____   **7.** _____

4. _____   **8.** _____

[CD 1, track 22] **LM 1-7** **¿Cuántas? ¿Cuántos?** Answer the following questions in complete sentences. Use the preposition **en** and an article **(el, la, los, las, un, una, unos, unas).** Follow the model.

MODELO: ¿Cuántas computadoras hay en la clase?
Hay una computadora en la clase.

1. _____

2. _____

3. _____

4. _____

5. _____

6. _____

VOCABULARIO Lenguas extranjeras, otras materias y lugares universitarios

[CD 1, track 23] **LM 1-8** **Los estudiantes internacionales de la profesora Muñoz** Listen to a brief description of eight international students in Professor Muñoz's class. Then complete the sentences that follow by writing their native language.

1. Felicitas Semprini habla _____.

2. Trini Whitmanabaum habla _____.

3. Miguel Paz d'Islilla habla _____.

4. Marilina Ribelina habla _____.

5. Kianu Tomasaki habla _____.

6. Stéphane Pagny habla _____.

7. Sergei Morosoff habla _____.

8. João do Maura habla _____.

LM 1-9 **¿Qué cursos?** Listen again to activity **LM 1-8** and identify what courses each student studies. List their courses in the spaces provided below.

1. Felicitas Semprini estudia _____.

2. Trini Whitmanabaum estudia _____.

3. Miguel Paz d'Islilla estudia _____.

4. Marilina Ribelina estudia _____.

5. Kianu Tomasaki estudia _____.

6. Stéphane Pagny estudia _____.

7. Sergei Morosoff estudia _____.

8. João do Maura estudia _____.

[CD 1, track 25] **LM 1-10** **En mi universidad** Listen to the following university places. Then write the proper name of the corresponding building at your university. Follow the model.

MODELO: la clase de español
Hellems Hall 202

1. _____

2. _____

3. _____

4. _____

5. _____

6. _____

ESTRUCTURA II Describing everyday activities:
present tense of regular *-ar* verbs

[CD 1, track 26] **LM 1-11** **¿Qué hacen?** *(What do they do?)* Listen to the sentences describing what each of the following people is doing. Then match the letter with the corresponding illustration.

1. _____

2. _____

3. _____

4. _____

5. _____

6. _____

[CD 1, track 27] **LM 1-12** **La vida de los estudiantes internacionales** Listen to a student's daily routine and compare it to your own by writing a sentence that describes your life. Follow the model.

MODELO: Sergei estudia mucho por la noche.
Estudio mucho en el día (during the day).

1. _____

2. _____

3. _____

4. _____

5. _____

6. _____

ASÍ SE DICE Expressing personal likes and dislikes: *me gusta* + infinitive

[CD 1, track 28] **LM 1-13** **Los gustos** You will hear some daily activities. Circle **me gusta** or **no me gusta** depending on your personal likes and dislikes.

1. me gusta   no me gusta   4. me gusta   no me gusta

2. me gusta   no me gusta   5. me gusta   no me gusta

3. me gusta   no me gusta   6. me gusta   no me gusta

ASÍ SE DICE Telling time and talking about the days of the week: *la hora y los días de la semana*

[CD 1, track 29] **LM 1-14** **¿Qué hora es?** Match the time you hear with the corresponding time written below.

_____ 1. 2:15 p.m.   _____ 4. 8:45 p.m.

_____ 2. 8:30 a.m.   _____ 5. 12:00 a.m.

_____ 3. 1:25 p.m.

[CD 1, track 30] **LM 1-15** **¿Qué día de la semana?** Tell which day of the week you do the following activities.

1. _____   4. _____

2. _____   5. _____

3. _____

PRONUNCIACIÓN I *a, e, i, o,* and *u*

Even though the letters **a, e, i, o, u,** and sometimes **y** are used to represent vowel sounds in both English and Spanish, the pronunciation of the vowel sounds is different. English vowels are generally longer than those in Spanish. In addition, English vowel sounds often merge with other vowels to produce combination sounds. As a general rule, you should pronounce Spanish vowels with a short, precise sound.

[CD 1, track 31] **LM 1-16** **¡A repetir!** Listen and repeat.

     a: armario   papel   lápiz   cuaderno   mochila
     Hay tres lápices en la mochila.

     e: reloj   mesa   secretaria   escritorio   pupitre
     En la clase hay un reloj, un escritorio y veinte pupitres.

i: libro   mochila   cinta   silla   televisor

En la universidad hay sillas, libros y televisores.

o: consejero   bolígrafo   biblioteca   profesor   borrador

Hoy el profesor no necesita el borrador.

u: nueve   universidad   Ud.   alumnos   única

Un profesor de la universidad tiene nueve alumnos.

PRONUNCIACIÓN II Spanish *e*, *i*, and *y*

Remember that Spanish vowels are always short, crisp, and tense. The Spanish **e** is pronounced like the **e** in *they*. The Spanish **i** and the word **y** are pronounced approximately like the **i** in *machine*.

[CD 1, track 32] | **LM 1-17** | **¡A repetir!** Listen and repeat.

—¿Cómo se llama tu compañera?
—Leonor. Es estudiante aquí.
—¿De dónde es?
—Ella es de Mérida, México.

—¿Qué estudias en la universidad?
—Estudio español, derecho e inglés.
—¿Qué días tienes clase, Elena?
—Los lunes, miércoles y viernes.

[CD 1, track 33] | **LM 1-18** | **¡A repetir!** Listen and repeat.

—¿Qué estudias aquí, María?
—Estudio inglés y filosofía.
—Y yo estudio medicina.
—¡Qué interesante! ¿Qué días tienes clase, Lucía?
—Los miércoles y viernes.
—Hay muchos estudiantes, ¿verdad?
—Sí. ¡En medicina hay muchos!

PRONUNCIACIÓN III *h* and *ch*

The letter **h** is the only silent letter in the Spanish alphabet; it is never pronounced: **historia.**
Ch is pronounced as in the English word *church:* **mochila.**

[CD 1, track 34] | **LM 1-19** | **¡A repetir!** Listen and repeat.

h: historia   hoy   hola   hamburguesa   Héctor

Hoy hay un examen en la clase de historia.

ch: mochila   ocho   chico   dieciocho   poncho

El chico tiene ocho ponchos y mochilas. ¡Son muchos!

SÍNTESIS

[CD 1, track 35] **LM 1-20** **¿Cierto o falso?** You will hear a narration about universities and university life in Spanish-speaking countries. Based on the narration, indicate if the following statements are true with **C (cierto)** or false with **F (falso).**

_____ **1.** Los fines de semana celebran fiestas, bailan, visitan a sus amigos, miran televisión o escuchan música.

_____ **2.** La asistencia a clase es obligatoria.

_____ **3.** Las clases son muy, muy grandes, donde el profesor habla y los estudiantes escuchan.

_____ **4.** Los estudiantes pagan mucho dinero por las clases.

_____ **5.** La vida estudiantil en los países hispánicos es similar a la vida estudiantil en los Estados Unidos.

[CD 1, track 36] **LM 1-21** **Faltan palabras _(Missing words)_** Ron and Sandy are roommates who go to the same university, but they are not taking the same classes. Ron studies Spanish and Sandy studies French. Listen to their dialog about their first day of classes. Then, you will be asked to complete the statements below with the correct information from the dialog. **¡OJO!** Listen to the dialog several times before you do activity **LM 1-21.**

1. La profesora de Sandy no es un hombre; es _____.

2. La profesora Balabeau es muy _____ y muy paciente.

3. En la clase de Sandy hay _____ estudiantes.

4. Las tizas de colores en la clase de Sandy son _____, _____, _____ y amarillas.

5. La profesora de español no es _____ y no es paciente.

En una reunión familiar: México

VOCABULARIO La familia

[CD 2, track 2] | **LM 2-1** | **Los miembros de la familia** Listen to each description and find the family relation to whom it refers. Then, write the letter of the description next to the correct relation.

_____ **1.** mi tío   _____ **6.** mi abuelo

_____ **2.** mi hermana   _____ **7.** mi tía

_____ **3.** mi abuela   _____ **8.** mi padre

_____ **4.** mi madre   _____ **9.** mi hermano

_____ **5.** mis primos

[CD 2, track 3] | **LM 2-2** | **No es de la misma (same) categoría** You will hear a list of family relationships. Repeat each pair and then write the one that does not belong in the series.

1. _____

2. _____

3. _____

4. _____

5. _____

[CD 2, track 4] | **LM 2-3** | **Tu familia** Listen to the sentences and circle the response that best fits your family situation.

1. a   b   c   **3.** a   b   c   **5.** a   b   c

2. a   b   **4.** a   b

ASÍ SE DICE Indicating ownership and possession: possession with **de(l)** and possessive adjectives

[CD 2, track 5] | **LM 2-4** | **¿De quién es?** Listen to the following questions and write your answers, following the model.

MODELO: El bebé es del hermano de Jill. ¿De quién es el bebé?
Es del hermano de Jill. Es su bebé.

1. _____

2. _____

3. _____

4. _____

5. _____

ESTRUCTURA I Describing people and things: common uses of the verb *ser*

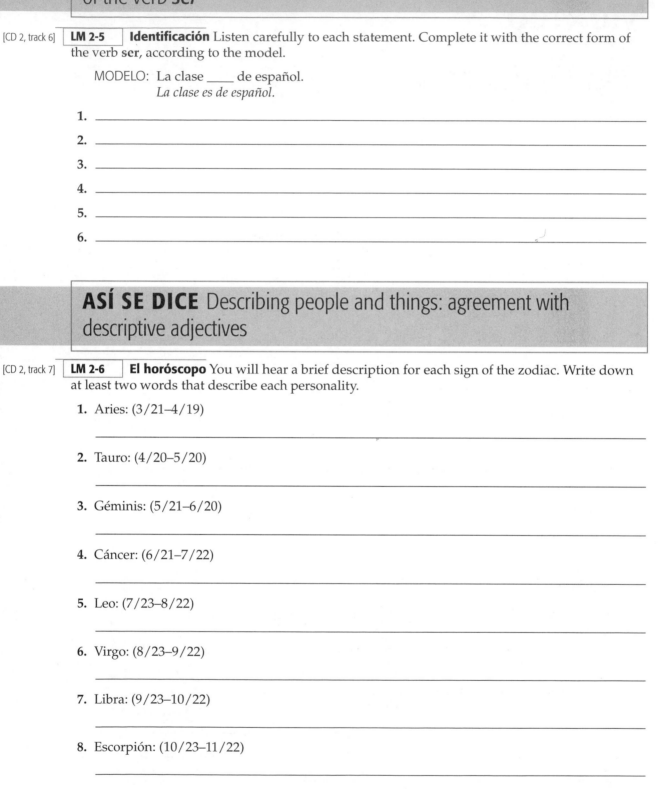

[CD 2, track 6] **LM 2-5** **Identificación** Listen carefully to each statement. Complete it with the correct form of the verb **ser**, according to the model.

MODELO: La clase ____ de español.
La clase es de español.

1. _____

2. _____

3. _____

4. _____

5. _____

6. _____

ASÍ SE DICE Describing people and things: agreement with descriptive adjectives

[CD 2, track 7] **LM 2-6** **El horóscopo** You will hear a brief description for each sign of the zodiac. Write down at least two words that describe each personality.

1. Aries: (3/21–4/19)

_____

2. Tauro: (4/20–5/20)

_____

3. Géminis: (5/21–6/20)

_____

4. Cáncer: (6/21–7/22)

_____

5. Leo: (7/23–8/22)

_____

6. Virgo: (8/23–9/22)

_____

7. Libra: (9/23–10/22)

_____

8. Escorpión: (10/23–11/22)

_____

9. Sagitario: (11/23–12/21)

_____

10. Capricornio: (12/22–1/20)

_____

11. Acuario: (1/21–2/18)

_____

12. Piscis: (2/19–3/20)

_____

CD 2, track 8]   **LM 2-7**   **Las descripciones** You will hear a description for each of the illustrations below. Match each one by writing the corresponding letter in the space provided.

1. _____

2. _____

3. _____

4. _____

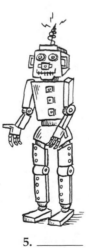

5. _____

6. _____

VOCABULARIO Las nacionalidades

[CD 2, track 9] **LM 2-8** **¿De dónde son?** You will hear the names of ten famous people. Following the model, write their nationality in the space provided.

> MODELO: Antonio Banderas
> *Es español.*

1. _____
2. _____
3. _____
4. _____
5. _____
6. _____
7. _____
8. _____
9. _____
10. _____

[CD 2, track 10] **LM 2-9** **¿Qué lengua(s) hablan?** You will hear the names of these famous people again, followed by the language(s) they may speak. Circle the letter(s) of the correct answer.

1. a   b
2. a   b
3. a   b
4. a   b
5. a   b

6. a   b
7. a   b
8. a   b
9. a   b
10. a   b

ESTRUCTURA II Describing daily activities at home or at school: present tense of *-er* and *-ir* verbs

[CD 2, track 11] **LM 2-10** **Mi suegra es una viuda *(widow)* alegre** Listen to the story and then write all of the regular **-er** and **-ir** verbs below.

1. _____
2. _____
3. _____
4. _____
5. _____
6. _____

7. _____
8. _____
9. _____
10. _____
11. _____
12. _____

LM 2-11 **La vida loca de Candela** You will hear a series of activities typical of Candela's life. After repeating each one, rewrite the same activity with the corresponding change of subject. **¡OJO!** Pay special attention to the verb conjugations.

> MODELO: Candela recibe muchos regalos. Uds. _____.
> Uds. *reciben muchos regalos.*

1. Nosotros _____.

2. Verónica _____.

3. Su hija y su esposo _____.

4. Sus amigas _____.

5. Tú _____.

6. Yo también _____.

ASÍ SE DICE Expressing possession and physical states: common uses of the verb *tener*

LM 2-12 **La propiedad** Identify each person's possession by matching the statement you hear with its corresponding illustration. Then draw yourself with your possession below.

1. _____

2. _____

3. _____

4. _____

LM 2-13 **Expresiones idiomáticas** Indicate the idiomatic expression used to properly react to the situations you will hear by writing the corresponding letter.

_____ 1. tenemos éxito

_____ 4. tienen hambre

_____ 2. tengo prisa

_____ 5. tienes sueño

_____ 3. tiene razón

ASÍ SE DICE Counting to 100: *los números de 30 a 100*

[CD 2, track 15] **LM 2-14** **Los números** Spell out the numbers as you hear them.

1. _____

2. _____

3. _____

4. _____

5. _____

PRONUNCIACIÓN I *r* and *rr*

In the middle of a word, the letter **r** in Spanish is pronounced with a single flap of the tongue on the ridge behind the upper front teeth. It is similar to the sound in the words *batter* or *ladder* in standard American pronunciation.

At the beginning of a word, **r** sounds like its counterpart in Spanish, the **rr,** which only occurs in the middle of a word. Its typical pronunciation throughout the Hispanic world is a sustained flapping of the tongue also known as "trilling."

[CD 2, track 16] **LM 2-15** **¡A repetir!** Listen and repeat.

r:	armario	comieron	caricia	mejor
r, rr:	rápido	rugido	racimo	romántico
	carriles	barrio	correo	Villarreal

r *and* **rr:** No queremos correr el riesgo de trabajar en esas precarias condiciones, señor Ramos.

Nombre _____ Fecha _____

PRONUNCIACIÓN II *d*

There are two basic pronunciations for the Spanish **d.** When it occurs at the beginning of a sentence or phrase, after a lateral or nasal sound **(l, n),** it is articulated by pressing the front portion of the tongue against the back of the upper teeth. The result does not have an equivalent sound in English.

A softer, fricative **d** is closer to the English *th* and occurs in the middle of a word, between vowels.

[CD 2, track 17] | **LM 2-16** | **¡A repetir!** Listen and repeat.

día   **d**ónde   **d**ándole   San **D**iego

a**d**iós   ra**d**io   A**d**ela   na**d**ar

A **D**arío le **d**uele el **d**e**d**o. A**d**ela na**d**a **d**espacio en la piscina **d**e **d**etrás.

SÍNTESIS

[CD 2, track 18] | **LM 2-17** | **Buscamos compañía** You will now listen to two personal ads from different Spanish-speaking newspapers. Mark the correct answer based on what you hear.

Anuncio A

_____ **1.** ¿Cómo se llama el perrito?
  a. Schnauzer
  b. Gino

_____ **2.** ¿Cómo es?
  a. un schnauzer miniatura blanco y negro
  b. un chihuahua de un año y medio que quiere Taco Bell

_____ **3.** ¿Qué busca el perrito?
  a. una novia chihuahua porque son irresistibles
  b. una perrita de su misma raza

Anuncio B

_____ **4.** ¿Cuál es su origen y qué lengua habla?
  a. Es de origen italiano y habla español.
  b. Es de origen alemán y habla español.

_____ **5.** ¿Quién es el viudo irresistible?
  a. Es un dentista apasionado por el arte.
  b. Es un artista: fotógrafo, pintor, bailarín de México.

_____ **6.** ¿Qué busca Carlos?
  a. una mujer de su edad, inteligente y creativa
  b. una hispana joven, moderna y algo tonta

_____ **7.** ¿Cómo deben comunicarse las señoritas interesadas?
  a. por teléfono
  b. por email

LM 2-18 | **Una visita de los abuelos** Listen to the following conversation between Juan Carlos and his grandparents in Mexico City. There they are meeting his American girlfriend, Jill. After listening to the conversation, you will hear a series of statements. Identify those that are true with **C (cierto)** and those that are false with **F (falso).**

1. _____   2. _____   3. _____   4. _____   5. _____

El tiempo libre: Colombia

VOCABULARIO Los deportes y los pasatiempos

[CD 2, track 20] **LM 3-1** **Los deportes, los pasatiempos y las actividades culturales** Do you remember the Incredible Juanjo? He enjoys all sports and leisure-time and cultural activities. Listen carefully and circle the right response indicating if it's a sport (**un deporte**), a leisure-time activity (**un pasatiempo**), or a cultural activity (**una actividad cultural**).

MODELO: A Juanjo le gusta mirar la tele.

un deporte (un pasatiempo) una actividad cultural

1. un deporte   un pasatiempo   una actividad cultural
2. un deporte   un pasatiempo   una actividad cultural
3. un deporte   un pasatiempo   una actividad cultural
4. un deporte   un pasatiempo   una actividad cultural
5. un deporte   un pasatiempo   una actividad cultural
6. un deporte   un pasatiempo   una actividad cultural
7. un deporte   un pasatiempo   una actividad cultural
8. un deporte   un pasatiempo   una actividad cultural
9. un deporte   un pasatiempo   una actividad cultural
10. un deporte   un pasatiempo   una actividad cultural

[CD 2, track 21] **LM 3-2** **Adivina, adivina** You will hear two clues. Select the activity associated with them and write the letter in the appropriate space.

_____ 1. la natación

_____ 2. sacar fotos

_____ 3. bailar

_____ 4. jugar al tenis

_____ 5. visitar un museo

[CD 2, track 22] **LM 3-3** **Mis actividades favoritas** Listen to the following sentences. Repeat each one and indicate if they are true with **C** for **cierto** or false with **F** for **falso** according to your daily routine.

1. _____ 2. _____ 3. _____ 4. _____ 5. _____ 6. _____ 7. _____

[CD 2, track 23] **LM 3-4** **¡Alguien quiere saber!** *(Someone wants to know!)* There is someone who is very interested in knowing how you spend your free time. Answer the questions orally in complete sentences, and then write your answers in the space provided.

1. _____

2. _____

3. _____

ESTRUCTURA I Expressing likes and dislikes: *gustar* + infinitive and *gustar* + nouns

[CD 2, track 24] **LM 3-5** **¿Qué les gusta?** Listen to the descriptions based on the seven illustrations below. Match each description with its illustration by writing the letter in the appropriate space.

1. _____

2. _____

3. _____

4. _____

5. _____

6. _____

7. _____

[○ 2, track 25] | **LM 3-6** | **Los gustos son gustos** Listen to what each person likes to do and write it in the space provided. Follow the example.

>   MODELO: Tiger Woods
>   *A Tiger Woods le gusta jugar al golf.*

1. Shakira y Carlos Vives

   _____

2. Carlos Valderrama

   _____

3. Serena Williams y yo

   _____

4. Felipe López (Timberwolves)

   _____

5. Lance Armstrong y tú

   _____

VOCABULARIO Los lugares

[○ 2, track 26] | **LM 3-7** | **¿Adónde vas?** Tell where you go for the following things. Follow the example.

>   MODELO: comprar papel
>   *Papelería.*

1. _____
2. _____
3. _____
4. _____
5. _____

ESTRUCTURA II Expressing plans with *ir: ir a* + destination and *ir a* + infinitive

[○ 2, track 27] | **LM 3-8** | **Los polos opuestos se atraen *(Opposites attract)*** Remember Gerardo, Catalina's friend, from the party? He and his mysterious girlfriend are soul mates. Although they like doing things together, their favorite activities don't always coincide. Listen to the dialog so that you may later complete activity **LM 3-9.**

[CD 2, track 28] **LM 3-9** **¿Qué van a hacer las almas gemelas?** After listening to the dialog, what will these soul mates in conflict do? Follow the example.

      MODELO: dar una fiesta
               Ella va a dar una fiesta.

1. _____
2. _____
3. _____
4. _____
5. _____
6. _____

[CD 2, track 29] **LM 3-10** **¿Quién tiene razón?** How would you reply to your soul mate's proposition? Write your response in a complete sentence following the example.

      MODELO: Vamos al museo.
               No, yo no voy al museo.
           o *Sí, vamos al museo.*

1. _____
2. _____
3. _____
4. _____
5. _____
6. _____

ESTRUCTURA III Describing leisure-time activities: verbs with irregular *yo* forms

[CD 2, track 30] **LM 3-11** **Más actividades** Listen closely to the following activities. Match each one to its drawing below. Follow the example.

      MODELO: *ver la televisión*

la familia

Mariana

1. _____

tú

2. _____

Laura

3. _____

los novios

4. _____

el disc jockey

5. _____

yo

6. _____

mis amigos y yo

7. _____

[CD 2, track 31]   **LM 3-12**   **Lo que la gente hace** Using the drawings in activity **LM 3-11,** write a complete sentence conjugating the verb. Follow the example.

> MODELO: la familia
> *La familia ve la televisión.*

1. _____
2. _____
3. _____
4. _____
5. _____
6. _____
7. _____

ASÍ SE DICE Expressing knowledge and familiarity: *saber, conocer,* and the personal *a*

[CD 2, track 32]   **LM 3-13**   **¿Saber o conocer?** Listen carefully to each sentence and write in the correct form of **saber** or **conocer.**

1. No me gusta correr las olas *(waves)* porque no _____ nadar.

2. Ellos _____ muy bien Cali, Colombia.

3. ¿_____ a Gerardo y a su novia?

4. A Leslie y a mí nos gusta mucho la música colombiana. _____ tocar la guitarra también.

5. Perdón, ¿_____ Ud. dónde está el Museo de Arte Contemporáneo?

ASÍ SE DICE Talking about the months, the seasons, and the weather

[CD 2, track 33]   **LM 3-14**   **¿Qué estación es?** Listen to the following months and circle the season to which they belong. Follow the example.

> MODELO: marzo
>
> invierno   primavera   verano   otoño

1. invierno   primavera   verano   otoño
2. invierno   primavera   verano   otoño
3. invierno   primavera   verano   otoño
4. invierno   primavera   verano   otoño
5. invierno   primavera   verano   otoño
6. invierno   primavera   verano   otoño

| **LM 3-15** | **¿Qué tiempo hace?** Listen to the questions related to the weather. Circle the most logical expression. Follow the example.

MODELO: ¿Qué tiempo hace en Canadá en invierno?

hace fresco   hace calor   (hace frío)

1. hace fresco   hace calor   hace frío

2. hace viento   hace calor   hace frío

3. hace fresco   hace buen tiempo   hace viento

4. hace fresco   hace calor   hace frío

5. hace fresco   hace viento   hace frío

| **LM 3-16** | **¿Cómo estás?** Complete the sentences using expresions with **tener** to state how you are. Follow the example.

MODELO: en invierno
Tengo frío.

1. _____

2. _____

3. _____

4. _____

5. _____

6. _____

PRONUNCIACIÓN I Diphthongs: *ia, ie, io,* and *iu*

The letter **i** (and also **y**) placed before the vowels **a, e, o,** and **u** sounds like the *y* in the English words *yacht, yet, yoke,* and *you.*

| **LM 3-17** | **¡A repetir!** Listen and repeat.

ia: familia   estudia   Amalia   residencia   universitaria

Amalia es estudiante y vive en la residencia universitaria, no con su familia.

ie: fiesta   bien   parientes   tiene   viene

¡Qué bien! Mis parientes vienen a la fiesta.

io: Antonio   Julio   novio   felicitaciones   quiosco

Antonio y Julio compran periódicos en el quiosco.

iu: viuda   ciudad   oriunda   ventiuno   diurna

El día ventiuno, la viuda va a venir a la ciudad.

PRONUNCIACIÓN II Diphthongs: *ua, ue, ui,* and *uo*

The letter **u** before the vowels **a, e, i/y,** and **o** sounds like the *u* in the English words *quit, quartz,* and *quench.*

[CD 2, track 37] | **LM 3-18** | **¡A repetir!** Listen and repeat.

ua: c**ua**dernos Ed**ua**rdo c**ua**tro G**ua**dalupe g**ua**pa

G**ua**dalupe es la más g**ua**pa para Ed**ua**rdo.

ue: b**ue**na p**ue**s P**ue**rto Rico Man**ue**l esc**ue**la

P**ue**s, Man**ue**l es un b**ue**n estudiante en P**ue**rto Rico.

ui/y: c**ui**dar r**ui**nas m**uy** c**ui**tas s**ui**cidio

Antonio está en la r**ui**na y sus c**ui**tas lo hacen andar con c**ui**dado.

uo: c**uo**ta

La c**uo**ta de la casa es muy alta.

[CD 2, track 38] | **LM 3-19** | **¿Cómo se pronuncia?** Before listening, pronounce the following words aloud. Then, listen and repeat using the correct pronounciation.

1. m**ue**ca, L**ui**s, g**ua**pa

2. aliv**ia**, aluv**io**, v**ie**ntre

3. h**ie**rba, b**ue**na, R**ui**z

SÍNTESIS

[CD 2, track 39] | **LM 3-20** | **Sábado de fiesta** It's Saturday, the day of the party. It is 9:30 p.m. and Catalina's friends are gathered in her apartment in Cali, Colombia. Listen to the following dialog so that you may later complete activity **LM 3-21.**

[CD 2, track 40] | **LM 3-21** | **La fiesta en casa de Catalina** Based on the dialog you just heard, indicate if the following statements are true with **C** for **cierto** or false with **F** for **falso.**

1. _____.

2. _____.

3. _____.

4. _____.

5. _____.

En la casa: España

[CD 3, track 2]   **LM 4-1**   **Un robo en el condominio** Take a look at the illustrations before and after the burglary. The police wants to know what's missing. Follow the model.

MODELO: ¿Qué falta *(is missing)* en el cuarto de baño?
En el cuarto de baño no está el espejo.

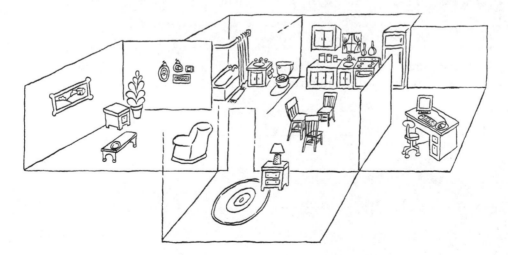

1. _____
2. _____
3. _____
4. _____

[CD 3, track 3] **LM 4-2** **¿Dónde están?** Listen and indicate in which part of the house you would find each thing. Follow the model.

MODELO: el armario
Está en el dormitorio.

1. _____

2. _____

3. _____

4. _____

5. _____

6. _____

[CD 3, track 4] **LM 4-3** **Mi vivienda** You will listen to a series of statements. Repeat each one and indicate if they are true with **C** for **cierto** or false with **F** for **falso.**

1. ____   2. ____   3. ____   4. ____   5. ____   6. ____   7. ____

[CD 3, track 5] **LM 4-4** **¿Cuál es?** Listen to the description and match it with the appliance that best fits it.

____ 1. la plancha

____ 2. el despertador

____ 3. el lavaplatos

____ 4. el horno de microondas

____ 5. la secadora

ESTRUCTURA I Describing household chores and other activities: present tense of stem-changing verbs (o → ue; e → ie; e → i)

[CD 3, track 6] **LM 4-5** **Un fin de semana en la casa de campo** Listen to a conversation among three friends. Pay attention to the irregular verbs and write in 10 of the 16 that are used.

1. _____   6. _____

2. _____   7. _____

3. _____   8. _____

4. _____   9. _____

5. _____   10. _____

3, track 7]   **LM 4-6**   **¿Quién lo hace?** Listen to the sentences and conjugate the verb according to the subject. Follow the model.

> MODELO: Yo prefiero comer aquí.
>   Uds. *prefieren* comer aquí.

1. Nosotros nos _____ por vivir aquí.

2. ¿Dónde _____ comer Uds.?

3. Nosotros no _____ a salir.

4. Él _____ un voto.

5. Ellas _____ la boca.

6. ¿Qué _____ yo?

ASÍ SE DICE Expressing physical conditions, desires, and obligations with *tener*

3, track 8]   **LM 4-7**   **¿Cómo reaccionas?** Listen to the following situations and indicate what your reaction would be by writing the letter of the situation in the appropriate blank.

____ **1.** Tengo sueño.   ____ **4.** Tengo miedo.

____ **2.** Tengo paciencia.   ____ **5.** Tengo hambre.

____ **3.** Tengo celos.

3, track 9]   **LM 4-8**   **Los deseos** You will hear four statements. Match each one with the expression that best describes the way you feel.

____ **1.** Tengo ganas de bailar.

____ **2.** Tenemos ganas de ver la película.

____ **3.** Ella no tiene ganas de lavar los platos.

____ **4.** Tengo ganas de un café.

3, track 10]   **LM 4-9**   **Las obligaciones** You will hear four situations. Match each one with an expression from the list below.

____ **1.** Tienes que limpiar la casa.

____ **2.** Tienen que comprar una aspiradora.

____ **3.** Tengo que alquilar un piso cerca de la uni.

____ **4.** Tenemos que estudiar mucho.

VOCABULARIO Los quehaceres domésticos

LM 4-10 **¿Ellas o ellos?** You will hear a list of household chores. Give your opinion as to who should be doing what.

	ellas	ellos	yo
1.			
2.			
3.			
4.			
5.			
6.			
7.			

ESTRUCTURA II Expressing preferences and giving advice: affirmative *tú* commands

LM 4-11 **Los diez consejos muy valiosos *(very valuable)*** Since Francisco moved out of the house to go to college, his mom has been reminding him constantly of all the things he ought to do. Listen to each sentence and conjugate the verb accordingly, following the example.

MODELO: Escribir seguido a casa.
Escribe seguido a casa.

1. _____
2. _____
3. _____
4. _____
5. _____
6. _____
7. _____
8. _____
9. _____
10. _____

ESTRUCTURA III Talking about location, emotional and physical states, and actions in progress: the verb *estar*

3, track 13] | **LM 4-12** | **¿Dónde están? ¿Cómo están?** You will hear a series of sentences. Match them with the illustrations below and write the sentences on the lines provided.

1. _____

_____

_____

2. _____

_____

_____

3. _____

_____

_____

4. _____

_____

_____

5. _____

_____

_____

_____

[CD 3, track 14] **LM 4-13** **¿Cómo estás cuando... ?** Respond to the following questions using **estar** + adjective.

1. _____
2. _____
3. _____
4. _____
5. _____

[CD 3, track 15] **LM 4-14** **Un espión *(Peeping Tom)* en el condominio** Miguel, Francisco's roommate, lives directly across from the two people on the balcony. With his telescope he can watch what the neighbors are doing this instant. Match what he sees by writing the appropriate letter on the line.

1. ____   2. ____   3. ____   4. ____   5. ____

ASÍ SE DICE Counting from 100 and higher: *los números de 100 a 1.000.000*

[CD 3, track 16] **LM 4-15** **Los números** Listen to each sentence carefully, paying close attention to the numbers. Then write the figure in both its numeric and written form.

1. _____
2. _____
3. _____
4. _____

Nombre _____ Fecha _____

PRONUNCIACIÓN *s, ce, ci,* and *z*

In most of peninsular Spain, the pronunciation of the **c** before **i** and **e,** and that of the **z** is inter-dental, resembling the English *th,* as in the word *thing.* The **s** sound is also stronger and is similar to the English *sh* in *shoe.*

[CD 3, track 17] | **LM 4-16** | **¡A repetir!** Listen and repeat.

s: casa Silvia estudiante universidad su

Silvia es una estudiante en la universidad. Vive en una casa con su amiga.

ce, ci: baloncesto cena residencia cine Cecilia

Cecilia es muy activa los fines de semana. Juega al baloncesto, va al cine y cena con su novio en la residencia.

z: feliz zapato azul corazón Zulma

Zulma está feliz con sus zapatos azules.

SÍNTESIS

[CD 3, track 18] | **LM 4-17** | **Se alquila cuarto** Francisco needs to rent a place close to the university. He sees an ad in the paper and decides to check it out. Listen carefully to what transpires so that you may later complete activity **LM 4-18.**

[CD 3, track 19] | **LM 4-18** | **¿Recuerdas?** Indicate if the statements are true with **C** for **cierto** or false with **F** for **falso,** according to the dialog.

1. ____ 2. ____ 3. ____ 4. ____ 5. ____ 6. ____

5 La salud: Bolivia y Paraguay

[CD 3, track 20] **LM 5-1** **Una lección de anatomía** Listen and repeat as you hear different parts of the body named. Mark each one on the drawing.

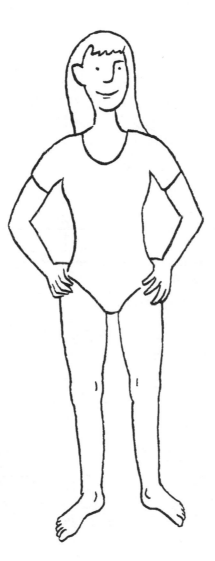

LM 5-2 **Monstruo** You will hear the description of a terrible monster. Listen carefully and draw what you hear.

LM 5-3 **Asociaciones** Listen to each word and write in the part of the human body with which you associate it.

1. _____
2. _____
3. _____
4. _____
5. _____
6. _____
7. _____
8. _____

ESTRUCTURA I Talking about routine activities: reflexive pronouns and present tense of reflexive verbs

CD 3, track 23] | **LM 5-4** | **El matrimonio Dardo Chávez** Listen to the dialog between Dr. Carlos Dardo Chávez, a doctor, and his wife, Dr. Nilda Calviño Guner, a dentist. Then write all the reflexive verbs you hear in the correct column. ¡OJO! There are 13 verbs.

Dra. Calviño Guner

_____

_____

_____

_____

_____

_____

Dr. Dardo Chávez

_____

_____

_____

_____

_____

_____

CD 3, track 24] | **LM 5-5** | **¿Cómo se dice?** Listen to the detailed description of what Drs. Dardo and Calviño do, and then write in the appropriate letter in the space provided.

_____ **1.** Se acuestan tarde.

_____ **2.** El Dr. Dardo no se afeita.

_____ **3.** Se despiertan muy temprano.

_____ **4.** La Dra. Calviño se pone la ropa después de bañarse.

_____ **5.** El Dr. Dardo no se pinta.

_____ **6.** La Dra. Calviño se peina todos los días.

_____ **7.** No se cuidan.

ASÍ SE DICE Talking about things you have just finished doing: *acabar de* + infinitive

CD 3, track 25] | **LM 5-6** | **¿Qué acabas de hacer?** Listen to the following actvities and write down that you just finished doing them. Follow the model.

MODELO: levantarse a las 7:00
Acabo de levantarme a las 7:00.
o *Me acabo de levantar a las 7:00.*

1. _____

2. _____

3. _____

4. _____

5. _____

VOCABULARIO La salud

[CD 3, track 26] **LM 5-7** **Doctora, ¿qué tengo?** Listen to the patient's symptoms and recommend a treatment. Write in the letter for the treatment you consider necessary.

_____ 1. a. Tiene que tomar jarabe y descansar.
   b. Tiene que dejar de hacer ejercicio.

_____ 2. a. Tiene que hacer ejercicio y comer bien.
   b. Tiene que guardar cama, beber muchos líquidos y tomar aspirina.

_____ 3. a. Tiene que tomar Pepto Bismol y cuidar su dieta.
   b. Tiene que ir al hospital inmediatamente.

_____ 4. a. Tiene que tomar unas medicinas y descansar.
   b. Tiene que bañarse y acostarse temprano.

[CD 3, track 27] **LM 5-8** **¿Qué le duele?** Fran overdoes it sometimes! Everything hurts! Listen to her and mark what part of her body is in pain.

_____ 1. Le duele la garganta.   _____ 4. Le duele la mano.

_____ 2. Le duele la cabeza.   _____ 5. Le duelen los ojos.

_____ 3. Le duele el estómago.   _____ 6. Le duelen las piernas.

ESTRUCTURA II Describing people, things, and conditions: *ser* versus *estar*

[CD 3, track 28] **LM 5-9** **¿Cómo es?** Listen to the description of Dr. Calviño Guner. Pay special attention to the uses of **ser** and **estar**. Write in the missing verbs as you hear them.

1. _____ la doctora Calviño Guner. 2. _____ de Bolivia.

3. _____ boliviana. 4. _____ dentista. 5. _____ casada.

6. _____ baja. Hoy 7. _____ 16 de febrero y 8. _____ mi

cumpleaños. Esta noche hay una fiesta para mí. La fiesta 9. _____ en mi casa.

En este momento 10. _____ en mi casa. Mi casa 11. _____ en Monteros.

Monteros 12. _____ en Bolivia. 13. _____ muy contenta.

14. _____ bailando y comiendo en la fiesta.

[CD 3, track 29] **LM 5-10** **Sobre la Dra. Calviño Guner** Based on what you heard in activity **LM 5-9,** answer the questions. Don't forget to use the correct forms of **ser** and **estar.**

1. _____

2. _____

3. _____

4. _____

5. _____

6. _____

ESTRUCTURA III Pointing out people and things: demonstrative adjectives and pronouns

LM 5-11 | **Escoge** Listen to the statements containing demonstrative adjectives and pronouns. Circle the ones you hear.

1. aquella   aquélla
2. este   éste
3. ese   ése

4. ese   ése
5. esa   ésa
6. Estos   Éstos

LM 5-12 | **¿Qué quieres, ésa, ésta o aquélla?** Answer the questions, substituting the demonstrative adjective for a demonstrative pronoun. Follow the example.

MODELO: ¿Prefieres esas pastillas?
Sí, prefiero ésas.

1. _____
2. _____
3. _____
4. _____
5. _____
6. _____

PRONUNCIACIÓN *p* and *t*

The letters **p** and **t,** when placed at the beginning of a word, are pronounced with more strength in English than in Spanish. In English, the sound is like the *p* in *Peter* or the *t* in *Tom*.
In Spanish however, the sound of these two letters is softer; it is very similar to the *p* in *spill* and to the *t* in *still*.

LM 5-13 | **¡Te toca a ti!** Listen, repeat, and write.

1. _____
2. _____
3. _____
4. _____

SÍNTESIS

[CD 3, track 33] **LM 5-14** **Lo contrario** Say and write the opposite of what you hear without using negation. Follow the example.

    MODELO: Me quito el maquillaje.
                Me pongo el maquillaje.

1. _____

2. _____

3. _____

4. _____

5. _____

[CD 3, track 34] **LM 5-15** **¿Ser o estar?** Circle the right verb in order to complete the sentence you hear.

    MODELO: de Bolivia
            (ser)   estar

1. ser   estar   5. ser   estar

2. ser   estar   6. ser   estar

3. ser   estar   7. ser   estar

4. ser   estar

¿Quieres comer conmigo esta noche?: Venezuela

6

[CD 4, track 2] **LM 6-1** **¡Qué hambre tengo!** Place your order according to what you hear. Make sure you match the food or beverage with the illustrations below.

1. _____   2. _____   3. _____

4. _____   5. _____

[CD 4, track 3] **LM 6-2** **En El Criollito** The Santos family is at the El Criollito restaurant for lunch. Pay attention to what they order and check it off as you hear it.

_____ una sopa de verduras

_____ las chuletas de cerdo en salsa de tomate

_____ las arepas

_____ unos camarones fritos

_____ unos refrescos

_____ el pollo asado

_____ unos calamares fritos

_____ el flan casero

_____ las manzanas y naranjas

[CD 4, track 4] **LM 6-3** **¡Buen provecho!** Listen carefully and repeat. Then write the item that does not belong to that group.

1. las comidas: _____

2. los mariscos y pescados: _____

3. los condimentos: _____

4. los platos principales: _____

5. los gustos y sabores: _____

ESTRUCTURA I Making comparisons: comparatives and superlatives

[CD 4, track 5] **LM 6-4** **Comparando alimentos** Compare the foods or drinks you hear following the symbols below to create your statement.

= (tan)   − (menos)   + (más)   ↑ (mejor)   ↓ (peor)

1. + _____

2. + _____

3. − _____

4. ↓ _____

5. = _____

6. = _____

7. ↓ _____

[CD 4, track 6] **LM 6-5** **¿Qué serán?** *(What could they be?)* Listen to the description and write the corresponding letter in the blank provided.

_____ **1.** el agua   _____ **4.** la langosta

_____ **2.** la banana   _____ **5.** el pavo

_____ **3.** la sangría

VOCABULARIO El restaurante

[CD 4, track 7] **LM 6-6** **Definiciones** Listen to the following definitions and match them with the concepts below.

_____ **1.** ¡Buen provecho!   _____ **7.** el menú

_____ **2.** picar   _____ **8.** desear

_____ **3.** ¡Salud!   _____ **9.** almorzar

_____ **4.** la especialidad de la casa _____ **10.** Estoy a dieta.

_____ **5.** la cuenta   _____ **11.** ligero

_____ **6.** la propina   _____ **12.** ¡Estoy satisfecho!

Nombre _____ Fecha _____

CD 4, track 8] | **LM 6-7** | **Una cena romántica** Listen to the dialog between Alejandro and Olga, a couple dining at a romantic restaurant in Caracas. Please listen carefully so that you may complete activity **LM 6-8.**

CD 4, track 9] | **LM 6-8** | **Una indigestión** Put each statement in the order in which it appeared in the dialog.

_____ ¡Ay, Olga, no puedo ir a la fiesta esta noche!

_____ Vamos a la fiesta de Manuel.

_____ ¡Tienes los ojos son más grandes que el estómago!

_____ Un vinito para mí, con un plato enorme de camarones.

_____ ¡Huele riquísimo y están para chuparse los dedos, como tú!

_____ Y yo quisiera una cervecita con carne de res bien asada, por favor.

ESTRUCTURA II Describing past events: regular verbs and verbs with spelling changes in the preterite

CD 4, track 10] | **LM 6-9** | **Un día muy ocupado** Marina will tell you all about her day yesterday. Match what she says with the illustrations below.

1. _____

2. _____

3. _____

4. _____

5. _____

LM 6-10 **¿Y tu día?** Marina will now ask you about your day. Respond in complete sentences.

1. _____
2. _____
3. _____
4. _____
5. _____
6. _____
7. _____
8. _____

ESTRUCTURA III Giving detailed descriptions about past events: more verbs with stem changes in the preterite

[CD 4, track 12] **LM 6-11** **Una romántica indigestión** Do you remember Olga and Alejandro's romantic dinner? After listening to what happened, identify the verbs with stem changes in the preterite and write them in the spaces provided.

1. _____
2. _____
3. _____
4. _____

[CD 4, track 13] **LM 6-12** **¿Cierto o falso?** Listen to each statement and indicate if it's true (**Cierto**) or false (**Falso**).

1. _____
2. _____
3. _____
4. _____
5. _____

PRONUNCIACIÓN *m*, *n*, and *ñ*

The letter **ñ** is a sound that does not exist in English, although it is used in foreign words as in the Italian word *gnocchi*. The letters **m** and **n** are pronounced in Spanish the same way they are in English, with one exception: the letter **n** before **p, b, v,** and **m** is pronounced like an **m;** for example, **un beso [umbeso].**

[CD 4, track 14] **LM 6-13**   **¡A escribir!** Listen and repeat. Then write what you hear.

1. _____
2. _____
3. _____
4. _____
5. _____
6. _____
7. _____
8. _____

SÍNTESIS

[CD 4, track 15] **LM 6-14**   **¡A comer!** Listen carefully to the description and circle what is being described.

1. la lechuga   la naranja   la banana   la manzana
2. el queso   la leche   el helado   el flan
3. el huevo   el pollo   el pavo   el pescado
4. la mantequilla   el azúcar   la pimienta   el vinagre

[CD 4, track 16] **LM 6-15**   **Ayer y hoy** You will hear a sentence in the present tense. Change it to the preterite and write it in the space provided. Follow the model.

MODELO: Hoy no como carne.
Ayer no comí carne.

1. _____
2. _____
3. _____
4. _____
5. _____
6. _____

Nombre _____ Fecha _____

De compras: Argentina

VOCABULARIO La ropa

[CD 4, track 17] | **LM 7-1** | **La ropa** You will hear the name of each article of clothing twice. First repeat it, and then write its letter under the correct illustration.

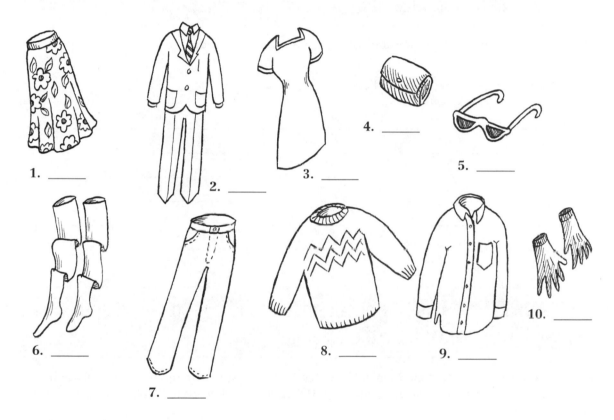

1. _____   2. _____   3. _____   4. _____   5. _____

6. _____   7. _____   8. _____   9. _____   10. _____

[CD 4, track 18] | **LM 7-2** | **¿Qué se ponen?** You will hear three brief conversations. Write how each character ought to dress in the space provided.

1. Silvia y su esposo deben llevar _____.

2. Claudia debe ponerse _____.

3. El señor debe comprar _____.

[CD 4, track 19] **LM 7-3** | **Los famosos y la ropa** You're listening to Joan Rivers on the radio as she interviews stars on the red carpet minutes before the Oscar ceremony. Pay attention to what they're wearing and indicate if it is **posible** or **imposible.**

1. posible   imposible   4. posible   imposible

2. posible   imposible   5. posible   imposible

3. posible   imposible   6. posible   imposible

ASÍ SE DICE Making emphatic statements: stressed possessive adjectives and pronouns

[CD 4, track 20] **LM 7-4** | **¿De quién es? ¿De quién son?** Listen to the sentence and then rewrite it using a pronoun. Follow the model.

> MODELO: Los pantalones son de Pepe.
> *Son suyos. Son los suyos.*

1. _____

2. _____

3. _____

4. _____

5. _____

6. _____

ESTRUCTURA I Talking about singular and/or completed events in the past: irregular verbs in the preterite

[CD 4, track 21] **LM 7-5** | **Un día de compras en Buenos Aires** Identify the irregular preterites in the story and write their infinitives in the spaces provided. **¡OJO!** There might be more than one irregular preterite in a sentence.

1. _____

2. _____

3. _____

4. _____

5. _____

6. _____

7. _____

[CD 4, track 22] **LM 7-6** **Más sobre las compras** You will listen to some questions based on the story in activity **LM 7-5.** Answer them in complete sentences.

1. _____
2. _____
3. _____
4. _____
5. _____

[CD 4, track 23] **LM 7-7** **La vida de una modelo famosa** You will listen to an imaginary, typical day in the life of famous Argentine model Valeria Mazza. Pay close attention so that you may then complete activity **LM 7-8.**

[CD 4, track 24] **LM 7-8** **¿Qué hizo Valeria?** Listen to the sentences and identify all stem-changing verbs in the preterite that you hear. ¡OJO! There might be more than one verb in a sentence.

1. _____
2. _____
3. _____
4. _____
5. _____
6. _____
7. _____

VOCABULARIO De compras

[CD 4, track 25] **LM 7-9** **Definiciones** Listen to the concept and write a definition for it in your own words.

1. _____
2. _____
3. _____
4. _____
5. _____
6. _____
7. _____
8. _____

ESTRUCTURA II Simplifying expressions: direct object pronouns

[CD 4, track 26] **LM 7-10** **Silvia Sepúlveda llama a una amiga** Silvia, who loves shopping, just found out about a tremendous sale at a famous boutique in La Florida. Listen to the dialog between her friend and her so that you may complete activity **LM 7-11.**

[CD 4, track 27] **LM 7-11** **Entre amigas** You will hear incorrect information. Based on the dialog you just heard, write the information correctly in the space provided.

1. _____

2. _____

3. _____

4. _____

5. _____

ESTRUCTURA III Describing on-going and habitual actions in the past: the imperfect tense

[CD 4, track 28] **LM 7-12** **Cuando Valeria Mazza era niña** Listen to the famous Argentine model, Valeria Mazza. Identify the verbs in the imperfect tense and write them in the spaces provided.

Cuando **1.** _____ niña **2.** _____ ser modelo. Años después

supe que *(found out)* que la vida de modelo **3.** _____ difícil y disciplinada.

Mi mamá me **4.** _____ que las modelos **5.** _____ y

6. _____ poco y **7.** _____ mucho. Todos los días

8. _____ con la ropa de mi madre, **9.** _____ y

10. _____ como las modelos ante el espejo. **11.** _____ muy

especial y siempre le **12.** _____ a mi madre sus revistas de moda. Mi madre

13. _____ y me **14.** _____: «Ay, hijita, qué especial que

eres». Ella siempre **15.** _____ conmigo; **16.** _____ mi com-

pañera. Las dos **17.** _____ modelos famosas. Después de un rato yo

18. _____ y **19.** _____ de hambre. Entonces mi madre

20. _____ el almuerzo y **21.** _____: «Ves, Valeria, ser modelo

no es tan fácil: mucho trabajo y poca comida». **22.** _____ razón, pero me gusta

mucho mi trabajo y mi madre es hoy mi «aficionada» número uno.

[CD 4, track 29] **LM 7-13** **¿Y tú?** Answer the following questions in complete sentences.

1. _____
2. _____
3. _____
4. _____
5. _____

PRONUNCIACIÓN I *c* and *qu*

The letter **c** before a consonant (except **h**) or the vowels **a, o, u,** and **qu** before **e** or **i** are represented by the sound [k]. The [k] sound is similar to the English [k] but without the puff of air that accompanies the [k] sound in *cat*.

[CD 4, track 30] **LM 7-14** **¡A repetir!** Listen and repeat.

c, qu: **c**liente pes**c**ado **c**omer **c**uchara **qu**eso **qu**iero

[CD 4, track 31] **LM 7-15** **¡A escuchar!** Listen and underline the [k] sounds you hear.

1. Y, ¿qué quiere Ud., señora?
2. El pescado con patatas fritas y después un café solo.

PRONUNCIACIÓN II *l, ll,* and *y*

The single **l** sound in Spanish resembles the *l* sound in English. The **ll** is pronounced like the consonant **y** in most of the Spanish-speaking world. The **ll/y** sound is like the *y* sound in the English words *yes* or *yellow*. In most of Argentina, the typical sound for **ll/y** is like the English *j* in the word *jump*.

[CD 4, track 32] **LM 7-16** **¡A repetir!** Listen and repeat.

l: sa**l**sa chi**l**e enchi**l**ada guacamo**l**e frijo**l**es

ll/y: torti**ll**a po**ll**o pae**ll**a Gui**ll**ermo **Y**olanda

[CD 4, track 33] **LM 7-17** **¡A escuchar!** Listen and underline the l and ll/y sounds you hear.

1. Tráigame enchiladas de carne con guacamole y frijoles.
2. ¿Y de postre?
3. El helado de chocolate, por favor.
4. Guillermo va a pedir pollo en mole con tortillas.
5. Yolanda y yo queremos paella.

SÍNTESIS

[CD 4, track 34] **LM 7-18** **¿Qué ropa llevan?** Listen to the description of what the Sepúlvedas are wearing. Draw at least three of the articles each of them have on.

[CD 4, track 35] **LM 7-19** **¿Qué ropa llevas hoy?** You will hear someone trying to guess what you're wearing to-day. Listen and mark **sí** or **no.** Then answer the last question.

1. sí no   6. sí no

2. sí no   7. sí no

3. sí no   8. sí no

4. sí no   9. sí no

5. sí no

10. _____

_____

Nombre _____ Fecha _____

Fiestas y vacaciones: Guatemala y El Salvador

| **VOCABULARIO** Fiestas y celebraciones |

[D 5, track 2] **LM 8-1** **¿Qué haces ese día?** Listen to the descriptions of a celebration or a holiday and indicate what you do on that day.

____ **1.** ¡Me asusto! ____ **4.** Me habla de cuando era joven.

____ **2.** Lo paso bien. ____ **5.** Hago un brindis.

____ **3.** Doy una fiesta.

[D 5, track 3] **LM 8-2** **¿Quién hace qué?** First, listen to six statements about a family. Then listen to the questions and check the right column to indicate who does each thing or reacts each way.

1. ¿Quién da una fiesta sorpresa?

2. ¿Quién se reúne con su familia?

3. ¿Quién se pone un disfraz?

4. ¿Quién hace un pastel el 24 de diciembre?

5. ¿Quién le desea muchas felicidades a su hermana?

6. ¿Quién tiene una celebración de cumpleaños?

	Ana	**Patricia**	**Victoria**	**Juan**	**Juan y Ana**
1.					
2.					
3.					
4.					
5.					
6.					

ASÍ SE DICE Inquiring and providing information about people and events: interrogative words

[CD 5, track 4]   **LM 8-3**   **¿Cuál es la pregunta?** You are going to listen to some answers. Based on the model write logical questions for each answer that you hear.

> MODELO: Estudio español para trabajar en Guatemala.
> *¿Para qué estudias español?*

1. _____

2. _____

3. _____

4. _____

5. _____

6. _____

ESTRUCTURA I Narrating in the past: the preterite vs. the imperfect

[CD 5, track 5]   **LM 8-4**   **Preguntas personales** Listen to the following questions about your childhood. Decide if the verbs in the questions are in the **pretérito** or **imperfecto.** Then, tell if the questions are based on a single, completed action or a habitual action or event.

> MODELOS: ¿Ibas a la playa de vacaciones cuando tenías nueve años?
> (imperfecto)   pretérito
> o ¿Comiste en un restaurante famoso?
> imperfecto   (pretérito)

1. imperfecto   pretérito

2. imperfecto   pretérito

3. imperfecto   pretérito

4. imperfecto   pretérito

5. imperfecto   pretérito

6. imperfecto   pretérito

7. imperfecto   pretérito

8. imperfecto   pretérito

9. imperfecto   pretérito

10. imperfecto   pretérito

[CD 5, track 6]   **LM 8-5**   **¡Contéstame!** Listen once again to the questions and answer them.

1. _____

2. _____

3. _____

4. _____

5. _____

6. _____

7. _____

8. _____

9. _____

10. _____

[CD 5, track 7] | **LM 8-6** | **La fiesta de Patricia y Victoria** First, listen to the story about a surprise birthday party that Victoria and Patricia are throwing for Javier, Victoria's boyfriend. Then, listen to each sentence from the story and write down the verbs that are in the **pretérito** or **imperfecto.** Then explain the use of the **pretérito** or **imperfecto**: single, completed action or habitual action or event; highlighted, main action, background action or description; beginning or end of an event or middle of an event; action that interrupts another action in the past; ongoing action that is interrupted. **¡OJO!** Some sentences have more than one verb!

MODELO: Victoria y Patricia prepararon una fiesta para Javier.
single, completed action: prepararon

1. _____

2. _____

3. _____

4. _____

5. _____

6. _____

7. _____

8. _____

9. _____

10. _____

11. _____

12. _____

13. _____

VOCABULARIO La playa y el campo

[CD 5, track 8] | **LM 8-7** | **¡De vacaciones!** Listen to the following descriptions of places to go on vacation and write the letter that best describes each place below.

____ **1.** la playa   ____ **4.** el balneario

____ **2.** la montaña   ____ **5.** la costa

____ **3.** el campo   ____ **6.** el mar

LM 8-8 **¿Posible o imposible?** Listen to the following statements and indicate if they are **posible** or **imposible.**

1. posible   imposible   4. posible   imposible
2. posible   imposible   5. posible   imposible
3. posible   imposible

ESTRUCTURA II Stating indefinite ideas and quantities: affirmative and negative expressions

[CD 5, track 10] **LM 8-9** **¡No estoy de acuerdo!** Listen to the following statements and write the contrary using affirmative or negative expressions logically.

1. _____
2. _____
3. _____
4. _____
5. _____
6. _____
7. _____

[CD 5, track 11] **LM 8-10** **¿Qué ves?** Look at the drawing and answer the following questions with the most logical affirmative or negative expressions.

1. _____
2. _____
3. _____
4. _____
5. _____
6. _____

ASÍ SE DICE Talking about periods of time since an event took place: *hace* and *hace que*

[D 5, track 12] **LM 8-11** **La nostalgia** Silvia Sepúlveda is very romantic. She thinks about her husband Julio, and wonders about a few things. Look at the drawings and identify the answers based on Silvia's thinking. Write down the answers.

1. _____
2. _____
3. _____
4. _____
5. _____

LM 8-12 **Hablando de tiempo** Answer the following questions with complete sentences.

1. _____

2. _____

3. _____

4. _____

5. _____

PRONUNCIACIÓN I *x*

In Spanish, the letter called **equis** is not very common at the beginning of a word, and it is pronounced like an **s,** as in **xenófobo.** Between two vowels it is pronounced like the English *x*, as in **examen.** However, when it is before a consonant the **x** is pronounced almost like an **s,** as in **extranjero.** In Mexico, **x** sounds like a Spanish **j** even if the word is written with an **x.** For example: **México** is written with an **x** but sounds like a **j: Méjico.**

LM 8-13 **¡Te toca a ti!** Listen, repeat, and write.

x: (between two vowels)

1. _____

x: (before a consonant)

2. _____

x: (initial position)

3. _____

x: (in Mexico)

4. _____

PRONUNCIACIÓN II La entonación

When we ask a question, the intonation changes—it rises or it falls—depending on the answer.

• In Spanish, the intonation rises if the answer to the question is affirmative or negative:
  ¿Tiene Victoria su traje de baño?
  ¿Se reúne Juan con su familia en Navidad?
  ¿Hay olas en el mar?

• The intonation also rises if the answer confirms something in the question:
  Toño es el novio de Patricia, ¿cierto?
  San Salvador es la capital de El Salvador, ¿no?
  Guatemala está al sur de México, ¿verdad?

• However, the intonation falls if the questions are informative ones:
  Por favor, ¿me puede decir qué hora es?
  Me gustaría alquilar un velero. ¿Cuánto cuesta una hora?

[CD 5, track 15] **LM 8-14** **¿Pregunta o respuesta?** Indicate if what you hear is a **question** or an **answer**. Pay particular attention to the intonation. Draw an arrow pointing up or down showing the intonation rising or falling.

1. pregunta respuesta 4. pregunta respuesta

2. pregunta respuesta 5. pregunta respuesta

3. pregunta respuesta 6. pregunta respuesta

SÍNTESIS

[CD 5, track 16] **LM 8-15** **¿Cuál no pertenece?** Listen to the following words and write the word that does not belong to the sequence.

1. _____

2. _____

3. _____

4. _____

[CD 5, track 17] **LM 8-16** **Y tú, ¿cómo te pones?** You are going to listen to different situations. Circle how you feel in each situation.

1. me pongo contento(a) me pongo furioso(a) me pongo triste

2. me pongo contento(a) me pongo furioso(a) me pongo triste

3. me pongo contento(a) me pongo furioso(a) me pongo triste

4. me pongo contento(a) me pongo furioso(a) me pongo triste

5. me pongo contento(a) me pongo furioso(a) me pongo triste

[CD 5, track 18] **LM 8-17** **¿Cuál es la pregunta?** You are invited to a big party. You really want to go to that party because a lot of famous personalities will be there. You are nervous and have lots of questions for your host. Listen to your host's answers and formulate the logical questions with the logical interrogative words.

MODELO: La fiesta se acaba después de las doce de la noche.
¿A qué hora se acaba la fiesta?

1. _____

2. _____

3. _____

4. _____

5. _____

6. _____

7. _____

De viaje por el Caribe: La República Dominicana, Cuba y Puerto Rico

VOCABULARIO Viajar en avión

[CD 5, track 19] **LM 9-1** **Un viaje en avión** Patricia and her sister are students from the University of Colorado. Last semester they studied abroad at the University of Puerto Rico in San Juan. Write the sentences that you hear in the spaces provided, and then put the sentences in a logical order by numbering them.

Oraciones   **Órden lógico**

1. _____ ____
2. _____ ____
3. _____ ____
4. _____ ____
5. _____ ____
6. _____ ____
7. _____ ____
8. _____ ____
9. _____ ____
10. _____ ____

[CD 5, track 20] **LM 9-2** **¡Ésa no!** Listen to the words associated with flights and traveling. First, repeat each word or expression that you hear. Next, write the word or expression that does not belong in the group.

1. _____
2. _____
3. _____
4. _____
5. _____

[CD 5, track 21] **LM 9-3** **Tus preferencias cuando viajas en avión** You are planning your next vacation. At the travel agency, the agent asks that you fill out a form indicating your preferences in order to find the ideal place for you. Circle your preferences: **sí, no,** or **es posible.**

1. sí no es posible	6. sí no es posible
2. sí no es posible	7. sí no es posible
3. sí no es posible	8. sí no es posible
4. sí no es posible	9. sí no es posible
5. sí no es posible	10. sí no es possible

ESTRUCTURA I Simplifying expressions: indirect object pronouns

[CD 5, track 22] **LM 9-4** **¿A quién le sucede?** Ester Carranza is assisting her clients at the travel agency. Listen to what she does for each client, and select the option with the indirect object pronoun that best reflects Ester's actions. Write its letter in the space.

1. _____ 2. _____ 3. _____ 4. _____ 5. _____

[CD 5, track 23] **LM 9-5** **Un viaje especial** Julio and Gloria went to the Caribbean on a romantic getaway. Listen to what they did, and answer the questions following the model.

MODELO: Julio y Gloria trajeron fotos para mí. ¿A quién le trajeron fotos Julio y Gloria?
Julio y Gloria me trajeron fotos a mí.

1. _____

2. _____

3. _____

4. _____

ESTRUCTURA II Simplifying expressions: double object pronouns

[CD 5, track 24] **LM 9-6** **¿Qué a quién?** Listen to what Ester Carranza did in activity **LM 9-4** once again. This time, replace both pronouns. Write your answers following the model.

MODELO: Ester les confirma el vuelo a ellos.
Ester *se lo* confirma.

1. Ester _____ _____ explica. 4. Ester _____ _____ recomienda.

2. Ester _____ _____ ofrece. 5. Ester _____ _____ promete.

3. Ester _____ _____ manda. 6. Ester _____ _____ pregunta.

[CD 5, track 25] **LM 9-7** **Más de qué a quién** Listen again to what Ester did in activity **LM 9-5.** This time, answer each question with direct and indirect object pronouns, as in the model below.

MODELO: Julio y Gloria trajeron fotos para mí. ¿A quién le trajeron fotos Julio y Gloria?
Julio y Gloria me las trajeron a mí.

1. _____

2. _____

3. _____

4. _____

VOCABULARO El hotel

5, track 26] | **LM 9-8** | **En el hotel** Manny and Teri are spending their honeymoon in a hotel in La Habana. Listen to their story and number each sentence in the space provided to put them in logical order.

____ Manny y Teri buscan un cuarto en un hotel.

____ Los recién casados prefieren una habitación con cama doble.

____ El señor en la recepción les dice que el cuarto está arreglado y es cómodo.

____ Los esposos hacen una reserva en un hotel de La Habana.

____ Manny y Teri prefieren un baño privado y limpio.

____ La pareja se registra para quedarse en el hotel.

ASÍ SE DICE Giving directions: prepositions of location, adverbs, and relevant expressions

5, track 27] | **LM 9-9** | **¿Dónde están?** Draw a map of the city that is described to you. Make sure that you do not forget anything!

[CD 5, track 28] **LM 9-10** **Durante un vuelo** Listen to the instructions that the flight attendant Silvia Vargas is giving to the passengers in the plane. Identify each command with the corresponding drawing.

1. _____

2. _____

3. _____

NO FUMAR

4. _____

5. _____

1. _____

2. _____

3. _____

4. _____

5. _____

[CD 5, track 29] **LM 9-11** **Las promociones para viajes especiales** Tere is listening to the radio when she hears a commercial from the travel agency Caribetel. Listen to the commercial at least twice and then write down the commands in the spaces provided.

1. _____   7. _____

2. _____   8. _____

3. _____   9. _____

4. _____   10. _____

5. _____   11. _____

6. _____   12. _____

| **LM 9-12** | **En el aeropuerto** Verónica and Juan are at the airport. They are both very excited about going to Aguadilla, Puerto Rico. But, Verónica is so afraid of flying that she is giving orders to Juan constantly telling him what not to do. Watch out! She is so nervous that some of her commands make no sense! Listen to the affirmative commands first and then write them in the negative form.

1. _____
2. _____
3. _____
4. _____
5. _____
6. _____

PRONUNCIACIÓN I *j*

The Spanish **j** has a sound somewhat like the *h* in *hill*, but harder. It is never pronounced like the English *j* in *jet*.

| **LM 9-13** | **¡A repetir y escribir!** Repeat and write each sentence.

1. _____
2. _____
3. _____
4. _____

PRONUNCIACIÓN II *g*

The Spanish **g** before an **e** or **i** is pronounced like the **j** in **Juan.** In all other cases, **g** is pronounced like the *g* in *go*.

| **LM 9-14** | **¡A repetir y escribir!** Repeat and write each sentence.

1. _____
2. _____
3. _____
4. _____
5. _____
6. _____

[CD 5, track 33] **LM 9-15** **¡A repetir y escribir!** Repeat and write each sentence.

1. _____

2. _____

3. _____

4. _____

SÍNTESIS

[CD 5, track 34] **LM 9-16** **¡Ay, las madres!** Do you remember Patricia and her sister from **Capítulo 8?** Well, her mother is very worried about their trip. Listen to each of her recommendations and transform them into commands.

1. ¡_____ los billetes de ida y vuelta!

2. ¡_____ sus respectivas maletas!

3. ¡_____ al aeropuerto!

4. ¡_____ el equipaje!

5. ¡_____ el vuelo en Denver!

6. ¡_____ escala en la ciudad de Miami!

7. ¡_____ en San Juan!

8. ¡_____ el equipaje!

9. ¡_____ por la aduana!

10. ¡_____ bien durante su estadía!

[CD 5, track 35] **LM 9-17** **¡Qué bien se lo pasa uno en el Caribe!** Listen to each sentence carefully. Then, replace the direct and indirect objects in the sentences with their direct and indirect object pronouns.

1. En Puerto Rico _____ _____ enseñaron.

2. El señor del hotel _____ _____ recomendó.

3. Tus padres _____ _____ prestaron.

4. Juan _____ _____ regaló.

5. El agente de viajes _____ _____ ofreció.

6. _____ _____ escribimos todos los días.

Las relaciones sentimentales: Honduras y Nicaragua

10

VOCABULARIO Las relaciones sentimentales

[CD 6, track 2] | **LM 10-1** | **¿Qué definición es?** Listen to the definitions. In the spaces below write the letter of the definition that matches each term.

_____ **1.** los recién casados

_____ **2.** el ramo

_____ **3.** los invitados

_____ **4.** la luna de miel

_____ **5.** la boda

_____ **6.** el divorcio

[CD 6, track 3] | **LM 10-2** | **Tú, ¿qué piensas?** First, listen to the following sentences. Next, complete the sentences with words from the vocabulary. Finally, give your opinion by selecting the expression **estoy de acuerdo** (*I agree*) or **no estoy de acuerdo** (*I disagree*).

1. No creo en el amor _____. ¡Es imposible!

estoy de acuerdo   no estoy de acuerdo

2. _____ es una institución anticuada y muy tradicional.

estoy de acuerdo   no estoy de acuerdo

3. Muchas veces _____ no es fácil.

estoy de acuerdo   no estoy de acuerdo

4. El _____ a alguien y que sea recíproco es una sensación muy bonita.

estoy de acuerdo   no estoy de acuerdo

5. Vivir en pareja y no _____ es la mejor situación.

estoy de acuerdo   no estoy de acuerdo

6. Después de muchos años de matrimonio, sólo hay _____ y no amor.

estoy de acuerdo   no estoy de acuerdo

ESTRUCTURA I Describing recent actions, events, and conditions: the present perfect tense

[CD 6, track 4] **LM 10-3** **Eva en una boda** Eva went to her cousin's wedding last week. Listen to her story and complete the sentences with verbs in the present perfect. **¡OJO!** Eva is a little girl, therefore she does not tell the story in order. Number the sentences from 1–10 in logical order.

_____ 1. Los novios se _____ al terminar la ceremonia religiosa.

_____ 2. Primero, los invitados _____ a la iglesia.

_____ 3. Las madres se _____ a llorar al ver a la novia entrar a la iglesia.

_____ 4. Después del «Ave María», la novia _____ con su padre a la iglesia.

_____ 5. La solista _____ el «Ave María» de Schubert.

_____ 6. Segundo, el novio _____ antes que la novia al altar.

_____ 7. Los novios _____ «sí, quiero».

_____ 8. Yo _____ detrás de la novia y _____ un ramo de flores.

_____ 9. Al final, el fotógrafo _____ muchas fotos.

_____ 10. Cuando los novios se _____, los invitados _____ .

ASÍ SE DICE Describing reciprocal actions: reciprocal constructions with _se, nos,_ and _os_

[CD 6, track 5] **LM 10-4** **¿Es recíproco?** You are going to listen to some statements about Victoria and Juan's relationship. Following the model below, change each sentence into a reciprocal action.

MODELO: Victoria mira a Juan con cariño.
Se miran.

1. _____

2. _____

3. _____

4. _____

5. _____

6. _____

7. _____

8. _____

324 Plazas, Second Edition, Lab Manual

VOCABULARIO La recepción

[CD 6, track 6] **LM 10-5** **Sinónimos** Listen to the definitions from the vocabulary. Write the letter of the definition next to the appropriate word below.

____ 1. terminar ____ 3. la pareja ____ 5. acompañar

____ 2. asistir ____ 4. la orquesta

[CD 6, track 7] **LM 10-6** **Tus definiciones** Listen to the following words and give a short definition. Follow the model.

MODELO: felicitar
¡Decir «felicidades»!

1. _____

2. _____

3. _____

4. _____

ASÍ SE DICE Qualifying actions: adverbial expressions of time and sequencing of events

[CD 6, track 8] **LM 10-7** **¿Cómo?** Qualify Victoria's and Juan's actions with the most logical adverbs. Follow the model.

MODELO: Victoria llama a Juan. frecuente
frecuentemente

1. _____ 5. _____

2. _____ 6. _____

3. _____ 7. _____

4. _____

[CD 6, track 9] **LM 10-8** **¡Radio chismes *(gossip)* increíbles de la imaginación!** First, listen to the program **"Radio chismes increíbles de la imaginación"** about the rich and famous. Then, answer the questions about the imaginary routine of the celebrities. Use the most logical adverbs of frequency.

1. ¿Quién se ha ido dos veces de luna de miel?

_____

2. ¿Qué actriz o actor se ha casado muchas veces?

_____

3. ¿Qué actriz sale siempre en la televisión los martes?

_____

4. ¿Quién se ha divorciado otra vez recientemente?

_____

5. ¿Qué actriz o actor no se ha casado nunca?

_____

ESTRUCTURA II Using the Spanish equivalents of *who, whom, that, and which*: relative pronouns

[CD 6, track 10] **LM 10-9** **¿Cuál es?** Listen to the sentences and circle the relative pronoun that you hear. Follow the model.

MODELO: La mujer que te mira es mi hermana.
(que) quien con quien a quien lo que

1. que quien con quien a quien lo que

2. que quien con quien a quien lo que

3. que quien con quien a quien lo que

4. que quien con quien a quien lo que

5. que quien con quien a quien lo que

6. que quien con quien a quien lo que

7. que quien con quien a quien lo que

PRONUNCIACIÓN I Review of accents

One easy rule to remember is that all words ending in **-ión** have a written accent on the **o**, for example, **atención** or **información.** The voice always rises with the accent, emphasizing its placement on the **ó.**

Listen to the following words ending in **-ión** and repeat: **interrogación, acumulación, constitución, argumentación, legión.**

All interrogative words have a written accent mark as well. The voice rises with the accent. Listen to the following interrogative phrases and repeat:

• **¿Cómo estás hoy?**
• **¿Qué tal estás hoy?**
• **¿Por qué fumas tanto?**
• **¿Cuándo llegas a casa?**

Now, compare **¿Por qué fumas tanto?** (interrogative) with **porque me gusta** (affirmative statement). Do you hear the difference?
Listen and repeat:

• **¿Por qué no vienes a clase?**
• **Porque estoy cansado.**

Some words have a written accent mark and are pronounced accordingly to distinguish one word from another: for example, **sí** and **si.**
Listen and repeat:

• **¡Sí, quiero!**
• **Si te casas conmigo, serás muy feliz.**

Nombre _____ Fecha _____

LM 10-10 **¿Puedes distinguir?** Listen to the sentences. Circle the word below that you hear in each sentence.

1. si   sí   4. se   sé
2. por qué   porque   5. cuándo   cuando
3. que   qué   6. como   cómo

PRONUNCIACIÓN II Review of pronunciation of vowels

[CD 6, track 12]   The vowel **a**: The Spanish **a** sounds like the English *a* found in the word *craft*.
mar   palabra   caja   puerta   mesa

The vowel **e**: The Spanish **e** sounds like the English *e* found in the word *get*.
Pepe   duele   meter   leer   pese

The vowel **i**: The Spanish **i** sounds like the English sound *ee* found in the word *India*.
Lili   Pili   mili   tía   mía   pistola

The vowel **o**: The Spanish **o** sounds like the English *o* found in the word *mother*.
por   amor   olor   agosto   oído

The vowel **u**: The Spanish **u** sounds like the English *oo* found in the word *choose*.
mula   muela   tutú   luz   suena

LM 10-11 **¡A escribir!** Repeat and write.

1. _____
2. _____
3. _____
4. _____
5. _____
6. _____
7. _____
8. _____
9. _____
10. _____

SÍNTESIS

[CD 6, track 13] **LM 10-12** **¿Qué palabra no pertenece en el grupo?** Listen to the following words and write the word that does not belong in the group.

1. _____
2. _____
3. _____
4. _____
5. _____

[CD 6, track 14] **LM 10-13** **¿Qué has hecho?** Answer the following questions about your day yesterday using the present perfect.

1. _____
2. _____
3. _____
4. _____
5. _____
6. _____

[CD 6, track 15] **LM 10-14** **¿Qué adverbio es?** Listen to the adjectives. Following the model, write down the corresponding adverb.

MODELO: difícil
difícilmente

1. _____
2. _____
3. _____
4. _____
5. _____
6. _____
7. _____

11
El mundo del trabajo:
Panamá

VOCABULARIO Profesiones y oficios

CD 6, track 16] **LM 11-1**   **Las profesiones** Listen to the descriptions. Match the descriptions that you hear with the appropriate professions below, by writing the corresponding letter.

_____   **1.** el (la) abogado(a)

_____   **2.** el (la) arquitecto(a)

_____   **3.** el (la) carpintero(a)

_____   **4.** el (la) contador(a)

_____   **5.** el (la) jefe

_____   **6.** el (la) maestro(a)

_____   **7.** el (la) periodista

_____   **8.** el (la) programador(a)

_____   **9.** el (la) traductor(a)

_____   **10.** el (la) veterinario(a)

CD 6, track 17] **LM 11-2**   **¿A quién llamas?** Listen to each situation and decide which person you need to call from activity **LM 11-1.**

1. _____

2. _____

3. _____

4. _____

5. _____

6. _____

7. _____

8. _____

9. _____

10. _____

ESTRUCTURA I Making statements about motives, intentions, and periods of time: *por* vs. *para*

[CD 6, track 18] **LM 11-3** *¿Por o para?* Listen to each sentence and decide which preposition you need to use. Write it in the space provided.

1. _____
2. _____
3. _____
4. _____
5. _____
6. _____
7. _____
8. _____
9. _____
10. _____

[CD 6, track 19] **LM 11-4** **Más preposiciones** Listen to the dialog carefully. Write the appropriate prepositions in the spaces provided.

1. _____
2. _____
3. _____
4. _____
5. _____
6. _____
7. _____

VOCABULARIO La oficina, el trabajo y la búsqueda de un puesto

[CD 6, track 20] **LM 11-5** **Buscando trabajo** You are at a temporary job agency looking for a job. You must fill out a form indicating your preferences to match your qualifications with the right position. Give your opinion (**sí, no,** or **no es importante**) after hearing each statement.

1. sí	no	no es importante	6. sí	no	no es importante
2. sí	no	no es importante	7. sí	no	no es importante
3. sí	no	no es importante	8. sí	no	no es importante
4. sí	no	no es importante	9. sí	no	no es importante
5. sí	no	no es importante	10. sí	no	no es importante

[CD 6, track 21] **LM 11-6** **Cosas de trabajo** Match the definition with its appropriate term. Write the letter of the definition in the space.

_____ **1.** pedir un aumento

_____ **2.** renunciar

_____ **3.** solicitar un empleo

_____ **4.** despedir

_____ **5.** la impresora

_____ **6.** contratar

_____ **7.** de tiempo completo

ESTRUCTURA II Expressing subjectivity and uncertainty: the subjunctive mood

[CD 6, track 22] **LM 11-7** **El jefe de mis pesadillas *(nightmares)*** Julián had a dream that his boss was great. However, that is not the case. When Julián woke up he remembered how awful his boss is. Listen to what Julián says about his boss. Then indicate whether you agree **(Estoy de acuerdo.)** or disagree **(No estoy de acuerdo.)** with his boss.

1. Estoy de acuerdo   No estoy de acuerdo

2. Estoy de acuerdo   No estoy de acuerdo

3. Estoy de acuerdo   No estoy de acuerdo

4. Estoy de acuerdo   No estoy de acuerdo

5. Estoy de acuerdo   No estoy de acuerdo

6. Estoy de acuerdo   No estoy de acuerdo

7. Estoy de acuerdo   No estoy de acuerdo

VOCABULARIO Las finanzas personales

[CD 6, track 23] **LM 11-8** **¡Empareja!** Listen to the following definitions and match them with the appropriate term. Write the letter of the definition in the space provided.

_____ **1.** el préstamo

_____ **2.** la tarjeta de crédito

_____ **3.** la cuenta corriente

_____ **4.** pagar en efectivo

_____ **5.** las facturas

_____ **6.** la cuenta de ahorros

_____ **7.** el cajero automático

_____ **8.** el cheque

[CD 6, track 24] **LM 11-9** **La administración de tu dinero** Answer the following questions with complete sentences.

1. _____

2. _____

3. _____

4. _____

ESTRUCTURA III Expressing desires and intentions: the present subjunctive with statements of volition

[CD 6, track 25] | **LM 11-10** | **El jefe de mis sueños** In activity **LM 11-7** Julián had a dream that his boss was the ideal boss, but in reality that was not the case. Now you have a chance to hear his dream about his ideal boss. Listen to each sentence and write the verbs that are in the subjunctive.

Yo quiero que mi jefe...

1. _____

2. _____

3. _____

4. _____

5. _____

6. _____

7. _____

8. _____

9. _____

10. _____

SÍNTESIS

[CD 6, track 26] | **LM 11-11** | **Asociaciones** Listen to the following expressions and select the one that does not belong in the sequence.

1. _____

2. _____

3. _____

4. _____

5. _____

6. _____

7. _____

[CD 6, track 27] | **LM 11-12** | **Mi trabajo ideal** What is your ideal job? Using the subjunctive, make a list of **five** characteristics your ideal job should have. Make sure to include job conditions, responsibilities, etc.

1. _____

2. _____

3. _____

4. _____

5. _____

12 El medio ambiente: Costa Rica

VOCABULARIO La geografía rural y urbana

[CD 7, track 2] **LM 12-1** **¿Rural o urbana?** Listen to the words from the vocabulary. Identify the words pertaining to urban or rural geography. Circle **rural** or **urbana** according to the word that you hear. Follow the model.

> MODELO: la fábrica
> rural   (urbana)

1. rural urbana	4. rural urbana	7. rural urbana	9. rural urbana
2. rural urbana	5. rural urbana	8. rural urbana	10. rural urbana
3. rural urbana	6. rural urbana		

[CD 7, track 3] **LM 12-2** **¿Es posible o imposible?** Listen to the following sentences and decide if the statements are possible or impossible. Circle **es posible** or **no es posible** depending on the information given.

1. es posible es imposible	4. es posible es imposible	6. es posible es imposible
2. es posible es imposible	5. es posible es imposible	7. es posible es imposible
3. es posible es imposible		

ESTRUCTURA I Expressing emotion and opinions: subjunctive following verbs of emotion, impersonal expressions, and *ojalá*

[CD 7, track 4] **LM 12-3** **¿Negativa o positiva?** You are about to listen to Mateo's opinions regarding lifestyles. Indicate if his opinions are positive **(positiva)** or negative **(negativa).**

1. positiva negativa	5. positiva negativa	8. positiva negativa
2. positiva negativa	6. positiva negativa	9. positiva negativa
3. positiva negativa	7. positiva negativa	10. positiva negativa
4. positiva negativa		

[CD 7, track 5] **LM 12-4** **Sugerencias** First, listen to some general statements. Then, give your friend your opinion based on the information found in the general statements. Follow the model.

> MODELO: Es una lástima no vivir en una metrópolis.
> *Es una lástima que tú no vivas en una metrópolis.*

1. _____
2. _____
3. _____
4. _____
5. _____
6. _____

[CD 7, track 6] **LM 12-5** | **¡Ojalá!** Your best friend just found a job in a big metropolitan area. Listen to the statements in present tense, and then, wish your friend the very best in the big city. Begin each of your sentences with the expression **ojalá** + subjunctive. Follow the model.

MODELO: La vida en una gran metrópolis te gusta.
¡Ojalá que la vida en una gran metrópolis te guste!

1. _____

2. _____

3. _____

4. _____

5. _____

VOCABULARIO La conservación y la explotación

[CD 7, track 7] **LM 12-6** | **¿Qué palabra es?** You are about to listen to some definitions. Match each definition with the appropriate word below by writing its letter in the space.

_____ 1. destruir

_____ 2. el petróleo

_____ 3. reforestar

_____ 4. acabar

_____ 5. recoger

_____ 6. el aire

[CD 7, track 8] **LM 12-7** | **¿Verdad o mentira?** The president of the country is speaking about conservation and exploitation. Listen carefully to the president's message and draw a circle around the word **verdad** or **mentira**, depending on the context.

1. verdad   mentira

2. verdad   mentira

3. verdad   mentira

4. verdad   mentira

5. verdad   mentira

6. verdad   mentira

ESTRUCTURA II Expressing doubts, uncertainty, and hypothesizing: the subjunctive with verbs, expressions of uncertainty, and with adjective clauses

[CD 7, track 9] **LM 12-8** | **¿Indicativo o subjuntivo?** Listen to the following sentences and circle the verbal mode that you hear. Follow the model.

MODELO: Creo que hay mucha contaminación en las grandes metrópolis.
subjuntivo   (indicativo)

1. subjuntivo   indicativo

2. subjuntivo   indicativo

3. subjuntivo   indicativo

4. subjuntivo   indicativo

5. subjuntivo   indicativo

6. subjuntivo   indicativo

7. subjuntivo   indicativo

8. subjuntivo   indicativo

LM 12-9 **¡Lo contrario!** You are going to listen again to the statements from activity **LM 12-8.** Following the model, write the opposite of what you hear.

MODELO: Creo que hay mucha contaminación en las grandes metrópolis.
No creo que haya mucha contaminación en las grandes metrópolis.

1. _____

2. _____

3. _____

4. _____

5. _____

6. _____

7. _____

8. _____

VOCABULARIO Los animales y el refugio natural

LM 12-10 **Asociaciones** Associate the following animals with the famous movies/cartoons where they appear. Follow the model.

MODELO: el elefante
Passage to India, Dumbo

1. _____

2. _____

3. _____

4. _____

5. _____

LM 12-11 **¡Adivina!** Listen to some animal and insect descriptions. Based on the descriptions, guess what animal or insect it is!

1. _____

2. _____

3. _____

4. _____

5. _____

[CD 7, track 13] **LM 12-12** **¿Dónde están?** Listen to the following words pertaining to the vocabulary for urban and rural geography. Circle the most logical place where each can be found.

1. el bosque la carretera la metrópolis la basura

2. la fábrica la selva la colina el tráfico

3. el arroyo el bosque la finca la metrópolis

4. la basura la tierra la selva el ruido

5. la catarata la colina la basura los rascacielos

[CD 7, track 14] **LM 12-13** **¿Estás de acuerdo?** Alex is going to give you his opinion regarding the environment. Listen to his statements and write the verbs that you hear. Then, give your opinion by circling **estoy de acuerdo** or **no estoy de acuerdo.**

1. _____

estoy de acuerdo   no estoy de acuerdo

2. _____

estoy de acuerdo   no estoy de acuerdo

3. _____

estoy de acuerdo   no estoy de acuerdo

4. _____

estoy de acuerdo   no estoy de acuerdo

5. _____

estoy de acuerdo   no estoy de acuerdo

6. _____

estoy de acuerdo   no estoy de acuerdo

7. _____

estoy de acuerdo   no estoy de acuerdo

13 El mundo del espectáculo: Perú y Ecuador

VOCABULARIO Programas y películas

[CD 7, track 15] | **LM 13-1** | **Las artes y los medios de comunicación** Listen to the descriptions, and then match them with the most logical category from the list below. Write the corresponding letter next to each category.

_____ **1.** película de acción

_____ **2.** canal de televisión

_____ **3.** película extranjera

_____ **4.** película romántica

_____ **5.** anuncio

_____ **6.** programa deportivo

_____ **7.** pronóstico del tiempo

_____ **8.** película de horror

_____ **9.** película clásica

_____ **10.** el cine

[CD 7, track 16] | **LM 13-2** | **Tus preferencias** Name the program that you prefer in each category. Justify your selection with a short sentence.

1. _____

2. _____

3. _____

4. _____

5. _____

6. _____

7. _____

8. _____

[CD 7, track 17] | **LM 13-3** | **¿Qué opinas?** You are a movie critic/TV program reviewer. Indicate your opinion regarding the shows or movies that you hear.

1. Me aburre.   Me molesta.   Siempre lo (la) miro.   No me gusta.

2. Me aburre.   Me molesta.   Siempre lo (la) miro.   No me gusta.

3. Me aburre.   Me molesta.   Siempre lo (la) miro.   No me gusta.

4. Me aburre.   Me molesta.   Siempre lo (la) miro.   No me gusta.

5. Me aburre.   Me molesta.   Siempre lo (la) miro.   No me gusta.

6. Me aburre.   Me molesta.   Siempre lo (la) miro.   No me gusta.

7. Me aburre.   Me molesta.   Siempre lo (la) miro.   No me gusta.

8. Me aburre.   Me molesta.   Siempre lo (la) miro.   No me gusta.

9. Me aburre.   Me molesta.   Siempre lo (la) miro.   No me gusta.

10. Me aburre.   Me molesta.   Siempre lo (la) miro.   No me gusta.

ESTRUCTURA I Talking about anticipated actions: subjunctive with purpose and time clauses

[CD 7, track 18] **LM 13-4** | **Ponte hipotético(a)** Listen carefully to each statement and circle the most logical conjunction to complete the sentence. Follow the model.

MODELO: La madre les permite ver el programa a sus hijos (sin que /(con tal de que) hagan la tarea.

1. para que / con tal de que
2. para que / sin que
3. cuando / a menos que
4. aunque / tan pronto como
5. Después de que / En caso de que

[CD 7, track 19] **LM 13-5** | **¿Subjuntivo o indicativo?** Listen and repeat the sentences that you hear. Then, decide if the verbs should be in the subjunctive or indicative. Circle your choice.

1. ve / vea
2. calmas / calmes
3. son / sean
4. canta / cante
5. podemos / podamos
6. preparo / prepare
7. vuelven / vuelvan
8. dicen / digan
9. comienza / comience
10. encanta / encante

VOCABULARIO Las artes

[CD 7, track 20] **LM 13-6** | **¿Qué género? ¿Qué artista? ¿Qué obra?** Listen to the names of the following personalities and their work. Identify them with the category they belong by writing the corresponding letter in the space provided.

_____ 1. la arquitectura, el arquitecto, el edificio

_____ 2. la pintura, el pintor, la obra maestra

_____ 3. la escultura, el escultor, la estatua

_____ 4. la música, el compositor, la ópera

_____ 5. la poesía, la poeta, el poema

_____ 6. el baile, el bailarín, el ballet

_____ 7. la fotografía, el fotógrafo, la foto

_____ 8. la literatura, la autora, la novela

_____ 9. el teatro, el dramaturgo, el drama

_____ 10. el rock, la cantante, el concierto

[CD 7, track 21] **LM 13-7** | **Cuéntanos de ti** Answer the following questions orally first. Then, write your answers in the spaces provided.

1. _____

2. _____

3. _____

4. _____

Nombre _____ Fecha _____

ESTRUCTURA II Talking about unplanned or accidental occurrences: no-fault *se* construction

[CD 7, track 22] | **LM 13-8** | **¿A quién le pasó?** Listen to the sentences and repeat them. Then, match each sentence with the appropriate drawing. Write the corresponding letter in the space provided.

1. _____

2. _____

3. _____   4. _____   5. _____

[CD 7, track 23] | **LM 13-9** | **¡No es culpa tuya!** Listen to the following sentences and write the expression with **se** that is the most logical. Follow the model.

> MODELO: No puedes beber leche porque tu hermana acabó la botella de leche.
> *Se acabó la botella de leche.*

1. _____

2. _____

3. _____

4. _____

5. _____

ASÍ SE DICE Describing completed actions and resulting conditions: use of the past participle as adjective

[CD 7, track 24] **LM 13-10** **¿Cómo están?** Match the past participle below with the sentence you hear by writing the corresponding letter of the sentence in the space provided.

_____ 1. cerrado   _____ 5. escrita

_____ 2. abiertas   _____ 6. cubiertas

_____ 3. muertos   _____ 7. resuelto

_____ 4. cancelado

[CD 7, track 25] **LM 13-11** **¿Quién fue?** Transform each sentence that you hear with **por** + the agent of the action.

      MODELO: el cuadro La artista pintó el cuadro.
              El cuadro fue pintado por la artista.

1. *La Gioconda*

_____

2. *Los heraldos negros*

_____

3. América

_____

4. La Sagrada Familia

_____

5. El concierto musical

_____

SÍNTESIS

[CD 7, track 26] **LM 13-12** **¿Qué les pasó?** Listen to the situations and write their letter next to the corresponding expression.

_____ 1. Se le mojó la ropa.   _____ 4. Se les quemó la comida.

_____ 2. Se te olvidaron las llaves.   _____ 5. Se me cayeron las pinturas.

_____ 3. Se nos dañó la tele.

[CD 7, track 27] **LM 13-13** **Hipotéticamente hablando** Listen carefully to each sentence. Complete the sentences logically using subjunctive when necessary.

1. _____

2. _____

3. _____

4. _____

5. _____

14 La vida pública: Chile

VOCABULARIO La política y el voto

[CD 8, track 2] | **LM 14-1** | **¿Qué va con qué?** Listen to the words from the vocabulary. Match the words with the sentences that better qualify them.

_____ 1. Tiene elecciones.

_____ 2. Tiene poder absoluto.

_____ 3. Gobierna con el gobierno.

_____ 4. Votan.

_____ 5. No permite elegir presidente.

_____ 6. Discute ideas.

_____ 7. Aprueba leyes.

_____ 8. Defiende al país.

_____ 9. Se firma.

[CD 8, track 3] | **LM 14-2** | **¿Con qué lo asocias?** Listen to each group of three words. Match the first word with one of the other two. Follow the model.

MODELO: el candidato: el voto   la dictadura
            el voto

1. _____

2. _____

3. _____

4. _____

5. _____

6. _____

7. _____

ESTRUCTURA I Talking about future events: the future tense

[CD 8, track 4] | **LM 14-3** | **Predicciones para mañana** The university newspaper, *The Informed Students*, is making some predictions about the upcoming student elections. Write the verbs that you hear in the future tense.

1. _____

2. _____

3. _____

4. _____

5. _____

6. _____

LM 14-4 **¿Qué pasará mañana?** Virginia is asking some questions of her friend Natalia, who is one of the candidates for the student body presidency. She wants to know what will happen in the future elections. Change the verbs that you hear in the questions into the future tense.

1. ¿_____ muchos votos?

2. ¿Cuándo _____ los resultados de las elecciones?

3. ¿_____ por ti misma?

4. ¿_____ nerviosa?

5. ¿_____ un discurso?

6. ¿_____ una campaña?

7. ¿_____ saber los resultados pronto?

8. ¿_____ un traje muy elegante?

9. ¿_____ muchas leyes?

10. ¿_____ muy ocupada?

VOCABULARIO Las preocupaciones cívicas y los medios de comunicación

LM 14-5 **En el futuro, ¿qué pasará?** Lilí can predict the future with her cards. Listen to her predictions and circle **es bueno** or **es malo** according to what Lilí sees in the cards.

1. es bueno   es malo

2. es bueno   es malo

3. es bueno   es malo

4. es bueno   es malo

5. es bueno   es malo

6. es bueno   es malo

LM 14-6 **¿Qué palabra es?** Listen to the definitions. Match them with the correct word or expression.

_____ 1. el analfabetismo

_____ 2. el Internet

_____ 3. el desempleo

_____ 4. el aborto

_____ 5. la libertad de prensa

_____ 6. los impuestos

_____ 7. la huelga

_____ 8. la drogadicción

ESTRUCTURA II Expressing conjecture or probability: the conditional

[CD 8, track 8] | **LM 14-7** | **¿Y tú?** Natalia is going to tell you how she envisions the ideal society. Listen to her statements and write the verbs that you hear. Then, give your personal opinion by circling **estoy de acuerdo** or **no estoy de acuerdo.** Follow the model.

MODELO: Los pobres tendrían dinero.
tendrían   estoy de acuerdo

1. _____

estoy de acuerdo   no estoy de acuerdo

2. _____

estoy de acuerdo   no estoy de acuerdo

3. _____

estoy de acuerdo   no estoy de acuerdo

4. _____

estoy de acuerdo   no estoy de acuerdo

5. _____

estoy de acuerdo   no estoy de acuerdo

6. _____

estoy de acuerdo   no estoy de acuerdo

7. _____

estoy de acuerdo   no estoy de acuerdo

8. _____

estoy de acuerdo   no estoy de acuerdo

9. _____

estoy de acuerdo   no estoy de acuerdo

10. _____

estoy de acuerdo   no estoy de acuerdo

[CD 8, track 9] | **LM 14-8** | **Especulaciones** You are about to hear some questions. Write down your own answers. Follow the model.

MODELO: ¿Adónde irían los estudiantes ayer por la mañana?
Los estudiantes irían a la universidad.

1. _____
2. _____
3. _____
4. _____
5. _____

ESTRUCTURA III Making references to the present: the present perfect subjunctive

[CD 8, track 10] **LM 14-9** **Un discurso** Natalia and her party have won the student elections. She is giving a speech. In her speech she is talking about her feelings and her wishes for her party. Following the model, write the verbs that you hear.

MODELO: Estoy muy contenta de que mi partido haya ganado las elecciones.
haya ganado

1. _____   4. _____

2. _____   5. _____

3. _____   6. _____

[CD 8, track 11] **LM 14-10** **¿Contento o triste?** What makes you happy? Start your sentences with **estoy contento(a) de que** or **estoy triste de que** to express what makes you happy or sad. Base your answers on the indications that you hear. Write the verbs in the present perfect subjunctive. Follow the model.

MODELO: mis padres / tener trabajo siempre
Estoy contento(a) de que mis padres hayan tenido trabajo siempre.

1. _____

2. _____

3. _____

4. _____

5. _____

6. _____

SÍNTESIS

[CD 8, track 12] **LM 14-11** **¡Con educación, por favor!** Alex is a small child who does not have proper manners yet. Following the model, change the orders he is giving by using the conditional tense. Repeat after the speaker and then write the correct answer.

MODELO: ¡Camarero, tráigame agua! *Camarero, podría traerme agua, por favor.*

1. _____   5. _____

2. _____   6. _____

3. _____   7. _____

4. _____

[CD 8, track 13] **LM 14-12** **Es lo contrario** Your grandmother is watching the special report on TV about the president. However, she does not get the details because she does not hear very well. Following the model, correct your grandma's opinions by writing the opposite of what she says. Repeat the correct answers after the speaker.

MODELO: Es improbable que el presidente haya tenido mucho apoyo.
No, abuelita, es probable que el presidente haya tenido mucho apoyo.

1. _____

2. _____

3. _____

4. _____

5. _____

6. _____

15 Los avances tecnológicos: Uruguay

VOCABULARIO Los avances tecnológicos

LM 15-1 **La tecnología es cosa de todos los días** Listen carefully to the definitions. Match the definitions with the corresponding words below, writing the letters in the blanks.

_____ **1.** el control remoto   _____ **4.** el teléfono celular

_____ **2.** la antena parabólica   _____ **5.** la cámara digital

_____ **3.** la alarma

LM 15-2 **Minia, la piba digital** First, listen to the description of a young Uruguayan woman. Then, based on the description, complete the sentences below with the appropriate words.

1. Minia es una chica del siglo XXI y sus amigos la llaman _____.

2. Siempre lleva su teléfono celular _____.

3. Cuando conduce va escuchando sus _____ o la radio; por los altavoces sale una música infernal.

4. A Minia le fascina la computadora y siempre está _____ _____ al Internet.

5. Usa su _____ para mandarle fotos a su novio en San Francisco.

6. La tele de Minia está equipada con _____ y

_____.

7. Por teléfono, los enamorados se mandan besos que recibe la

_____.

8. Los amigos de Minia le preguntan si el suyo será el primer

_____.

LM 15-3 **¿Eres un(a) chico(a) digital?** Compare your lifestyle with Minia's. Based on your lifestyle give the most appropriate answers by circling **siempre, a veces, depende,** or **nunca.**

1. siempre   a veces   depende   nunca

2. siempre   a veces   depende   nunca

3. siempre   a veces   depende   nunca

4. siempre   a veces   depende   nunca

5. siempre   a veces   depende   nunca

6. siempre   a veces   depende   nunca

7. siempre   a veces   depende   nunca

8. siempre   a veces   depende   nunca

9. siempre   a veces   depende   nunca

10. siempre   a veces   depende   nunca

ESTRUCTURA I Making statements in the past: past (imperfect) subjunctive

[CD 8, track 17] **LM 15-4** **Mis padres me decían** Listen carefully to what Minia's parents wanted her to do. Then, complete the sentences with the most appropriate option below.

_____ **1.** la llamara todos los días por teléfono.

_____ **2.** escuchara mis discos compactos cuando estuviera en el coche.

_____ **3.** instalara una alarma en la casa porque vivo sola.

_____ **4.** me comunicara con chicos por el Internet.

[CD 8, track 18] **LM 15-5** **¿Qué te decían tus padres?** Do you remember what Minia's parents were telling her to do? Now it is your turn to share how your parents wanted you to use technology. **¡OJO!** Do not forget to use the subjunctive.

1. _____

2. _____

3. _____

4. _____

VOCABULARIO La computadora

[CD 8, track 19] **LM 15-6** **Ciberespacios en la sociedad del siglo XXI** First, listen to the scenarios. Then, use the words and expressions below to complete them in a logical manner. Don't forget to write the letters that correspond to the appropriate scenario.

_____ **1.** Internet

_____ **2.** salón de charla

_____ **3.** abrir un documento, impresora

_____ **4.** correo electrónico

_____ **5.** navegar la Red

_____ **6.** teletrabajaremos

_____ **7.** archivar

_____ **8.** escáner

LM 15-7 **¿Cuán cibernauta eres?** You will hear some questions about how much of a technological person you are. First, answer the questions orally and then write your answers.

1. _____

2. _____

3. _____

4. _____

5. _____

ESTRUCTURA II Talking about hypothetical situations: *if*-clauses

LM 15-8 **Resuelve la hipótesis** Listen carefully to each sentence. Then, complete it by selecting one of the three choices.

_____ 1. **a.** la buscaba en el Internet.

            b. la buscaría en el Internet.

            c. la buscaré en el Internet.

_____ 2. **a.** habría menos accidentes.

            b. había menos accidentes.

            c. habrá menos accidentes.

_____ 3. **a.** ahorrarás tiempo y dinero.

            b. ahorrarías tiempo y dinero.

            c. ahorrabas tiempo y dinero.

_____ 4. **a.** no habrá suficiente tiempo para hacer otras cosas.

            b. no habría suficiente tiempo para hacer otras cosas.

            c. no había suficiente tiempo para hacer otras cosas.

_____ 5. **a.** la comunicación internacional era más difícil.

            b. la comunicación internacional sería más difícil.

            c. la comunicación internacional será más difícil.

LM 15-9 **¿Qué harías si pudieras?** Tell what you would do in an ideal world by completing the sentences you hear.

1. _____

2. _____

3. _____

4. _____

5. _____

[CD 8, track 23] | **LM 15-10** | **¿Cuánto sabes de tecnología?** How much technological vocabulary do you know? Write the names in the drawing corresponding to each word from the vocabulary that you hear.

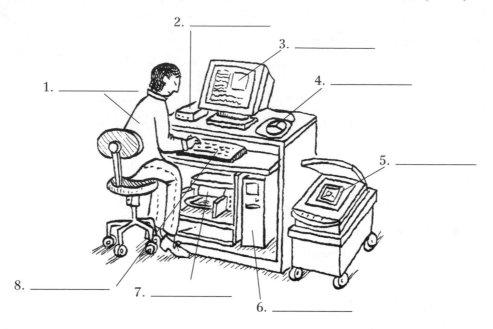

1. _____
2. _____
3. _____
4. _____
5. _____
6. _____
7. _____
8. _____

[CD 8, track 24] | **LM 15-11** | **¡Si fuera posible!** Listen to the beginning of the sentences and complete them expressing your own opinion.

1. _____

2. _____

3. _____

4. _____

5. _____

Autopruebas Answer Key

CAPÍTULO PRELIMINAR

WB P-13 Una conversación típica

1. Hola 2. Qué 3. estás 4. gracias 5. gusto
6. es mío 7. dónde 8. Soy 9. Adiós 10. Adiós
11. Nos

WB P-14 Números

1. quince / catorce
2. uno /cero
3. treinta / veintinueve
4. diecisiete / dieciséis
5. veinticinco / veinticuatro

WB P-15 Presentaciones

1. eres 2. Soy 3. es 4. son 5. somos

WB P-16 ¿Sois de España?

1. vosotros 2. nosotros 3. Yo 4. él 5. Ud.
6. Yo 7. Ella 8. tú 9. Yo 10. Uds.

WB P-17 ¿Cuántos años tienen?

1. Lourdes tiene veintiún años.
2. Olga y Nidia tienen diecinueve años.
3. Mariana tiene dieciocho años.
4. Carmen y tú tienen veinte años.

CAPÍTULO 1

WB 1-18 Los cursos

1. Letras: matemáticas
2. Lenguas: historia
3. Ciencias sociales: zoología
4. Arte: biología

WB 1-19 ¿Qué hora es?

1. Son las tres menos cuarto de la tarde.
2. Es la una y veintidós de la tarde.
3. Es la una menos veintinueve de la tarde. /
   Son las doce y treinta y un minutos de la
   tarde.
4. Son las cinco y cuarto de la mañana.
5. Son las nueve y media de la mañana.

WB 1-20 Está muy ocupada

1. Los martes Nancy estudia alemán a las
   cuatro menos cuarto de la tarde.
2. Los miércoles Nancy estudia chino a la
   una menos cuarto de la tarde.
3. Los jueves Nancy estudia ruso a la una y
   media de la tarde.
4. Los viernes Nancy estudia italiano a las
   cinco y cuarto de la tarde.
5. Los sábados Nancy estudia portugués a
   las siete y media de la noche.
6. Los domingos Nancy estudia japonés a
   las diez de la mañana.

WB 1-21 Los colores

1. amarillo
2. negro
3. rojo
4. marrón
5. blanco
6. verde

WB 1-22 Lupe y Lalo

First paragraph: una; la; una; la; las; el; el

Second paragraph: los; el; una

Third paragraph: La; las; la; los; la; los

WB 1-23 Las actividades del día

1. Ramón trabaja todos los días.
2. Teresa y Evelia estudian matemáticas por
   la tarde.
3. Yo practico deportes por la mañana.
4. Nosotros descansamos a las 4:00 de la
   tarde.
5. Tú enseñas ejercicios aeróbicos por la
   noche.
6. Uds. regresan a la casa a las 6:00 de la
   tarde.

CAPÍTULO 2

WB 2-20 Los miembros de la familia

1. esposa
2. primo
3. apellido
4. sobrina
5. nietos

WB 2-21 Descripciones

1. es, mexicana
2. somos, simpáticas
3. son, tontos
4. eres, atlética
5. es, paciente

WB 2-22 Probablemente son...

Answers will vary. Examples are:

1. trabajadores
2. inteligente / estudiosa
3. tacaño
4. irresponsable
5. perezosa
6. gordos

WB 2-23 Los números

1. treinta y dos
2. noventa y nueve
3. veinticuatro
4. doce
5. quince

6. diecisiete
7. cuarenta y seis
8. setenta y nueve

WB 2-24 Una conversación

1. Tienes 2. Mi 3. tengo 4. tienes 5. mis
6. tienen 7. tienen 8. su 9. Su 10. Tienes
11. tengo 12. Tienes 13. tengo

WB 2-25 En la universidad

1. vives 2. vivo 3. vive 4. Escribes 5. escribes
6. recibo 7. debo 8. tienes 9. creo

CAPÍTULO 3

WB 3-19 Los meses y las estaciones

1. diciembre, el invierno
2. febrero, el invierno
3. enero, el invierno
4. octubre, el otoño
5. mayo, la primavera
6. noviembre, el otoño

WB 3-20 En la ciudad

1. a 2. g 3. b 4. d 5. c 6. f 7. e

WB 3-21 Pasatiempos

1. Me gusta ver películas en video.
2. Me gusta sacar fotos.
3. Me gusta jugar al tenis.
4. Me gusta tocar la guitarra.
5. Me gusta bailar con música rock.
6. Me gusta visitar a mis abuelos.

WB 3-22 Entre amigos

1. vas 2. Voy 3. vas 4. vamos 5. va 6. van

WB 3-23 Un joven contento

1. salgo 2. Hago 3. voy 4. hago/doy
5. Pongo 6. Conozco 7. sé 8. veo 9. estoy

WB 3-24 ¿Qué vas a hacer?

1. Voy a practicar deportes.
2. Voy a jugar al tenis.
3. Voy a nadar en la piscina.
4. Voy a montar a caballo.
5. Voy a levantar pesas.

WB 3-25 ¿Qué tiempo hace?

A. Hace sol. Hace buen tiempo.
B. Hace sol.
C. Hace mucho calor.
D. Hace fresco.
E. Hace viento.
F. Hace frío.

CAPÍTULO 4

WB 4-26 Los muebles

1. un escritorio
2. un armario
3. mi cama
4. el inodoro
5. el jardín

WB 4-27 Los electrodomésticos

1. una lavadora
2. un horno de microondas
3. una aspiradora
4. un despertador
5. el refrigerador

WB 4-28 Los quehaceres

1. el comedor
2. la cocina
3. el patio
4. la sala

WB 4-29 Entre novios

1. tienes 2. Tengo 3. quieres 4. quiero
5. Prefiero 6. comienza 7. Comienza
8. queremos 9. preferimos 10. pienso

WB 4-30 La hora del almuerzo

1. almuerzo 2. sirve 3. dice 4. almorzar
5. duermo 6. vuelven 7. vuelvo 8. jugamos
9. juego

WB 4-31 En otras palabras

1. Tengo ganas de bailar.
2. No tengo paciencia.
3. Tengo celos de...
4. Tengo miedo de...

WB 4-32 ¿Qué hago?

1. Haz tu cama todos los días.
2. Quita la mesa después de comer.
3. Saca la basura todos los días.
4. Ve al supermercado todos los sábados.

WB 4-33 ¿Cómo están todos?

1. Lolita está emocionada. Está jugando en el patio.
2. Teresita y Javi están ocupados. Están regando las plantas.
3. Miguelín está aburrido. Está leyendo un libro.
4. Ángel y yo estamos sucios. Estamos preparando un pastel.

WB 4-34 ¿Cuántos son?

1. mil setecientos treinta y ocho
2. mil ciento sesenta
3. mil cuatrocientos dieciséis

CAPÍTULO 5

WB 5-19 El cuerpo humano

1. el ojo
2. el pelo
3. las orejas
4. la nariz
5. la boca / los dientes
6. el estómago
7. la pierna
8. el pie
9. la mano
10. el brazo

WB 5-20 Los problemas médicos

1. alergia / estornudo
2. catarro
3. enfermedad
4. congestionado
5. escalofríos / síntomas
6. sano / enfermo
7. examina
8. fiebre / toma la temperatura
9. náuseas / guardar cama

WB 5-21 La rutina diaria

1. Se despierta a las seis.
2. Se levanta a las seis y media.
3. Se ducha y se lava.
4. Se seca.
5. Se viste.
6. Se pinta. / Se maquilla.
7. Despierta a su hijo a las siete.
8. Se acuesta a las once.

WB 5-22 ¡Cómo vuela el tiempo!

1. Acaba de despertarse.
2. Acaba de levantarse.
3. Acaba de ducharse y lavarse.
4. Acaba de secarse.
5. Acaba de vestirse.
6. Acaba de pintarse / maquillarse.
7. Acaba de despertar a su hijo.

WB 5-23 Lorena Bobada

1. es 2. Es 3. está 4. está 5. está 6. está
7. Es 8. es 9. está 10. ser 11. es 12. es

WB 5-24 Gemelos distintos

1. No quiero ésta, prefiero esa medicina.

2. No quiero pedir a éste, prefiero pedir a ese médico.
3. No prefiero ésta, prefiero ésa.
4. No quiero pedir éstos, prefiero esos jarabes.
5. No prefiero esto, prefiero eso.

CAPÍTULO 6

WB 6-17 La comida

Carnes: jamón, res, pollo, bistec, pavo, chuletas de cerdo

Pescado/Mariscos: calamares, camarones

Bebidas: café, vino, agua mineral, té helado, leche, cerveza, jugo

Postres: flan, queso

Frutas: naranja, manzana, banana

Verduras: lechuga, papas

Condimentos: mantequilla, sal, pimienta, vinagre, aceite

WB 6-18 En el restaurante

1. c 2. c 3. a 4. a 5. b 6. a

WB 6-19 ¡Viva la igualdad!

1. Beti come tantas verduras como Martín.
2. Beti almuerza en restaurantes tanto como Martín.
3. Beti está a dieta tanto como Martín.
4. Beti es tan amable como Martín.
5. Beti toma tanto café como Martín.

WB 6-20 El más...

1. Guillermo es el hijo mayor.
2. Alejandro es el más paciente de los dos primos.
3. El jugo es la bebida más dulce.
4. Michael Jordan es el mejor jugador.

WB 6-21 Un sábado por la tarde

1. almorzó 2. almorcé 3. comimos 4. tomé
5. bebió 6. terminaste 7. terminé 8. comencé
9. leí 10. leyó 11. busqué 12. compré

WB 6-22 Padre e hijo

1. se divirtieron 2. pidió 3. sirvió
4. se durmió

CAPÍTULO 7

WB 7-19 La ropa

1. el traje de baño
2. el sombrero
3. los zapatos, los calcetines, las sandalias, las botas

4. la blusa, la falda, las medias, el vestido
5. los pantalones, el traje, la corbata
6. el impermeable

WB 7-20 En la tienda

1. En qué puedo servirle 2. probarme 3. talla
4. queda bien 5. Hace juego 6. moda 7. le
debo 8. ganga 9. tarjeta de crédito

WB 7-21 ¿Son tuyos?

1. ¡El sombrero es tuyo! / Éste es un
   sombrero tuyo.
2. ¡Son suyos! / Éstos son unos cinturones
   suyos.
3. ¡Son suyos! / Éstos son unos zapatos
   suyos.
4. ¡Son mías! / Éstas son unas gafas de sol
   mías.
5. ¡Es suyo! / Éste es un paraguas suyo.

WB 7-22 A la hora de la cena

1. La 2. lo 3. Me, te 4. las

WB 7-23 La pequeña Elena

1. vivía 2. Tenía 3. sacaba 4. limpiaba
5. íbamos 6. compraba 7. gustaba
8. comíamos

WB 7-24 Paca y Peca

1. trabajábamos 2. llamó 3. conociste
4. quería 5. invitó 6. Fue 7. recibiste 8. dijiste
9. dije 10. podía 11. invitaron 12. dijo
13. oyó 14. fue 15. invitó 16. acepté

CAPÍTULO 8

WB 8-17 Una celebración especial

1. cumplió 2. entremeses 3. invitados 4. dis-
frazarse 5. máscara 6. disfraz 7. se reunieron
8. celebrar 9. brindis 10. gritaron 11. Felicidades 12. pastel 13. velas 14. recordar
15. regalos 16. llorar 17. lo pasaron
18. anfitriona

WB 8-18 En la playa y en el campo

1. f 2. a 3. d 4. h 5. c 6. g 7. b 8. e

WB 8-19 Más preguntas

1. De dónde 2. Dónde 3. Cuál 4. Adónde
5. Qué 6. Cuántas 7. Qué

WB 8-20 Un viaje inolvidable

1. era 2. hice 3. Fui 4. tenía 5. tenía 6. decidieron 7. vivíamos 8. era 9. había 10. podía
11. sabía 12. fui 13. empezó 14. nadaba
15. mordió 16. sentí 17. grité 18. se metió
19. salvó 20. tuve 21. fue 22. asustó

WB 8-21 Significados especiales

1. tuvimos 2. supo, sabía 3. quise 4. pudo
5. tenía

WB 8-22 En el mercado

1. algo 2. algunos 3. algunas 4. también
5. ninguna 6. algunos 7. tampoco 8. ni 9. ni
10. nada

WB 8-23 ¿Cuanto tiempo hace?

1. Hace tres meses que Lucía no trabaja.
2. Hace un año que Santi y Silvina no están
   casados.
3. Hace una semana que nosotros no vamos
   al centro comercial.
4. Hace demasiado tiempo que yo no tengo
   novio(a).
5. *Answers will vary. Example:* Hace dos años
   que yo no estoy en la secundaria.

CAPÍTULO 9

WB 9-17 Viajes

1. c 2. b 3. d 4. a 5. f 6. g 7. e

WB 9-18 En el hotel

1. cuatro estrellas 2. cuartos 3. limpios
4. sucios 5. dobles 6. sencillas 7. privado
8. aire acondicionado 9. ascensor 10. recepción 11. cómodo

WB 9-19 ¿Dónde está todo?

1. al lado 2. delante 3. a la izquierda 4. entre
5. a la derecha 6. enfrente 7. detrás

WB 9-20 Indicaciones

1. cruce 2. siga 3. Doble 4. suba 5. Siga
6. hacia

WB 9-21 Una carta

1. les 2. les 3. le 4. le 5. les 6. me 7. te 8. me
9. me 10. les

WB 9-22 Elena, la buena

1. Sí, te la presto.
2. Sí, se la preparo.
3. Sí, se lo escribo.
4. Sí, me la pueden pasar. *or* Pueden
   pasármela.
5. Sí, se lo puedo comprar. *or* Puedo
   comprárselo.

WB 9-23 Antes de salir del mercado

1. Perdone 2. deme 3. Tome 4. Dígame
5. Salga 6. vaya 7. Tenga 8. Vuelva

CAPÍTULO 10

WB 10-17 El noviazgo

1. noviazgo 2. amor 3. nos enamoramos
4. cariño 5. nos llevamos 6. enamorados
7. matrimonio 8. casados

WB 10-18 La boda

1. novios 2. casarse 3. se besan 4. recién
casados 5. aplauden 6. tiran 7. recepción
8. tienen lugar 9. banquete 10. brindis
11. felicitan 12. orquesta 13. ramo de flores
14. agarrar 15. luna de miel 16. se separan
17. se divorcian

WB 10-19 ¿Qué han hecho?

1. Pablo ha leído tres libros.
2. Teresa y Ángela han visto una película nueva.
3. Mamá y yo le hemos escrito cartas a la familia.
4. Yo me he divertido con mis amigos.
5. Tú has vuelto de un viaje largo.

WB 10-20 El romance de Ken y Barbie

1. Ken y Barbie se conocieron en Malibú.
2. Ellos se miraron intensamente.
3. Ellos se abrazaron fuertemente.
4. Ellos se enamoraron inmediatamente.
5. Ellos se casaron en junio de ese año.

WB 10-21 Miguel lo hace así

Answers will vary. Examples include:

1. Miguel lee el periódico detenidamente.
2. Miguel habla con las chicas nerviosamente.
3. Miguel come rápidamente.
4. Miguel saca buenas notas fácilmente.
5. Miguel va a las fiestas frecuentemente.

WB 10-22 La rutina

1. Todos los días 2. Siempre 3. Solamente
4. A veces 5. Una vez 6. Nunca 7. siempre

WB 10-23 ¿Cómo lo hago?

Primero te consigues una cuenta electrónica
de Internet. Después, te compras software
para el email. Luego le pides a tu novia su
dirección electrónica y entonces puedes
escribir el mensaje que quieres mandar. Finalmente, le envías el mensaje.

WB 10-24 ¿El nuevo novio de Valeria?

1. que 2. que 3. lo que 4. quien

CAPÍTULO 11

WB 11-17 ¿Qué debe hacer?

1. arquitecto 2. peluquero 3. veterinario
4. periodista 5. programador 6. maestro
7. traductor 8. policía 9. siquiatra 10. dentista

WB 11-18 Solicitando trabajo

1. solicitar 2. currículum 3. computadora
4. imprimir 5. impresora 6. fotocopias
7. solicitud 8. llamar 9. entrevista
10. proyectos 11. beneficios 12. empleados
13. sueldo 14. contratar 15. tiempo parcial
16. tiempo completo 17. jubilarte 18. despedir

WB 11-19 Consejos financieros

1. ahorrar 2. deposites 3. cuenta de ahorros
4. cajero automático 5. presupuesto 6. tarjeta
de crédito 7. cheques 8. facturas 9. prestar
10. en efectivo 11. a plazos

WB 11-20 De vacaciones

1. por 2. por 3. Por 4. para 5. para 6. Para
7. por 8. para 9. por 10. para

WB 11-21 El amor y los negocios

1. escribas 2. llames 3. tengas 4. mire
5. pienses 6. te enamores 7. pierdan
8. mandes 9. vayamos 10. nos divirtamos

WB 11-22 Entre amigos

1. salir 2. ir 3. sigamos 4. trabajemos 5. ir
6. vuelva 7. acompañes

CAPÍTULO 12

WB 12-14 La geografía rural y urbana

1. metrópolis, acelerado, sobrepoblación, ruido, tráfico, contaminación, medio ambiente, basura, recogen
2. tranquila, campesinos, cultivar, regar, colinas, arroyos
3. resolver, recursos naturales, petróleo, reforestar, capa de ozono, desarrollar / explotar, energía solar, desperdicio, destrucción, reciclar, escasez

WB 12-15 Trivia animal

1. el mono 2. la culebra 3. el ave 4. el elefante 5. el gorila 6. el león 7. el lobo 8. el oso
9. el tigre

WB 12-16 Entre amigos

1. estemos 2. poder 3. venir 4. estén 5. digas
6. acompañen 7. pienses 8. vayan 9. tengan
10. sea

WB 12-17 Hablando del viaje

1. TERE: Yo creo que estas vacaciones son excelentes.
   CARMEN: Sí, pero dudo que David quiera venir este año.
2. TERE: Gabriela no está segura que el hotel sea bueno.
   CARMEN: Yo estoy segura que todos los hoteles van a ser muy buenos.
3. TERE: En San José nosotros tenemos que buscar un restaurante que sirva gallo pinto.
   CARMEN: Yo conozco un buen hotel que sirve gallo pinto.
4. TERE: Yo quiero visitar una reserva biológica que tenga muchas especies exóticas.
   CARMEN: Manuel Antonio es una reserva preciosa que tiene todo tipo de animales exóticos.

CAPÍTULO 13

WB 13-14 Las películas y los programas

1. e 2. c 3. d 4. f 5. g 6. b 7. h 8. i 9. j 10. a

WB 13-15 El mundo de las bellas artes

1. literatura 2. concierto 3. fotografía, fotógrafo 4. director 5. actriz 6. arquitectura
7. cuadro 8. dramaturgo 9. bailarín
10. danza 11. compositor 12. cantante

WB 13-16 Consejos para la cita

1. limpie 2. venga 3. se asuste 4. llegue
5. está 6. guste 7. vas 8. invites / invites
9. diga 10. guste 11. decida

WB 13-17 Pero ¡NO FUE CULPA NUESTRA!

1. Se nos cayó una escultura.
2. Se le escaparon los niños.
3. Se me olvidó la cita.
4. Se nos acabó el dinero.
5. Se me perdió la llave de mi coche.

WB 13-18 ¿Ya está hecho?

1. Los estudiantes ya están invitados.
   Fueron invitados por Jaime y Juan.
2. El entretenimiento ya está confirmado.
   Fue confirmado por Analisa.
3. La lista de música ya está organizada.
   Fue organizada por Rosa y Eva.
4. La comida ya está preparada.
   Fue preparada por Marta y Esteban.
5. Las decoraciones ya están colgadas.
   Fueron colgadas por Julio.

CAPÍTULO 14

WB14-14 Políticamente hablando

1. partidos políticos, republicano, liberales, conservadores
2. candidatos, campaña, debates, ciudadanos
3. dictadura, democracia, elegimos, deber, votar
4. ejército, paz, defender

WB14-15 Las preocupaciones cívicas

1. f 2. i 3. k 4. e 5. a 6. c 7. h 8. l 9. n 10. d
11. j 12. m 13. o 14. g 15. b

WB14-16 El primer día

1. tendrás 2. comenzará 3. será 4. vendrán
5. sabrán 6. querrá 7. dirás 8. habrá 9. durará 10. veré 11. podremos 12. haré 13. serás
14. irá

WB14-17 Puros sueños

1. harías 2. viajaría 3. gustaría 4. Podría
5. saldríamos 6. iríamos 7. tomaríamos
8. Pasaríamos 9. querríamos 10. volaríamos
11. tendríamos

WB14-18 No lo creo

1. Es imposible que te hayas quedado en hoteles de cuatro estrellas.
2. No creo que tú y tu novia hayan conocido al presidente de los Estados Unidos.
3. Estoy seguro de que tu novia lo ha pasado bien en Washington.
4. No dudo que has participado en tres manifestaciones políticas.
5. No pienso que tu novia te haya dicho que no quiere volver a Chile.

CAPÍTULO 15

WB 15-12 Los domingueros modernos

1. cámara 2. videocámara 3. teléfono celular
4. caseta de video 5. videocasetera 6. antena parabólica 7. satélite 8. desconectar
9. equipo 10. estéreo 11. enchufado

WB 15-13 ¿Estás al tanto?

1. c 2. b 3. h 4. d 5. i 6. g 7. a 8. f 9. e

WB 15-14 Las instrucciones

1. abrir el programa 2. hacer click 3. pantalla
4. quitar 5. archivar 6. disquete 7. página web 8. navegar

WB 15-15 Buenas amigas

1. me recordaras **2.** nos pusiéramos **3.** nos casáramos **4.** fuéramos **5.** nos metiéramos **6.** dieran **7.** pudiera **8.** estudiara **9.** se graduara

WB 15-16 ¿Qué harían?

1. Si Juan no tuviera que trabajar, pasaría todo su tiempo en la computadora.

2. Si Carlos y Marga compraran una mejor computadora, podrían usar el Internet.

3. Si Tomás no fuera tan tímido, podría conocer a más chicas en los salones de charla.

4. Si Nancy se graduara con un título en informática, ganaría mucho dinero.

5. Si Óscar me ofreciera un trabajo con su compañía, yo cambiaría de carrera.